Strolling Through Time:

A Chronology of Beaver County, PA, History to 2016

Compiled by Roger Applegate

Published by:
Beaver County Historical Research & Landmarks Foundation
The Captain William Vicary Mansion
1235 3rd Ave.
Freedom, PA 15042

Beaver County Historical Research & Landmarks Foundation
Copyright © 2016
All Rights Reserved
ISBN: 978-0-9674749-1-5

First Edition
Updated and Expanded July, 2017

Printed in the USA by:
CreateSpace, An Amazon.com Company

Cover Art by:

Daniel Harper
Daniel Harper Design
646.824.8609
dan@daniel-harper.com

All Proceeds from this book benefit the Beaver County Historical Research & Landmarks Foundation

This book is dedicated to my wife Brenda.

God couldn't have given me a better companion for my stroll through history and life.

"History is the witness that testifies to the passing of time; it illumines reality, vitalizes memory, provides guidance in daily life and brings us tidings of antiquities."

— Cicero

Introduction

This chronology of Beaver County, Pennsylvania history has been a project that has been on the proverbial "back burner" for many years, and owes its final existence to the efforts of the many dedicated historians on whose work it was built. The idea for its basic structure came from an article that was published in "*Milestones*" Volume 31, Number 3 by Foundation historian James Kelbaugh, and includes the dates and other information relating to county history and industry which he faithfully recorded. No serious publication would be complete without drawing on the work of Denver Walton and Charles Townsend who both edited our "*Milestones*" magazine for many years, and who also produced many books and writings on county history.

Thanks is due in no particular order to: Charles Townsend, Wayne Cole, Don Inman, Brenda Applegate, Jeff Snedden, Sandy Davis, Gino Piroli, Bernie Catalucci, Pat Riley and Emily Crum who contributed ideas and who also helped to correct what was written here. I would be remiss not to mention my favorite English teacher Ellen Glasser who spent many hours wielding her legendary red pen while trying to fix my many grammatical errors. To all of these dedicated historians I owe a great debt. Also, I would like to give a very special "Thank You" to Dan Harper for creating the cover art.

Drawing on many resources, it has been my intention to keep each entry as short but as complete as possible within the limitations of a timeline. In order to avoid as much as possible having multiple date entries for the same person/event, each entry may contain past as well as future dates and information. However, it is not the intention of this book to be a complete reference for each date in itself, but rather a synopsis that points the reader to more in depth information elsewhere. To help accomplish this, reference listings will appear at the end of each entry so that that date's information may be tracked back to its source via the "Key to Sources" pages near the end. In the case of web sources, I simply listed the link for them with each entry, and added a "QR Code" for convenience. Unfortunately, there were many interesting facts/occurrences for which we could find no specific dates or reliable information or sources for, and as a result, those items were not included here.

As you read through the chronology, it is important to keep in mind the changes to geographical and/or place names that have occurred over the years. In the earlier chapters as I write the words "Beaver County" it is done with the understanding that these events occurred within the geographical confines of what was to become the county of Beaver in 1800. Also, it is important to remember that the 1800 version of Beaver County included a part of present day Lawrence County until that county's formation in 1849. In addition, keeping track of the changes in the names of the boroughs and townships can be very confusing. Please refer to the diagrams in Appendices "A" & "B " to help avoid any confusion as to place names and corresponding dates.

As you stroll through the chronology, please remember that it was never meant to be comprehensive, but only to give the reader a starting point for historical reference and further research. Additions and corrections are always welcome.

Table of Contents

I. Pre-history to 1771 1

II. Early Settlement 1772 to 1799 10

III. Creating Beaver County 1800 to 1829 19

IV. Early Industrial Period 1830 to 1860 28

V. Civil War & its Aftermath 1861 to 1889 45

VI. Small Business & Big Dreams 1890 to 1904 68

VII. Big Steel Brings Big Changes 1905 to 1919 80

VIII. The "Roaring Twenties," "Depressed Thirties" & WWII 1920-1945 94

IX. The Post War Years 1946 to 1980 112

X. Death of Big Steel 1981 to 1989 130

XI. A New Era Begins 1990 to 2016 135

Appendix A – Evolution of Boroughs and Townships 150

Appendix B – Evolution of Beaver County 152

Appendix C – National Register Listings 153

Appendix D – State Historical Markers in County 154

Appendix E – Beaver County Historical Markers 155

Appendix F – Original Depreciation Land Owners 158

Key to Sources 164

Index 173

Strolling Through Time: A Chonology of Beaver County, PA History to 2016

I. Pre-history to 1771

Nearly 900,000 years ago, an ice age covered the land with great glaciers which moved and reshaped the landscape in what is now northern Beaver County. Early man appeared on the scene as Paleo-Indians came to hunt ice age animals, until they eventually gave way to other more settled cultures. During the Late Prehistoric Period, the Monongahela People, the last known people to live in this area, appeared about 900 A.D. but were gone by approximately 1600 A.D. Around one hundred years or so later, other native tribes such as the Delaware and Shawnee began to immigrate here from Eastern Pennsylvania. After the tribes had established themselves at such places as Sawkunk and Logstown, French and English traders appeared and their respective countries began competing for control of Western Pennsylvania, leading to the French & Indian War. Shortly after the end of the French & Indian War, Pontiac's Rebellion would explode across the frontier as a number of native tribes banded together to attempt to destroy British forts and settlements. The end of those two conflicts led to a flood of settlers who came west with an insatiable desire to own land, a concept which was totally foreign to the Indian way of life. This more than anything else would spark the nearly continuous warfare between Europeans and native tribes during this period of our history.

- **900,000 Years Ago** – The Ice Age began and blanketed parts of the county with great sheets of ice. Before it was over, it was to cause a great deal of change to the county's river systems as they were affected by the presence of glaciers blocking rivers and streams, thus diverting them in direction and flow. Over time, glaciers caused the formation of our present Ohio River, then an insignificant tributary, from the ancient and massive pre-glacial Monongahela River (also called the "Pittsburgh River") which flowed northward through part of the present Ohio and Beaver River channels into Canada. When the Monongahela River along with the Teays River in Ohio were dammed by the glaciers, a massive lake also named Monongahela was formed that covered parts of Eastern Ohio, Northern West Virginia and Western Pennsylvania including parts of Beaver County. The drainage from this lake began the process of creating the modern Ohio River system.
(http://www.dcnr.state.pa.us/cs/groups/public/documents/document/dcnr_00682 7.pdf)

- **10,000 – 20,000 Years Ago** – The glacial period had ended and the farthest advance of the glaciers stopped at a line extending from Big Beaver (near Koppel) southwestward through South Beaver Township. As the world became warmer, the glaciers began to melt and retreat allowing Lake Monongahela to drain itself into the new river channels. **21(3), (http://www.dcnr.state.pa.us/cs/groups/public/documents/document/dcnr_00682 7.pdf)**

Strolling Through Time: A Chonology of Beaver County, PA History to 2016

- **14,000 B.C – 7,000 B.C.** – The earliest arrivals to Beaver County were almost certainly nomadic people from the Paleo-Indian period who hunted Ice Age animals and lived in caves and rock shelters or established rude camps along water sources. No Paleo-Indian camps have so far been identified in Beaver County, but one of the oldest in America was discovered at Meadowcroft Rock Shelter in nearby Avella, Washington County, PA. Large Ice Age mammals like the Wooly Mammoth became extinct during this period. **34("Another era ends at Ohio View dig," June 25, 1978)**

- **7000 B.C. to 1500 B.C.** – Known by archaeologists as the Archaic Period, early Indian inhabitants of Beaver County were still hunter-gatherers, but their technology became more sophisticated to keep up with a changing environment following the retreat of the glaciers. Their groups were most likely composed of extended family bands. Large numbers of artifacts for this period were found in local archaeological digs along the rivers.
  (http://explorepahistory.com/story.php?storyId=1-9-14&chapter=1), 34("Another era ends at Ohio View dig," June 25, 1978), (http://pspb.org/archaeology/media/Archaic_Period_TextV2.pdf)

- **1,500 B.C. to 1,000 B.C.** – This was known as the Transitional Period. Local archaeologists discovered camp sites along the Ohio River that contained net sinkers and stone anchors which indicated that fishing and river travel were primary occupations.
  34("Another era ends at Ohio View dig," June 25, 1978)

- **1000 B.C. to 100 B.C.** – Inhabitants of this Early Woodland Period, the Adena, learned to grow crops which allowed them to be able to establish permanent villages and increase populations. In Beaver County, they grew things like sunflowers and squash. They were also believed to be great travelers and traders based on the exotic flints found in county sites. The Adena also began the use of burial mounds and held elaborate burial ceremonies. **(http://explorepahistory.com/story.php?storyId=1-9-14&chapter=1), 34("Another era ends at Ohio View dig," June 25, 1978)**

- **100 B.C. to 900 A.D.** – The early Indian inhabitants of the Middle Woodland Era, the Adena-Hopewell did some farming - growing corn and squash, but also relied heavily on hunting and fishing. Artifacts found in local archaeological digs were things like: side and corner notched points, drills, knives, anvil stones and pottery. Burial mounds and elaborate burial ceremonies were still in use.
  (http://explorepahistory.com/story.php?storyId=1-9-14&chapter=1), 34("Another era ends at Ohio View dig," June 25, 1978), (http://www.phmc.state.pa.us/portal/communities/archaeology/native-american/early-middle-woodland-period.html)

Strolling Through Time: A Chonology of Beaver County, PA History to 2016

🍃 **900 A.D. – 1600 A.D.** – During what is known as the Late Prehistoric Period, the Monongahela people, were living here. Archaeologists believe that they derived in part from the Mississippian Culture and were the most highly advanced Indians to have inhabited the Ohio and Beaver Valleys to that time. They were an agricultural people who lived in small circular houses and their villages sometimes numbered close to several hundred people. Their villages were surrounded by a stockade fence indicating that they sought safety from neighboring tribes. Their main weapon and hunting instrument was the bow and arrow. Large numbers of artifacts have been found locally including: spear and arrow points, blades, knives, drills and scrapers, hammers, choppers, elk and bear teeth, pottery, beads, pendants and fish hooks. The Monongahela people, like the cultures before them, disappeared before the arrival of the white man. The area remained unoccupied until the Delaware Indian migration in 1725. **21(4), 125(13-15), 21(Chronology), 34("Another era ends at Ohio View dig," June 25, 1978), (http://www.phmc.state.pa.us/portal/communities/archaeology/native-american/late-woodland-period.html),** *See entry for Ca. 1725*

Indian Petroglyphs at Smith's Ferry - Courtesy of Charles Townsend

🍃 **Up to 1,000 Years Ago** – A group of Indian rock carvings known as petroglyphs were made near Smith's Ferry on a rock shelf that extended into the Ohio River. Scientists are unsure who made them and when they were made. The carvings are now completely covered by the Ohio River due to the dams increasing the water depth. The petroglyphs were first documented in depth by Harold Barth in 1908. **2(933-934),** *See 1739*

🍃 **1609** – The London Company patent was revised to include land "from sea to sea, west and northwest," becoming the basis of Virginia's later claim to the Ohio Country which included the south side of Beaver County. **21(Chronology)**

🍃 **1650's** – This region south of Lake Erie was controlled but not inhabited by the Erie or "Cat Nation." Following a devastating war with the powerful Iroquois Nation, control of this area passed to the victorious Iroquois. For the next seventy years or so, the Ohio River Valley continued to remain mostly uninhabited. **122(32-33)**

🍃 **Spring, 1670** – Rene Robert Cavelier, Sieur de La Salle, was credited by most history books with the discovery and exploration of the Ohio River. La Salle never kept a journal and only related the story to a friend in Paris years later. The French government, wishing to claim the Ohio Valley, promoted the story. **122(30)**

1681 – King Charles II granted a charter to William Penn to include land extending westward five degrees of longitude from the Delaware River; this was the basis of Pennsylvania's claim to future Beaver County. **21(Chronology)**

1694 – Arnout Viele, a Dutch trader, accompanied by a band of Shawnee, explored the Ohio Valley; He was the first known colonial to visit future Beaver County. **21(Chronology)**

1720s – The French were the first known European traders to arrive in the Ohio country, with Jacques LeTorte, arriving around this date. He was soon followed by several other French traders. It was not until the 1740s that Pennsylvanian George Croghan arrived and built his storehouse and trading post at Logstown. **139(9)**

Ca. 1725 – Parts of the Delaware Indian tribe began migrating to this area from the eastern part of the state and settled at Sawkunk near present-day Bridgewater. Sawkunk was also known as Shingas' Town or King Beaver's Town, and it was situated at the intersection of the Great Trail with two other important Indian paths. **21(Chronology), 122(44)**

Ca. 1727 – The Shawnee tribe established the first village of Logstown on a narrow plain on the north side of the Ohio River in present day Harmony Township and became known by the French as "Chiningue," pronounced "Shenango." A later town was built on the second terrace by Shawnee Chief Kakowatchiky in about 1744, and it was inhabited by both Delaware and Shawnee. Logstown was burned by Monacatootha (Scaroudy) and other Indians loyal to the British in 1754. The French re-built some thirty houses there in 1756. A large cornfield existed on the south side of the river. **122(39, 4-6),** *See entry for 1740's*

1727 – French agent Joncaire was sent to the Ohio Country to promote French interests. **21(Chronology)**

Ca. 1728 – The Shawnee nation joined the Delaware in Sawkunk Village (present day Beaver). **21(Chronology)**

1739 - The Baron de Longueiul French military expedition traveled from Quebec down the Allegheny and Ohio Rivers to attack a troublesome Chickasaw tribe living on the Mississippi River. While floating through Beaver County, a young French engineer, Lt. Joseph Gaspard Chaussegros de Lery, the expedition's engineer, became possibly the first known white man to record the existence of the mysterious Indian carvings known as petroglyphs near the mouth of Little Beaver Creek (present-day Smith's Ferry). de Lery noted that there were "many marks and figures of men and animals cut out on the rocks, as if with chisels". **122(37-39,72)**

- **1740's** – Logstown (present Harmony Township) became the principle Indian town and trading center in the area. Living there were Delaware, Shawnee, Wyandot and the remains of various other displaced tribes. **2(970-980)**, *See entry for Ca. 1727*

- **1740's** – The main body of the Delaware Indian tribe came westward. **46(18)**

- **1748** – George Croghan, British Indian Agent, established a trading post at Sawkunk (Beaver). **21(Chronology)**

- **August 27, 1748** – Pennsylvania agent Conrad Weiser visited the Indian village of Logstown (Harmony Township), then explored the entire Beaver Valley. **2(38, 970ff), 4(8,9), 6(111), 8(55), 9(72)**

- **July, 1749** – In response to their petition to the English crown, the Ohio Company, a joint partnership based in Virginia, was granted rights to survey and to settle certain land west of the Allegheny Mountains and south of the Ohio River that had been granted earlier to the Colony of Virginia by royal charter. **8(56ff)**

- **August 8, 1749** – French officer Pierre Celeron de Blainville visited the Indians at Logstown while traversing the region to place lead markers at the mouths of major rivers in order to lay claim to the area for France. **8(58), 9(73), 16(128), 29(65), 2(413, Note 1)**

- **August 8, 1749** – Reverend Joseph Peter de Bonnecamps of the Society of Jesus performed the first public religious ceremony (a Catholic Mass) at Logstown as a member of the Celeron Expedition. **8(58), 9(73), 16(128), 29(65), 2(413, Note 1)**

- **1750** – Cumberland County was established including the south side of future Beaver County. **21(Chronology)**

- **1750** - Trader Philippe Thomas de Joncaire was sent to the Ohio country to establish a French trading post at Logstown. Within two years, a number of other French traders were established there as well as other spots along the Ohio River. Many had been trading in the country for a number of years, but this time they were licensed and had the full blessing of the French government. **138(10-11)**

- **1750's** – Iroquois Half-King Tanacharison had a hunting camp in the Cannelton area. When Washington visited Logstown in 1753, a runner was sent after Tanacharison to bring him from this camp to the Logstown conference. **21(78), 2(945)**

- **May 18, 1751** - George Croghan visited Logstown to give presents from the Governor of Pennsylvania to the tribes settled there. A French officer and interpreter were present to try to turn the Indians against the English. **137(136-137)**

- **1752** – Christopher Gist, Ohio Company agent, made a treaty at Logstown where the Indians pledged not to molest any settlements of the company on the southeast side of the Ohio River. **2(970-980, 40)**

- **1752** – Shingas was recognized by the Pennsylvania and Virginia Colonies as the King of the Delaware tribe. **46(18)**

Washington at Logstown painted by Andrew Knez, Jr.

- **February 1753** – William Trent and several other traders from Virginia arrived at Logstown to find over a dozen French workmen building what they were told were store rooms meant for trading purposes. Captain Trent and company distrusted that explanation and felt that the builders had other plans in mind. **140(29-30)**

- **November 24, 1753** – Major George Washington visited Logstown while on a mission from the Governor of Virginia to warn the French to leave this area. The Indian name for Logstown was "Maugh-wa-wa-me" which means broad plains or plateaus. **2(971), 16(140), 29(65)**

- **Spring, 1754** – French troops from Canada forced the Virginians to abandon their partially completed fort at the forks of the Ohio (Fort Prince George), bringing the entire region under French control. The French then built their own fort nearby and named it Fort Duquesne. **6(112), 8(73ff), 29(67)**

- **Spring 1754** – According to "The French Invasion of Western Pennsylvania" by Donald H. Kent, "The original plan had been to build Fort Duquesne at Logstown, further down the Ohio, but now it was felt that the Forks of the Ohio was a better location to halt English traders, and–perhaps–an English army. Another reason given was the lack of wood at Logstown. Apparently the Indians and the traders had used up all the trees for miles around, so that there was a shortage of logs at Logstown, and it would be difficult to build a fort there." **138(81-82)**

- **June 24, 1754** – Prior to the Battle of Fort Necessity and expecting a British defeat, Tanacharison (Half-King) sent word to Scaroudy (also known as Monacatootha) to abandon Logstown and retreat to Aughwick (present day Shirleysburg, Pa.) where Pennsylvania trader George Croghan was living. Scaroudy carried out his instructions and Logstown was evacuated and burned to the ground. **139(75)**

- **Autumn 1754** – Contreceour, the commander at Fort Duquesne sent a working party to rebuild Logstown on a hill overlooking the old town. The new town consisted of thirty log cabins with stone chimneys. **139(83)**

Strolling Through Time: A Chonology of Beaver County, PA History to 2016

- **1754** – The Pennsylvania – Virginia border controversy began. **21(Chronology)**

- **1754** – Queen Aliquippa, a Seneca leader who had met with Major George Washington as he passed by her village at the mouth of the Youghiogheny River in 1753, died at Aughwick, Pennsylvania. **122(34)**

- **1756** – A second village of Sawkunk, consisting of thirty eight log cabins, was built by the French about a mile down the Ohio River on the western end of present-day Beaver, following the outbreak of the French & Indian War. Smaller Sawkunk still existed, but the larger one became predominant. **(NOTE: the book "Beavertown" 46(18) puts the date of the establishment of the second Sawkunk at 1748) 122(44), 46(18)**

- **1757** – Jesuit Father Claude Francis Virot established the first Catholic mission at Sawkunk among the Delaware Indians. At some point, Chief Pakanke of the Wolf Clan drove him off. Father Virot was killed by the Iroquois while serving as chaplain to a French force attempting to relieve Fort Niagara during the French and Indian War. **21(Chronology), 2(413,Note 2)**

- **1758** – Christian Frederick Post was sent by Pennsylvania authorities to the Ohio Indians to draw their friendship away from the French. Post visited both Sawkunk and Logstown during his trip and was well received. French officers from Fort Duquesne unsuccessfully attempted to turn the assembled chiefs against him. **21(Chronology), 137(106-111)**

- **November 24, 1758** – After dark, the French abandoned and burned Fort Duquesne, and withdrew from the forks of the Ohio (present day Pittsburgh). A contingent of about 100 retreating French soldiers camped overnight at Beaver Creek (Beaver River) before continuing their withdrawal down the Ohio River. The next day, a British army commanded by General John Forbes occupied the deserted ruins of Fort Duquesne effectively ending French control in this portion of western Pennsylvania. **8(95), 9(78), 29(67), 122(93)**

- **1758** – Logstown and Sawkunk were abandoned by the Indian tribes following the French retreat from Fort Duquesne. **21(Chronology)**

- **1760/1761** – Delaware Chief White Eyes established his town along the Beaver River at the Great Trail crossing where the first village of Sawkunk was formerly located. It was known as "White Eye's Town." **122(279)**

- **1762** – Moravian missionary John Heckewelder, along with Christian Frederick Post, conferred with Delaware Chief "White Eyes" at his settlement near the mouth of the Beaver River and received permission to setup a school and mission house. **21(Chronology)**

Strolling Through Time: A Chonology of Beaver County, PA History to 2016

1763 – The British Royal Proclamation of 1763 restricted settlement west of the Allegheny Mountains. **21(Chronology)**

1763 – Shingas, also known to the British as "King Shingas" died in 1763 where the Moravian Village of Gnadenhutten was established years later in present day Tuscarawas County, Ohio. Tamaqui, younger brother of King Shingas assumed the title of King of the Delaware upon his brother's death. **NOTE: The Great Trail claims his death at 1769, but this appears to be an error. 46(19), 123(292)**

May, 1763 – Indian Trader Thomas Calhoun and his fourteen men were ordered out of the Tuscarawas Village (present day Ohio) by Shingas (King Beaver) and instructed to leave their weapons while three Indians would conduct them safely to Fort Pitt. Perhaps led into a trap, the party was ambushed while passing Beaver Creek (now Beaver River) and only Calhoun and three of his party escaped to Fort Pitt. **122(111)**

June, 1763 – Amid general uprisings, Indians from many tribes seized nine English forts west of the Allegheny Mountains and lay siege to Fort Pitt. This conflict became known as "Pontiac's Rebellion." **2(64)**

August 5 & 6, 1763 – An expedition led by Colonel Henry Bouquet defeated Indian forces at the battle of Bushy Run (Jeanette, Pennsylvania), that helped to break the siege of Fort Pitt. Most of the remaining Indian settlements within the present boundaries of Beaver County were abandoned soon afterward. **21(Chronology)**

Fall, 1764 – British Colonel Henry Bouquet, then commander of Fort Pitt, led an army of 1,500 militia and regulars into the heart of the Ohio country to finally help to quell the recent Indian uprising known as "Pontiac's Rebellion." During its march, the army encamped along the Tuscarawas Trail (in what is now Ohioville Borough). **21(Chronology)**

1768 – The Purchase of 1768 was made by the Pennsylvania Proprietary government from the Indians at Fort Stanwix (New York) which included the south side of future Beaver County. **21(Chronology)**

Prior to 1769 – Alexander McKee lived opposite Logstown near present day Aliquippa as an Indian trader. His land was seized and sold when he became a renegade during the Revolution. **21(Chronology), 2(156-157)**

1770 – George Washington travelled through the county on the Ohio River and stopped at the remains of Logstown for breakfast. **21(Chronology), 97(248)**

1770 – A Moravian mission was established at Friedenstadt (formerly Beaver County, now present day Moravia, Lawrence County) on the Big Beaver River by Rev. David Zeisberger to convert the local Indians. **21(Chronology)**

- **July 14, 1770** – Rev. David Zeisberger was adopted by Delaware Indians along the Beaver River. **2(420)**

- **1770** – Mingo Chief Logan maintained a hunting lodge near present day Rochester known as "Logan's Town" or "Mingo Town." **2(26-27)**

- **June 12, 1770** – The first baptism in the county occurred at Friedenstadt (formerly Beaver County, now present day Moravia, Lawrence County) when it was administered to the wife of the blind Delaware chief Solomon. **2(420)**

- **1771** – Bedford County was erected including the future south side of Beaver County. **21(Chronology)**

- **1771** – John Gibson built a house at the former Logstown site as an Indian trader and not as a permanent settler. During the Revolution, he was the Colonel of the 13th Virginia Regiment and was at times in temporary command at both Forts Pitt and Laurens. He was also a member of the convention which later framed the Pennsylvania constitution. **21(Chronology), 2(156-157, Note 1)**

- **June 20, 1771** – The Moravian Church at Friedenstadt was dedicated, and was built for and by the Indian converts living there. It was most likely the first church building dedicated to the worship of God west of the Allegheny Mountains. (formerly Beaver County, the location is now present-day Moravia, Lawrence County). **2(422)**

II. Early Settlement 1772 to 1799

During this period of our history, European settlers were beginning to discover the rich land and other natural advantages provided by the rivers and streams of what was to later become Beaver County. The first settlers arrived to claim land on the southside of this area only to discover that not only did Pennsylvania claim this territory, but Virginia did as well. Land deeds issued by both states caused a great deal of confusion and the result of overlapping claims caused many problems until both states reached an agreement as to their permanent boundaries. Settlement on the north side or "Indian side" of the Ohio River began with the purchase of the land at the Treaties of Fort Stanwix and Fort McIntosh. These purchases allowed the state to survey the area into what were called Depreciation and Donation Lands that were used to attempt to pay off debts to soldiers and other participants in the Revolutionary War.

- **Circa 1772** – The earliest recorded permanent white settlers in the county were established on King's Creek and Raccoon Creek (now Hanover Township) by Levi Dungan and others. Dungan brought two slaves with him from Philadelphia named Fortune and Lunn and who remained in his service until they died. A part of Dungan's original farm is now the Ponderosa golf course. Mary Dungan became one of the first medical practitioners in the county although she was not formally trained, Mary had Studied medicine with Dr. Benjamin Rush and brought her library over the mountains with her. **6(106, 107)**

- **1772** – Missionary David McClure visited Friedenstadt (a Moravian mission set up for Christianized Native Americans) and wrote a diary. **2(423)**

- **1772/1773** – The George Baker family settled in present-day Center Township. **21(Chronology), 2(148-149), 21(70)**

- **1773** – Westmoreland County was established with the county seat at Hanna's Town, including future south side Beaver County. **21(Chronology)**

- **April 13, 1773** – Friedenstadt was abandoned and the mission and followers were moved to Gnadenhutten and Schoenbrun Villages in the Tuscarawas Valley in present day Ohio. **2(425)**

- **April 19, 1775** – The Revolutionary War began with the battles of Lexington and Concord.

- **1776** – The George Baker family was captured by Indians and sold to the British garrison in Detroit where they were held as prisoners of war until 1777. **21(Chronology)**

- **1776** – The Thomas Moore family settled in present-day Greene Township. **21(Chronology)**

Strolling Through Time: A Chonology of Beaver County, PA History to 2016

🍂 **1776** – The Virginia County of Yohogania, District of West Augusta was erected, including south side of Beaver County. The county seat was at Fort Dunmore (Pittsburgh). **21(Chronology)**

🍂 **1778** – General Edward Hand marched through Beaver County on the "Squaw Campaign." **21(Chronology)**

White's Mill – BCHRLF Collection

🍂 **October 8, 1778** – During the Revolutionary War, General Lachlan McIntosh officially moved his Western Department headquarters from Fort Pitt to Fort McIntosh. Fort McIntosh became the first United States military post built on the north or "Indian" side of the Ohio River. The fort was built under the supervision of a military engineer named Le Chevalier De Cambrary. **46(24), 2(86)**

🍂 **1778** – A supply road named after Colonel Daniel Brodhead was built between Forts Pitt and McIntosh. **2(86,237), 6(126)**

🍂 **1778/1779** – The David Kerr family settled at the head of King's Creek. (It is now Hanover Twp.). **21(Chronology)**

🍂 **1779** – The first land patent in what is now Beaver County was issued by the state of Virginia and signed by then Governor Thomas Jefferson to Robert Rutherford. It was located near present day Hookstown and consisted of 1,300 acres of land. **(NOTE: both Pennsylvania and Virginia claimed this area at the time.) 94(22)**

🍂 **1779** – William Anderson, while living along Raccoon Creek, was shot and wounded by Indians while building a calf pen. Bleeding profusely, he ran to Beeler's Blockhouse several miles away. Meanwhile, his wife and infant child hid in the cornfields until night and escaped to the blockhouse. Mr. Anderson recovered and lived a long life. **9(93)**

August 31, 1779 – The formerly disputed Pennsylvania/Virginia boundary was resolved and the state lines were permanently established. **2(139ff)**

Before 1780 – Thomas White built a three story grist mill on Raccoon Creek near the mouth of Potato Garden Run. White's mill marked the boundary with Washington County in 1800 and became part of the Village of Murdocksville. Apparently, the burrs for the mill were quarried from the Seine River in France. It was the oldest mill in what is now Beaver County. This huge log structure stood until 1950 when it was "carted away" and only ruins remain. **50(138-139), 2(289), 100(124)**

1780 – The Pennsylvania legislature passed a law for the gradual end to slavery in the state. The law prohibited importing slaves into the state and any children born to slaves were to be emancipated when they reached the age of 28. In 1800 there were four slaves in the county; In 1810 there were eight and in 1820 there were five. By 1830 all slaves in the county had been liberated. **2(NOTE 2, page 152; Dr. Bausman uses the incorrect date of 1790 for this law)**

1780 – Sam Brady's rescue of Jennie Stoops from the Indians. **21(Chronology)**

1780 – An Indian massacre happened on Raccoon Creek. The Foulkes family was attacked at their sugar camp on a tributary called Reardon's Run. **21(Chronology)**

July, 1780 – Thirty Wyandot Indians crossed the Ohio River five miles below Fort McIntosh and killed four out of five men reaping in a field, taking the fifth prisoner. Captain McIntyre's company from the fort pursued and attacked the Indians, killing and wounding many, and recapturing the prisoner. **9(89)**

1781 – Washington County was erected, including south side of future Beaver County. **21(Chronology)**

1781 – Andrew Poe's legendary battle with the Indian "Bigfoot" happened on the Ohio River bank near Tomlinson's Run in Virginia (present day West Virginia). **21(Chronology), 19(201)**

1782 – George McElhaney, Indian scout, settled in present-day Independence Twp. **21(Chronology)**

March 12, 1783 – The Pennsylvania Legislature set apart lands north and west of the Ohio and Allegheny Rivers for the purpose of redeeming Depreciation Certificates issued to the troops to cover the runaway inflation of Continental currency. **2(182), 8(205), 9(143)**

🍂 **September 3, 1783** – The Revolutionary War ended with the signing of the Treaty of Paris.

Point of Beginning – Courtesy Brenda Applegate

🍂 **1784** – The "First American Regiment" took up permanent quarters in Fort McIntosh that would last approximately one year. It was the forerunner of the Third Infantry Regiment (The Old Guard) that today serves as the Presidential honor guard. **46(27)**

🍂 **1784** – Mill Creek Presbyterian Church, the oldest religious institution in the county, was established in present day Greene Township. **NOTE; THE BICENTENNIAL ATLAS PUTS THIS DATE AS 1785. 1(84), 21(100), 2(899)**

🍂 **1784** – In the Treaty of Fort Stanwix, Pennsylvania purchased land from the Six Nations including the north side of future Beaver County. **2(183)**

🍂 **January 21, 1785** – The Treaty of Fort McIntosh with the Delaware, Wyandot, Ottawa and Chippewa nations opened up the Northwest Territory for settlement. **21(Chronology)**

🍂 **Summer, 1785** – Depreciation & Donation Lands surveys were underway. **2(1227)**

🍂 **August 23, 1785** – The "Point of Beginning" was established on the north bank of the Ohio River on the border of Pennsylvania for use in surveying all lands in the Northwest Territories. The original marker is now covered by the Ohio River. **19(67-68)**

🍂 **1785** – Virginia (now West Virginia) and Pennsylvania sent a joint survey team to mark the permanent north-south boundary line between the states which came to be known as the "Ellicott Line" that ended at the Ohio River. The leaders of the survey team were David Rittenhouse from PA and Andrew Ellicott from VA, but the boundary has become known historically as the "Ellicott Line." Stones were placed at intervals along the boundary line and one was placed on the border just west of present

Pennsylvania-Virginia Border 1785 – Courtesy Brenda Applegate

day Georgetown where it resides today. The Stone was stolen in 1960 and recovered and returned in 1976 by Jack Lanam of the East Liverpool Historical Society. **109("How History was Stolen," Saturday December 5, 1987)**

September 30, 1785 – Thomas Hutchins began the first survey of U.S. public lands at the "Point of Beginning" on the north bank of the Ohio River where it crosses the western border of Pennsylvania. This point was established on August 23, 1785, for use in measuring all lands in the Northwest Territory. **12(2), 19(68)**

January 25, 1786 – Three deserters from Fort McIntosh were captured, returned to the fort and shot in front of a firing squad. They were buried in what is now the northwest park in Beaver, making it the first cemetery in what was to become the town of Beaver. **NOTE: the article claimed this as the first graveyard in the county, but that is highly unlikely with settler cemeteries around. 25("First Cemetery was at McIntosh," August 25, 1959),** *See entry for March 14, 1814*

1786 – Surveyors Andrew Porter and Andrew Ellicott extended the north-south Virginia (now Ohio) – Pennsylvania border line north from the Ohio River, thus completing the establishment of the permanent state border line. **2(142)**

1786 – James Moore, the earliest settler on the east side of the Beaver River, established a ferry on the Beaver River in present-day Rochester Township. **21(149)**

1786 – Hanover Township was incorporated as a township in Washington County and transferred to Beaver County upon its establishment in 1800. **21(102)**

1786 – Benoni Dawson built a settler fort on the site of present-day Georgetown. **2(171)**

1787 – The town of Montmorin was surveyed (in what is now Harmony Township) by Isaac Melchior but never developed or settled. It was the earliest town site in the county. During a 1776 meeting of the Continental Congress, Isaac Melchior stood in front of the assemblage and proceeded to "damn" both the Continental Congress and its President, John Hancock for only offering him a Captain's commission when he believed that he deserved a higher rank. Later called back before Congress to answer for his conduct, Melchior, apologized but claimed not to remember having behaved as charged. After purchasing several Depreciation lots, Melchior laid out the plan for a town called "Montmorin" on the site of former Logstown. The proposed town was named after French Minister of Foreign Affairs, Count Montmorin, who as a child was a playmate of the King of France. Due to economic issues and Melchior's untimely death, the town was never built and the land was eventually sold to the Harmony Society in 1824 which built its own town on the site. **21(Chronology), 49("Beaver County's Depreciation Land Owners" Vol. 40 No. 2, Spring, 2015)**

1788 – Allegheny County was erected; included north side of Beaver County, and in 1789 part of the south side as well. **21(Chronology)**

1789 – Fort McIntosh was abandoned and the garrison was withdrawn to a new blockhouse built at the present site of New Brighton on a small stream emptying into the Beaver River known as "Blockhouse Run." **1(114), 4(13), 6(121), 9(87), 2(114)**

November 17, 1789 – Major General Samuel H. Parsons drowned in the Beaver River rapids several miles above the Big Beaver Blockhouse while returning from an expedition to purchase land in the Western Reserve. Formerly from Connecticut, Parsons participated in many of the major battles of the Revolutionary War. He also served on the military board which tried British Major John André and sentenced him to death. Following the Revolution, Parsons was well known on the frontier as the first judge of the Northwest Territory and officer of the Ohio Company. Parson's badly decomposed body was found six months later and buried along the river bank near the blockhouse. **2(Appendix IX, pgs. 1271-1278)**

1790 – Service United Presbyterian Church was founded. After Mill Creek Presbyterian Church, it was one of the oldest of any denomination in the county. **21(Chronology), 2(915), 4(485)**

1790 – First King's Creek United Presbyterian Church was founded in Frankfort. **21(Chronology)**

March, 1790 – Mary Colvin and her infant were the last victims of the last Indian attack in Beaver County. They are buried in Swearingen Cemetery, Hanover Township. **21(Chronology), 2(166),** *See entry for 1792-James Clark.*

September 28, 1791 – The Pennsylvania Legislature authorized the governor to direct the Surveyor-General to survey two hundred acres of land in town lots, near the mouth of the Beaver Creek (now River) along with one thousand acres adjoining. **2(614)**

1791 – The murder of an Indian party occurred at the Big Beaver Blockhouse Trading Post (present-day New Brighton) by Captain Sam Brady and his men. **21(Chronology)**

1792 – James Clark, who built the first house in the village of Smith's Ferry, was killed by Indians and was the first person buried in the graveyard at Georgetown. **(NOTE: There is an apparent contradiction here with the murder of Mary Colvin in 1790 being claimed by Dr. Bausman as the last Indian murder in the county. Although in this case, there is no mention of where Clark was killed. Warner lists him as the FIRST white man killed in the county, but uses 1792 as the date which cannot be correct.) 2(932), 9(585),** *See entry for March, 1790*

April 3, 1792 – Pennsylvania passed the "Land Act" which provided for the sale of vacant public lands to persons who would "cultivate, improve, and settle the same, or cause the same...[to be done]." **2(186)**

Strolling Through Time: A Chonology of Beaver County, PA History to 2016

- **April, 1792** – The earliest settlements north of the Ohio River included those of Nicholas Dawson, a brother of Benoni Dawson of Georgetown, and Neal McLaughlin, who started settlements on the north side of the Ohio River about four miles back from the river and west of the Beaver River. William Foulkes is thought to have made an early settlement in what is now Ohioville between Salem Church and the Little Beaver. Benoni Dawson was also known to have begun improvements north of the Ohio at about that same time. **21(Chronology), 2(41,168)**

- **November, 1792** – General Anthony Wayne established Legion Ville near the former Logstown site to begin training his troops for war against the Indians. It was the first training camp for the United States Army. **1(129), 11(65ff)**

- **November, 1792** – Surveyor Daniel Leet laid out the town of Beavertown (later called Beaver). **9(275)**

- **1793** – General Anthony Wayne's army left on its western campaign which ended at the battle of Fallen Timbers. *See entry for August 20, 1794.* **21(Chronology)**

- **January 13, 1793** – Benoni Dawson laid out the town of Georgetown. It was incorporated as a borough in 1850. **21(97)**

- **March 5, 1793** – The first non-permanent Freemasonry lodge existed in the county as early as this date when the Grand Lodge of Pennsylvania granted Warrant #58 to a number of officers and men camping at Legion Ville. The Warrant itself was thought to be lost during the battle of Fallen Timbers. **52(23)**

- **March 12, 1793** – The legislature of Pennsylvania passed a law opening up for sale and settlement the lands lying north of the Ohio River, which were formerly known as the Depreciation and Donation Lands. **9(404)**

- **April, 1793** – A soldier was shot at Legionville for conspiring to rob and murder two paymasters. **126(No Title, April 27, 1793)**

- **1793** – James McGuire became the first Catholic settler in the county when he settled on a large tract of land immediately north of present-day New Brighton. He built one of the largest log cabins ever erected in Beaver County. **2(414)**

- **1793** – Big Beaver Blockhouse was abandoned. **21(Chronology)**

- **1793** – Mt. Carmel Presbyterian Church was established in White Oak Flats (present-day New Sheffield). **56(15), 5(486)**

- **July 2, 1793** – First sale of lots in the Beaver Reserved Tract began and continued until August 12, 1793. Ninety lots were sold. The very first lot sold was on the northwest corner of River Road and Market Streets to Alexander Wright for $16.33. **46(38)**

- **April 21, 1794** – Founded by Dr. John Anderson, Service Theological Seminary (Eudolphia Hall) became the first seminary west of the Allegheny Mountains and only the second in the nation at that time. It was located in southern Beaver County near Service Creek Church. **1(79), 6(125), 15(5)**

- **August 20, 1794** – U.S. Army troops commanded by General Anthony Wayne defeated a large force of Indians at Fallen Timbers (Toledo, Ohio) greatly reducing the threat of further attacks against settlers on the frontier. **2(130), 11(113), 17(395)**

- **1795** – Early Little Beaver settlers George Foulks, Samuel McCaskey and John Hughes make the first mention of "candle (Cannel) coal for lights in place of candles." Cannel Coal burned hotter and gave off more and much brighter light than regular coal. This was the same area where Tannacharison had his hunting camp in 1752. **19(136)**

- **August 3, 1795** – The Treaty of Greenville (Ohio) with the Shawnee and Wyandot Indians marked the pacification of the frontier. This treaty allowed safe settlement of lands north of the Ohio River. **2(192), 8(203), 11(114)**

- **1796** – One of the earliest teachers in the territory that is now Beaver County was John Bean who taught two years near the mouth of Beaver Creek (River). **2(401)**

- **1796** – The first Methodist religious convocation in Beaver County was held at the James Powers home in what is now present day Chippewa. *See entry for 1810.* **91(79)**

- **1797** – The Mount Pleasant Presbyterian Church was founded in present-day Darlington. It was first mentioned in the records of the Ohio Presbytery, and this date was accepted as its date of establishment since the actual date was lost in time. **2(818), 21(Chronology), 1(75)**

- **1797** – Foulkes Mill was established on Little Beaver Creek by George Foulkes, who was a one-time Indian hostage and later served under Captain Sam Brady; later known as Watts Mill (in present-day South Beaver Township). **21(Chronology)**

- **1797** – Ennion Williams, an agent for the Pennsylvania Population Company, began selling land at Beaver Creek. **51(6)**

- **1798** – New Salem Presbyterian Church was founded in present-day Ohioville. **21(Chronology)**

- **Ca. 1799** – John Wolf established a flour mill on the east bank of the Beaver River at the middle falls (present day New Brighton), and David Townsend erected a saw mill at the lower falls (present day Fallston). **(NOTE: BAUSMAN PUTS THE DATE FOR THE TOWNSEND MILL AT 1800.) 2(701ff), 4(87), 6(121), 2(727)**

1799 – The Rev. Francis Reno, an Episcopal minister from Washington County, became one of the earliest settlers in Rochester and the first Episcopal clergyman west of the Allegheny Mountains. His cabin was located just below the spot on which the Passavant Memorial Hospital was built. **2(736), 9(231), 5(491)**

III. Creating Beaver County 1800 to 1829

Beaver County as we know it today didn't exist until March 12, 1800 when it was formed from parts of Allegheny and Washington counties and was divided into six townships, few of which we would recognize today. The Borough of Beaver, then called Beavertown, had been surveyed nearly eight years earlier by Colonel Daniel Leet and was designated by the State of Pennsylvania as our county seat.

Several events of national importance occurred during this era of our history. Meriwether Lewis and the Corps of Discovery passed through our county in the very early stages of their trek across the country. Former Vice President Aaron Burr had a flotilla of boats built in Bridgewater to transport men down the Ohio River in support of his western conspiracy. Also, the War of 1812 roused local patriots to form militia companies that aided in the defense of the key lake port of Erie.

Meanwhile, various churches and communities were established and the seeds of early industry were planted along the Beaver River. With the rise of these first industries, many of our towns were laid out to attract a supply of labor. The German Communal Harmony Society (aka the Harmonists) moved into the county to found their final home in what is present-day Ambridge. They brought with them knowledge, expertise, and a strong work ethic, which resulted in industries that prospered and helped the county to grow.

- **Ca. 1800** – Dr. Samuel Adams settled at the upper falls of the Beaver River (Eastvale), most likely becoming the earliest physician to practice in the county. **2(371)**

- **1799/1800** – Miss Electa Smith opened the first school to charge tuition in Beavertown. Her school was built of timber from Fort McIntosh. **2(401-402)**

- **March 12, 1800** – Pennsylvania established Beaver County from parts of Allegheny and Washington Counties. The 14th Section of this act appointed Jonathan Coulter, Joseph Hemphill and Denny McClure Trustees of Beaver County. The six original townships established within the county were First Moon, Hanover, North Beaver, Second Moon, Sewickley and South Beaver. **2(193, 863), 6(106), 8(214)**

- **1800** – There were four slaves living in the county. **2(152 note)**

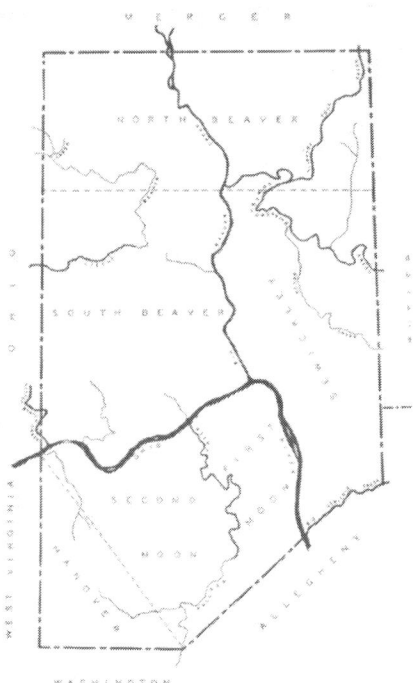

Beaver County Original Townships – 1976 Bicentennial Atlas

Strolling Through Time: A Chonology of Beaver County, PA History to 2016

🦫 **1800** – St. Luke's Protestant Episcopal Church was organized in Georgetown. **2(836)**

🦫 **1800** – Frankfort opened the first post office in the county which operated between 1800 -1900. **2(832)**

🦫 **Early 1800's** – Dr. Samuel Adams built the first Eastvale Dam to power a gristmill, sawmill and forge. **1(22)**

🦫 **1800** – Population of Beaver County was 5,776. **2(275), 3(50), 8(215)**

🦫 **Ca. 1801** – Daugherty Cemetery was established as the first Roman Catholic cemetery in the county. **2(1034)**

🦫 **1801** – New Sewickley Township was formed from Sewickley Township. **21(132)**

🦫 **1801** – North Sewickley Township was formed from Sewickley Township. Ezekial and Hanna Jones are said to be the earliest settlers in North Sewickley Township arriving from New Jersey in 1801. **2(957)**

🦫 **1801** – Hoopes, Townsend & Co. set up a water powered sawmill near the site of the present Patterson Dam at Beaver Falls. **1(28)**

🦫 **November 14. 1801** – The first Baptist church in the county, Providence Baptist Church, was established in present North Sewickley Township. **1(40), 6(120), 2(957), 5(489)**

🦫 **March 29, 1802** – Town of Beaver or "Beavertown" was incorporated as a borough. It had been surveyed by Daniel Leet in 1792, and was confirmed by an act of assembly in 1793. Beavertown became our county seat in 1800 upon the formation of the county. **6(108), 8(434)**

Greersburg Academy - Courtesy Charles Townsend

🦫 **1802** – Greersburg Academy in Darlington was established by the Erie Presbytery, becoming the first academy west of the Alleghenies. William McGuffey, author of the McGuffey readers, was the most famous student. **1(12), 8(397), 6(122), 19(160)**

🦫 **1802** – The River Hotel in Georgetown was built by Thomas Foster and was licensed as a tavern in 1805. It is believed to be the oldest public building in the county. It is now a private residence. **1(87)**

- **March 18, 1803** – The first will recorded in the county was made by George Riddle **2(178)**

- **August 19, 1803** – The first deed recorded in the county was for Lot #74 at McIntosh (Beaver) for $150 by Joseph and Mary Pentecost to merchants Wilson, Porter and Fulton. **2(198).**

- **September 2 to 4, 1803** – Meriwether Lewis and the Corps of Discovery traversed Beaver County via the Ohio River on their way to explore the Louisiana Purchase. **18(2-5)**

- **1803** – Jesse Moore was appointed the first President Judge in the Sixth District, including Beaver County. **2(195)**

- **1803** – Messrs. Hoopes, Townsend & Co. erected the second building in Sharon for Isaac Wilson for general merchandising purposes. It was known as the "Old Red Front." The first building was erected by Major Robert Darragh for use as a place of public entertainment and boarding for the managers who built Aaron Burr's boats for his expedition. **9(503-504)**

- **1803** – William Henry became the first county sheriff; James Allison, district attorney; Guion Greer, first treasurer; David Johnson, first prothonotary – a position which included register and recorder; Ezekial Jones was the first coroner. **2(196-198)**

- **February 6, 1804** – First county court was held on the upper floor of a building on Third Street in Beavertown (present day Beaver) owned by Abner Lacock. Court was presided over by Judge Jesse Moore. **2(202, 195)**

- **1804** – Pugh family established a flour mill in what is now Fallston. **2(727)**

- **May 13, 1804** – Abner Lacock laid out the present town of Darlington. **21(76)**

- **1805** – Ohio Township was formed from part of South Beaver Township. It was incorporated as a borough (Ohioville) in 1960. **21(136)**

- **1805 – 1806** – Aaron Burr arranged for construction of a flotilla on the west bank of the Beaver River in support of his conspiracy to establish a western empire. **2(770ff), 11(137)**

- **1806** – Thomas Ashe, an Englishman visiting the county, tested some of the oil from a spring on the Ohio River nearly opposite Georgetown and predicted its profitable production in this county. This was 53 years before Edwin Drake drilled his famous oil well in Titusville. **2(287)**

- **1806** – Isaac Wilson & Co. laid out a town plot for what was to become Beaver Falls (formerly the Brighton District of Brighton Township) and began lot sales. The actual survey was made by the Constable brothers from Brighton, England, and they were allowed to name it after their hometown. When the Harmony Society took over the town site in 1866, they renamed it Beaver Falls. **21(60)**

- **1806** – The first school that opened in Patterson Township was taught by two Quaker ladies, Mary Reeves and Mary Townsend, and it occupied an old log house near the site of Patterson Block. **9(588)**

- **1807** – The Little Beaver Congregation of the Reformed Presbyterian Church was organized about one mile from New Galilee. **9(590)**

- **November 4, 1807** – The *Minerva* was the first known newspaper published in the county. It was published every Saturday in the town of Beaver by John Berry. **2(454)**

- **November 5, 1807** – The first trial for murder in Beaver County occurred when Nathaniel Eakin was charged with the shooting death of James Hamilton. He was acquitted by a jury. **2(356-357)**

- **1808** – Wilson, Barker & Gregg built an iron blast furnace along the Beaver River at the point of Beaver Falls. **2(667), 8(304)**

- **1808** – David Townsend erected a mill in what is now Fallston to produce linseed oil and also a mill to spin cotton. **2(727)**

- **1810** – The second county courthouse was built in Beaver. It was two stories of white painted brick and was topped by a twenty foot bell tower. After the completion of the courthouse, the building was also used as a place of worship by Presbyterian and other denominations until their churches were built. In 1840 an east wing was added, and in 1848 a west wing was added to the structure. **5(212), 2(202), 46(44), 2(645)**

- **1810** – The first physician to practice on the southside of Beaver County was a Dr. McCullough in Georgetown. His practice did not make enough money for him to survive on it alone, so he began running a tavern on the side. **94(50)**

- **1810** – A major flood hit the county causing widespread damage. It was also known as a "pumpkin flood" similar to the future flood of 1832, since it occurred in the fall and hundreds of pumpkins could be seen floating in the rivers. **58(67)**

- **1810** – "Old Stone" Methodist Church, was built in present-day Chippewa on the Thomas Stratton farm. The church was originally founded by Abraham Powers and his home served as the meeting house

beginning in 1796. It was considered the oldest Methodist Church north of the Ohio River and the first on the "Mother Circuit" or Shenango Circuit. In 1857, it became the Chippewa United Methodist Church at its present location. **1(30), (http://www.chippewaumc.org/about/our-history), 91(79)**

- **1810** – The population of the county was 12,165. **2(275), 3(50)**

- **1812** – Greene Township was formed from parts of Hanover and Second Moon Townships. **21(100)**

- **1812** – Hopewell Township was formed from a part of First Moon Township. **21(110)**

- **June 18, 1812** – The War of 1812 began when Congress declared War on England.

- **July, 1812** – Four Mile United Presbyterian Church was organized and met in the woods of George Barclay. The first services were held by the Rev. David Imbrie. **9(579)**

- **November 4, 1812** – St. James' Lodge in Beaver became the first Masonic Lodge physically established in Beaver County. This lodge dissolved about 1837 and was replaced by Rochester Lodge #229 on April 11, 1848. **52(23-27)**

- **1813** – General Abner Lacock was elected to the United States Senate. **2(323)**

- **1813** – During the War of 1812, Commodore Oliver Hazard Perry's Great Lakes fleet was rigged with rope produced by William Quinn's Rope Walk located in Phillipsburg (now Monaca). The rope was made from flax grown locally in the county, and Perry bought it all and sent it north by ox team. William Quinn supervised all of the work and was present at the battle. Perry went on to beat the British fleet at the Battle of Lake Erie. **19(135), 60(May 25, 1940, pg. 10)**

- **June 8, 1813** – The *Beaver Gazette* was started by Andrew Logan. **2(455)**

- **August 1, 1813** – The first settler in what is now Monaca was considered to be a Polish nobleman named Francis Helvedi. Helvedi was exiled from Poland and here bred and raised Merino sheep. **2(797, 797 Note 1)**

- **January, 1814** – During the War of 1812, the county had formed eight militia companies consisting of 587 officers and men. All of those companies marched by way of Meadville and served a tour of duty at Erie during the months of January, February and March of the very severe winter in 1814. **2(481)**

- **January 21, 1814** – A charter was approved for a toll bridge at Wolf Lane in Beaver to be built over the Beaver River to Rochester. The bridge was completed by 1816, and was blown down by a severe wind in 1821. It was re-built in 1826 and swept away in the flood of 1884. **2(241), 5(75)**

March 14, 1814 – The (old) Beaver Cemetery was established by an act of Assembly in the northwest public square (Clark Square on Fifth and Buffalo Streets). The first burial in this graveyard was Rev. Ezekiel Glasgow, the first pastor of the Presbyterian Church of Beaver in April, 1814. The present Beaver Cemetery was opened on August 15, 1866. **2(659-660),** *See entry for January 25, 1786*

March 21, 1814 – The Bank of Beaver was incorporated by an act of the Pennsylvania Assembly. **2(665), 8(304)**

1814 – Bassenheim Furnace was built in Franklin Township by Baron Detmar Basse and John Glasser. It was the second iron furnace built in the county, and lasted until 1824. **1(35), 6(120)**

1814 – St. Luke's Episcopal Church was organized in Georgetown, the first Episcopal Church in the county. **5(491)**

December 24, 1814 – The War of 1812 ended with the signing of the Treaty of Ghent.

November 11, 1815 – A wooden truss toll bridge over the Beaver River was opened between Brighton (lower Beaver Falls) with New Brighton becoming one of the earliest bridges over a large stream in western Pennsylvania. It was torn down in 1900 and replaced by a modern steel bridge by the Penn Bridge Company. **2(239), 4(167), 8(239)**

1816 – Brighton Township was formed from South Beaver and Ohio Townships. The name came from Brighton, England. **21(68)**

1816 – Chippewa Township was established when the original South Beaver Township was split into four parts. **21(72, 153)**

1817 – The James Nelson house was built in Hookstown, Greene Township. It was considered the first Underground Railroad station encountered when entering Beaver County from the south. **19(30)**

April 11, 1818 – The first post office in Brighton (Beaver Falls) was established in John Dickey's store. **44(29)**

May 9, 1818 – N.B.F. McBeats opened a store in Frankfort, Hanover Township on the road between Georgetown and the Cross Roads where he was selling China, groceries, coffee, tea, chocolate and a variety of spices. **128("A Large and General Assortment....," May 26, 1818)**

September 1, 1818 – James Logan began publication of the *Western Argus*. **2(456-459)**

Strolling Through Time: A Chonology of Beaver County, PA History to 2016

- **May 6, 1819** – James Nicholson, a farmer in Big Beaver, deeded his land to his three slaves (Pompey Frazier, Tamar Frazier and Betty Mathers) to be conveyed to them upon the deaths of him and his wife. Betty, the remaining heir, sold the land in 1872 and the greater part of New Galilee was built upon it. **9(154)**

- **Early 1820's** – John Boles established perhaps the first boatyard in the county on the Beaver River at Bolesville (Pulaski Township) for building flatboats, keelboats and finally steamboats. **2(296)**

- **Ca. 1820's** – James Beach Clow, a prominent abolitionist and brother-in-law of John Brown of Harper's Ferry fame, built his house in North Sewickley Township. The house served as a station on the Underground Railroad, and it was listed on the National Register of Historic Places in 1989. **1(37)**

- **March 28, 1820** – The Borough of Greersburg (present day Darlington) was incorporated. It was originally named "Greersburg" after George Greer who owned part of the land used for the borough, and the name was changed to "Darlington" on April 6, 1830 because of the confusion of names with the town of Greensburg and the subsequent problems with accurately sending and receiving mail. Greersburg/Darlington had once been an important stagecoach stop between Pittsburgh and Cleveland. **21(76), 2(811)**

- **1820** – John Roberts of Hanover Township brought two slaves, Henry and Henley Webster with him when he arrived from Fauquier County, Virginia, and they remained with him for many years. **9(154)**

- **1820** – The U.S. Census reports the county population totaled 15,340. **2(275), 3(50), 8(316)**

- **1820/1821** – The earliest Methodist congregation in Sharon (now Bridgewater) was established, utilizing a small frame church on land which they didn't own. They eventually merged with the Bridgewater Methodist group. **2(445)**

- **1822** – Stephen Phillips and Charles Graham purchased land from the Harmonists and established a boat building operation in Phillipsburg. In 1892, the town would be renamed "Monaca." **2(297)**

- **1825** – Having relocated from Harmony, Indiana, the German communal Harmony Society established the village of Economy at the present site of Ambridge. **2(292)**

- **Spring, 1826** – Merchant Sea Captain William Vicary began construction of his mansion in present-day Freedom, and finally completed it in 1829. **(bchrlf.org)**

Strolling Through Time: A Chonology of Beaver County, PA History to 2016

Captain William Vicary Mansion – BCHRLF Collection

🖋 **April 10, 1826** – By an act of the Pennsylvania Assembly, the Methodist Episcopal Church in Beaver was given a grant of land to establish itself on the southeast section of the public square. **2(649)**

🖋 **Ca. 1827** – St. John's Lutheran Church was built by the Harmony Society (present day Ambridge) and was used as their principle place of worship until the society dissolved in 1905. **47(69)**

🖋 **1827** – The Rocky Spring United Presbyterian Congregation of New Galilee was organized. **9(590)**

🖋 **1828** – David Townsend laid out the town of New Brighton in anticipation of the new canal to be built along the Beaver River by the state. **21(125)**

🖋 **1828** – David Townsend built a flour mill on the bank of the Beaver River in New Brighton near present day Fifth Street. **57(10)**

🖋 **1828** – The Townsend Company relocated to present-day Fallston from Pittsburgh where it became one of the first industrial enterprises. The company at one time produced over 20,000 different types of fasteners. It was founded in 1816, and grew to twelve plants in the United States and Canada. It closed in the 1970's. **1(70), 57(11)**

🖋 **1829** – James Patterson built a dam across the Beaver River (current Patterson Dam) to run his flour and cotton mills. **1(31), 2(668)**

🖋 **1829** – Fallston Borough was established from a part of Brighton Township. **2(279)**

🖋 **1829** – The name of Beavertown was shortened to "Beaver." **2(662)**

🖋 **1829** – President Andrew Jackson stopped at Stone's Point in present-day Bridgewater on his way to his inauguration in Washington, D.C. **58(18)**

🖋 **1829** – Archibald Robertson built a steam paper mill in Brighton (now Beaver Falls) which manufactured an excellent quality of printing and wall paper until 1849. Realizing that water power was more economical, he built a second mill at the head of the falls. **2(668)**

- **June 25, 1829** – The first Fallston Post Office was established with Hall Wilson as postmaster. **2(732)**

- **August 15, 1829** – A meeting of the citizens of Hanover and Greene Townships who were opposed to Freemasonry, was held at the house of Thomas McGuire. This was in response to an anti-Masonic movement that was sweeping the country at the time. **9(251-252)**

IV. Early Industrial Period 1830 to 1860

Great changes occurred during this period, causing county growth to move forward at a rapid pace. Canals were being built and replacing the slower wagons as a quicker and more efficient way to move both freight and passengers across the county. The canals, however, had their own drawbacks, as they were expensive to build, maintain, and keep open during the winter and times of low water. The coming of the railroads signaled the end of the canal era, since freight and passengers could be moved at an even greater pace and helped to accelerate industrial and population growth.

In addition, early bridges were being built and the infrastructure for greater growth was being put into place. Education became important as schools and academies were established to give both male and female students more than just a rudimentary education.

During this time, the institution of slavery was a controversial national issue and became a topic which galvanized abolitionist sentiment among our citizens. Beaver County had a large anti-slavery contingency, and people banded together at great risk to themselves to hold abolitionist conventions and to form and operate various stations on the "Underground Railroad" which helped many slaves escape to freedom.

- **Ca. 1830** – Edward McGinnis developed Frankfort Mineral Springs into a health resort and built a large three story hotel called the "Frankfort House" which closed in 1912. Raccoon Creek State Park purchased the springs area in the early 1960's. **50(13-20)**

- **1830s** – Gertrude Rapp, granddaughter of George Rapp head of the Harmony Society, became head of the society's silk mill. She was the first to introduce the use of freezing silk cocoons to kill the larvae. Harmonist mills produced very high quality silk under her guidance.

- **1830** – Beaver County Associate Judge John H. Reddick, a well-known eccentric passed away and asked to be buried astride the line between Pennsylvania and Virginia (now West Virginia). According to legend, he asked to be interred that way so that the Devil wouldn't be able to locate him. Following the Civil War when that part of Virginia became West Virginia the state lines were re-surveyed, and his tomb was found to have been located wholly in Pennsylvania. It is unknown whether or not the Devil finally caught up with him. In 1987, his grave was vandalized and repaired by volunteers. **19(229), 33("Judge's Gravesite Repaired," October 1, 1987)**

- **Ca. 1830** – St. Paul's Episcopal Church was organized at Fairview in Ohio Township (Present Ohioville) to accommodate people who could not attend church at Georgetown. **9(585)**

Strolling Through Time: A Chonology of Beaver County, PA History to 2016

- **1830** – The oldest commercial brickyard in the county was established on Oak Hill (New Brighton) near the entrance to present St. Joseph's Cemetery. **2(709)**

- **1830** – The Georgetown Methodist Episcopal Church was formed in Georgetown. **9(563)**

- **1830** – St. John African Methodist Episcopal Church in Bridgewater was established. It was the oldest African-American church in the county. In 1868 members of this church who lived in New Brighton formed Wayman Chapel A.M.E. Church. **2(778), 5(496), 58(61)**

- **1830** – The first school building in Chippewa Township was erected by private subscriptions. **9(587)**

- **1830** – County population had grown to 24, 183. **2(275), 3(50)**

- **Prior to 1831** – William Grimshaw, a noted historian and the author of a series of popular histories of the United States and of several European countries, was an early landowner near present-day Homewood. He apparently never lived there, but in 1831, he sold land to Joseph M. Smith who, in turn, laid out the borough of Homewood. **2(927)**

- **1831** – Darlington post office was established. **2(823)**

- **July 26, 1831** – Ground was broken for the Beaver Division of the Pennsylvania Canal, by Revolutionary War soldiers and a great celebration was held in a grove opposite Fallston. The canal originally extended from Rochester to New Castle, and the cost was over $500,000. **2(246-248), 4(87)**

- **1832** – A major flood hit the county that was so devastating that it completely washed away the Darragh and Stow Foundry in Sharon. It was also known as a "pumpkin flood" since it occurred in the fall and hundreds of pumpkins could be seen floating in the rivers. Stone Island in the Beaver River below Bridgewater dam was almost entirely washed away. **2(9), 58(67)**

- **1832** – Joseph Pugh began manufacturing window sash in Fallston under the name of Pugh & Bacum's Sash Factory. He later made flour barrels. **2(728)**

- **1832** – Phillips & Graham sold the town of Phillipsburg to seceders from the Harmony Society led by Count Maximilian DeLeon who established the New Philadelphia Society. **1(94), 2(781)**

- **1832** – The Fallston Academy was built for school purposes, but was also open to all denominations for church purposes. In 1897, it was used for a lumber yard run by H.M. Burns. **2(728)**

Ca. 1832 – Douthitt house was built north of Darlington by Joseph Douthitt and served as a stagecoach stop between Cleveland and Pittsburgh. **1(9)**

 March 6, 1832 – St. Peter's Evangelical Church was established in Phillipsburg (Monaca). **(28)**

Boatyard in Freedom – BCHRLF Collection

 May, 1832 – Stephen Phillips & Jonathan Betz laid out the town of Freedom and relocated their boat building business there from Phillipsburg. A number of families relocated from Phillipsburg to Freedom, and it was composed of rude board "shanties" giving the town its unofficial first name of "Shantytown." **2(781-782), 6(114)**

 November 22, 1832 – A fire broke out at Old Economy Village destroying one large barn full of grain, three stables along with their contents, a flax breaking machine and building, three other out buildings and a large quantity of flax. The loss was estimated at $100,000. **120(November 27, 1832, Page 3)**

 1833 – Raccoon Township was formed from parts of Moon and Greene Townships. **21(144)**

 April 24, 1833 – The Beaver County Temperance Society was officially organized to revive and encourage temperance societies where they existed and established them where they did not. **9(244-245)**

 July 4, 1833 – Marcus T. C. Gould from Rome, New York, established the New Brighton Female Seminary "wherein the young ladies were taught all of the useful branches of modern female education." It was chartered in 1840 with Robert Townsend as President. Mr. Gould was the originator of a system of stenography and the inventor of one of the first self-supplying fountain pens. **2(704-705, 738-740),** *See entries for 1836 and October 19, 1860*

 August 10, 1833 – The New Philadelphia Society, comprised of followers of Count Maximillian DeLeon who broke away from the Harmony Society, dissolved in Phillipsburg (Monaca). **55(92)**

 April 1, 1834 – The Pennsylvania assembly passed a bill establishing free public schools. **9(221),** *See Entry for November 4, 1834*

 May 1, 1834 – Dr. James Sloan and Thomas Nicholson opened the Frankfort Springs Academy to prepare male students as teachers. The Academy closed in 1847 and became a private residence. **50(32)**

- **May 28, 1834** – Freight and passenger service on the Beaver Division of the Pennsylvania Canal was opened to New Castle. **4(89), 10(13), 14**

- **July, 1834** – A cholera epidemic broke out in Fallston carried by a steamboat returning from the lower Mississippi. The village was nearly de-populated. The disease returned to the county in both 1845 and 1851. **5(306)**

- **September 27, 1834** – The first school board in Sewickley Township was organized. **9(604)**

- **October 20, 1834** – Smith's Ferry established its first post office with Samuel Smith as postmaster. **2(932)**

- **November, 1834** – The First Presbyterian Church of New Brighton was formed. **9(461)**

- **November 4, 1834** – In accordance with the Act passed by the state legislature on April 1, 1834, to establish free public schools, commissioners from each district held a meeting during which an agreement was made to assess taxes to establish the common public schools in the county. **2(398)** *See Entry for April 1, 1834*

- **1834** – The Frankfort Springs Presbyterian Church was organized. **9(559)**

- **1834** – The North Branch Presbyterian Church was erected in Center Township, which was formerly a part of Moon Township. **9(574)**

- **1834** – The Concord Methodist Episcopal Church in North Sewickley was organized in the house of Thomas Elliott. **9(606-607)**

- **1834** – Tomlinson's Run Presbyterian Church was organized in Greene Township. The first pastor was Reverend Marcus Ormond. **49("Greene Celebrates 200 Years: 1812-1912, Vol. 37, No. 4, Fall, 2012)**

- **1835** – The Beaver School District was formed. It consisted of Beaver, Vanport, Bridgewater and Sharon. **2(644)**

- **1835** – The first public school house in New Brighton was built. The small brick building had seats of rough planks and boards nailed to the wall as writing desks. **2(705-706)**

- **1835** – The Old Brighton Paper Mill Company was founded in Brighton (present-day Beaver Falls) by Robertson, Lee & McElroy and was powered by steam. In 1840 under new owners, the name was changed to the Pittsburgh Wall Paper Company. **2(672)**

Strolling Through Time: A Chonology of Beaver County, PA History to 2016

- **Spring 1835** – A new covered wooden toll bridge was built over the Beaver River at New Brighton, opposite Brighton, replacing the 1815 bridge. **2(240), 4(168)**

- **April 2, 1835** – Bridgewater was established and named for a city in England. It was incorporated in 1868. **2(771)**

- **August 5, 1835** – Dr. E.K. Chamberlain & N.P. Fetterman published the *Fallston & Brighton Gazette*. **2(465-466)**

- **January 28, 1836** – The Greersburg Resolution against slavery was drafted at a meeting at Greersburg Academy. **9(247), 49(Vol. 30 No. 2, Insert page 1)**

- **February 6, 1836** – Townsend, Baird and Company was incorporated. **5(132-134)**

- **July, 1836** – James Dungan opened the Frankfort Springs Hotel on the southern end of Frankfort. It was later sold to the Vance family and renamed the Vance Hotel. **50(29)**

Frankfort Springs Hotel

- **September 14, 1836** – The village of Industry was surveyed by William McCallister. **9(582)**

- **October 1, 1836** - A contract was let for a covered wooden bridge over the Beaver River at Fallston. The bridge opened in 1837 and was swept away by flood on February 6, 1884. **2(242), 4(169)**

- **1836** – Moses Metheny built the Metheny Tavern, a frequent stop for canal travelers, next to the Beaver Division Canal at the mouth of Connoquenessing Creek. **7, 20**

- **1836** – Surveyor Sanford C. Hill laid out Glasgow, and it was incorporated in 1854. Glasgow was to become a canal town on the Sandy and Beaver Canal, but due to low travel, Glasgow never grew much beyond its original small size. **21(99)**

- **1836** – *Morus Multicaulis*, a species of Chinese mulberry tree was introduced into Beaver County in order to raise silkworms. This caused a "boom" in real estate speculation, as land was laid out in lots and sold at exorbitant prices where the mulberry was planted. The plan failed causing the speculators to lose money. **9(262-263),** *See entries for July 4, 1833 and October 19, 1860*

- **1837** – The Beaver County Institute was established in New Brighton with the object of teaching science, literature and natural history. **2(704)**

- **February, 1837** – Captain William Vicary laid out the village of St. Clair, later a part of Freedom, and began selling building lots. **2(795), 24**

- **May 1, 1837** – Richard Leech and his wife opened a second female seminary in New Brighton which taught the English branches (reading, writing and arithmetic), French, Latin and higher mathematics. **2(704-705)**

- **June 29, 1837** – S.S. Peter & Paul Church, the first Roman Catholic Church in Beaver County, was dedicated in Bridgewater on land donated by James Hemphill. The church was dedicated by the Very Reverend Francis Patrick Kenrick, Bishop of Philadelphia, the only bishop in Pennsylvania at the time. **1(68), 2(415), 55(111)**

- **November 30, 1837** – The Beaver County Colonization Society was formed in Beaver to aid the state society to purchase slaves, free them and return them to Africa as colonists. **49(Vol. 30 No. 2, Insert page 1)**

- **December 1, 1837** – The Beaver Falls Colonization Society, an auxiliary to the Pennsylvania Young Men's Colonization Society, was organized in New Brighton. These courageous people helped to establish the "Underground Railway" in Beaver County. (NOTE: Dr. Bausman speaks in generalities, but he most likely means within the county & not the country) and helped slaves to escape to freedom. **2(718)**

- **1837/1838** – The Methodist Episcopal Church was established in New Brighton by Rev. Z.H. Caston. **9(464)**

- **April 16, 1838** – Freedom Borough was incorporated. In 1896, Freedom merged with Vicary Extension and St. Clair. **2(783)**

- **May, 1838** – Town of Baden was laid out by William McCallister on lots #22 and #26 of Depreciation Tract No. 2. Christian Burkhardt, the proprietor, named the town "Baden" for a city and state in Germany. **21(54)**

- **1838** – Borough of New Brighton was incorporated. It was originally laid out by David Townsend in 1828. **2(722), 14**

- **1838** – Jonathan Chapman, also known to history as "Johnny Appleseed" for his efforts at planting apple seeds throughout this area. It was said that his main route was down the Ohio River. He is said to have also landed his canoe at Rochester and walked across country into Ohio over the route which later became the Darlington Road from Fallston to East Palestine, Ohio. In 1838, Johnny Appleseed abandoned this region and moved further west. While staying at a farmer's home near St. Joseph, Indiana, he fell ill and passed away on March 11, 1845. He was buried in Fort Wayne, Indiana. **19(230)**

1838 – The Female Reform Society was founded in New Brighton to oppose licentiousness. It was an auxiliary to the New York Female Moral Reform Society. **19(37)**

1838 – The public school system in the Borough of Beaver was established when two one story buildings were built. **5(255)**

1838 – A group of men in what is now New Brighton formed the Mechanics Fire Company, and were the only firemen in the county at that time. **5(335)**

January 6, 1840 – The first Bible Society was organized in the county with the object of distributing Holy Scriptures without note or comment. **49("Beaver County History: An overview from 1931," Vol. 36 No. 1, Winter, 2011)**

Ca. 1840 – William L. Hamilton established one of the first pottery making industries in the county when he formed the Hamilton Brothers Company in present-day Bridgewater (formerly Sharon). **58(31)**

1840 – County population grew to 29,368. **2(275), 3(50)**

1840 – The New Brighton Female Seminary was chartered and taught Greek, Latin, Hebrew, French and Italian along with music and drawing. **2(704-705)**

1840 – Rochester Township was created from a part of New Sewickley Township, following the development of Rochester Village as a canal and river port. **21(149)**

May 6, 1840 – The Borough of Phillipsburg (Monaca) was incorporated. **2(801), 6(127)**

October 15, 1841 – Patterson Township was formed from Brighton Township and one farm in Fallston. Citizens had petitioned the court to erect their district into a township since it was neither a borough, town or a township. **21(139)**

1842 – The Methodist Episcopal Church was organized in Freedom. **9(530)**

1842 – Sarah Jane Clark moved to New Brighton with her father from Rochester, New York, and in 1844, her first prose appeared in the *New York Mirror* under the pseudonym of "Grace Greenwood." Most sources agree that she most likely adopted the pen name from the Greenwood Institute in New Brighton which she attended. In 1853, she married Leander K. Lippincott and moved to Philadelphia where she became a famous writer and lecturer. **49("Greenwood Institute of New Brighton", Vol. 30 No. 4), 9(448),** *See entries for 1852, October 17, 1853*

Between 1842 &1845 – The first Abolition Society in Chippewa was formed. **2(1143)**

🦫 **May 9, 1843** – The Presbyterian Church was established in Freedom. **9(530)**

🦫 **April 18, 1843** – Hookstown Borough was incorporated. It was named for Matthias Hook, an early settler. It is interesting to note that Hookstown was earlier known as "Nineveh," "Moscow" and "Newton" but the names disappeared and it became known only as "Hookstown." **21(109), 2(826-827), 94(15)**

🦫 **December 15, 1843** – The *Western Star* newspaper was started by Washington Bigler and William Denlinger in Beaver. **2(462)**

🦫 **January 19, 1844** – Beaver Academy was opened for the reception of female students in Beaver. About ten years later, the school was divided, the boys reciting in the Academy building, and the girls in a building in another part of town. The Academy closed about 1867 or 1868. **2(639 - 643)**

Beaver Division Canal through New Brighton – BCHRLF Collection

🦫 **1844** – The Beaver Division Canal was finally extended to Erie. **1(45)**

🦫 **1844** – The Evangelical Association of Freedom was organized. **9(531)**

🦫 **1844** – John and William Bonbright established a starch factory in Rochester and manufactured three grades of starch. **2(746)**

🦫 **1844** – The Town of Frankfort Springs was established in Hanover Township and incorporated in 1847. It had the first post office with a circulating library in the county. **21(91), 1(79)**

🦫 **November 9, 1844** – First Teacher's Association met in Beaver Academy and was preliminary to the formation of a permanent organization. This association was short-lived. **2(401)**

🦫 **March, 1845** – "Hookstown Fever" epidemic broke out in the town of Hookstown and every family except three were infected. It was later diagnosed as "Enteric Fever," a variation of typhoid. **5(306)**

Strolling Through Time: A Chonology of Beaver County, PA History to 2016

- **January 29, 1845** – The First Presbyterian Church of Bridgewater was established as an outgrowth of the Beaver church. **9(512)**

- **November 14, 1845** – The A.M.E. Church of Bridgewater was incorporated. It was later disbanded and its congregation attended the Baptist Church in Rochester. **9(513)**

- **1845** – Marion Township was formed from New Sewickley Township, and named after General Francis Marion, the "Swamp Fox" of the American Revolution. **21(118)**

- **1845** – Squire John Glass started the Globe Fire Brick Works in New Brighton. It later became the A.F. Smith & Co. **9(455-456)**

- **1845/1846** – The North Sewickley Academy was established through the influence of Rev. James S. Henderson and the trustees of the Presbyterian Church of North Sewickley. Classes had been held in a log cabin until the actual building was constructed in 1850. **2(959)**

- **December 21, 1845** – Famous abolitionists Abby Kelly and Stephen Symond Foster (NOT the famous composer Stephen Collins Foster) were married in a Quaker ceremony at the home of fellow abolitionists Milo and Elizabeth Townsend in New Brighton. They were considered by many to have been the "dynamic duo" of abolition and the women's rights movements. **75(39)**

- **Spring, 1846** – In the town of New Philadelphia (formerly Phillipsburg, now Monaca), a man from Ohio named Keil proclaimed himself as Christ and announced that he would be crucified on a certain day. The cross was made and set up on a hillside on the farm of George Frank with a large crowd gathered only to find out that the false Christ had fled to Oregon. **2(800)**

- **1846** – The United Presbyterian Church was organized in Hookstown. **9(565)**

- **1847** – Darlington Township was formed from Little Beaver Township. **21(78)**

- **1847** – Darlington Free Presbyterian Church was founded by Arthur Bullus Bradford over the question of slavery. He was a descendent of William Bradford who arrived on the "Mayflower" in 1620. In 1861, Bradford was appointed by President Lincoln as the United States Consul to the Chinese port of Amoy. Due to an inhospitable climate which caused him health problems, Bradford returned home after about eight months. **2(819, 1149), 9(625-626)**

- **1847** – Future President James Garfield (then a teenage boatman) fell off the "Evening Star" canal boat when it was approaching the locks at Rock Point near Ellwood City, and nearly drowned. **36(12)**

Strolling Through Time: A Chonology of Beaver County, PA History to 2016

- **February 23, 1847** – In response to the great Irish potato famine, Beaver County held a public meeting to take donations for Irish relief. The county shipped 4,366 ½ bushels of corn, 145 barrels of flour, 10 barrels of wheat, 18 ¾ bushels of wheat, 1 barrel barley and 140 barrels of dried corn meal. **9(254-255)**

- **August, 1847** – Abolitionists Frederick Douglass and William Lloyd Garrison spoke at two meetings in New Brighton in the upper storeroom of a general store because the local churches were closed to them. Despite the cramped conditions, the meetings were well attended by several hundred people. **49("Abolitionists and the Underground Railroad," Vol. 30 No 2, Spring 2005), 69(Pg. 237 Note 14).**

- **August 7, 1847** – Leader of the Harmony Society, George Rapp died and was buried in an unmarked grave like his followers. **47(19)**

- **January 9, 1848** – The Sandy and Beaver Canal was completed between Glasgow, Beaver County and Bolivar, Ohio – a distance of 73 miles with 30 dams and 90 locks. Problems with low water flow and structural problems caused the death of the canal by 1854. **19(106-107)**

- **March 27, 1848** – A former candidate in three Presidential elections, Henry Clay reached Beaver Point on the Steamer "Monongahela" and stayed at the home of Stephen and Sherlock Stone. **9(238)**

- **1848** – "Water Cure Sanitorium" was founded in Phillipsburg (Monaca) by Dr. Acker and offered hydrotherapy treatment as was popular at that time. **2(800), 68(7)**

- **1848** – Independence Township was formed from Hopewell Township. **21(112)**

- **1848** – The Blount House was built and became one of the earliest hotels in New Brighton. **2(718)**

- **June 1, 1848** – Lot sales began for the new town of Monterey which was laid out by Amos Dawson, William Dawson and Willian Rupell adjacent to Glasgow at the mouth of Little Beaver Creek. **33("Monterey," May 23, 1848)**

- **July 11, 1848** – Surveys began for the route of the Ohio & Pennsylvania Railroad through Beaver County. Advocates from New Brighton and Brighton (Beaver Falls) persuaded railroad representatives to run the route through those towns. Ground was broken near East Palestine, Ohio, on July 4, 1849. **7(20), 2(254)**

- **1848/1850** – The Evangelical Lutheran Church was established in Freedom. **9(531)**

- **1849** – Edwin Stanton, many years before becoming President Lincoln's Secretary of War during the Civil War, represented the Harmony Society in the Nachtrieb case where a member who had left the Harmony Society tried to claim a share of the society's assets. The case was sent to the United States Supreme Court which in 1856 overturned the settlement awarded to Nachtrieb by a lower court, effectively ending the case. **70(85-86)**

1849 – The Presbyterian Church was established in Glasgow. **9(546)**

1849 – Rochester Borough was formed from a part of Rochester Township. It was previously known as "East Bridgewater," "Beaver Point," and "Fairport," but was finally named "Rochester" by a local merchant named Mitchell Hammond sometime between 1837 and 1840. This was the early site of Chief Logan's Town. **21(146), 2(738)**

March 20, 1849 – The two northernmost townships of Beaver County (North Beaver and Shenango) were detached and joined with a portion of Mercer County to form Lawrence County **21(11)**

March 20, 1849 – The Borough of Rochester was incorporated. **2(735)**

August 21, 1849 – President Zachary Taylor and Pennsylvania Governor Johnston visited Old Economy and were entertained by the Harmony Society. Following dinner, the President stayed at the Shepherd's Point Hotel in Bridgewater. **9(241)**

November 12, 1849 – The first post office in New Brighton was established with B.B. Chamberlin as postmaster. Mr. Chamberlin had worked in the office of Vice-President Millard Fillmore and through his influence, the post office was obtained. In 1899, Congress authorized the erection of a post office building at a cost of $60,000. **2(721)**

1850 – The first reaping machine in the county was said to have been used on the farm of John Wolf. It was a Hussey machine and was considered to be an innovation on the method of cutting grain at that time. **2(278), 19(128)**

1850 – The United States Congress passed the Fugitive Slave Act of 1850.

1850 – The Ohio and Pennsylvania Railroad was extended from Pittsburgh to Rochester. **1(49)**

1850 – Franklin Township was established. It was formed from parts of Perry and Marion Townships. **21(92)**

1850 – Christ Church (Episcopal) was organized in New Brighton and was an offspring of the old St. Peter's of Fallston. **9(466)**

1850 – St. Peter's German Lutheran Church in Phillipsburg (Monaca) installed the first pipe organ in Beaver County. The organ was built by Johannes Mueller of Zelienople for $240. The organ was in use until 1929. **55(95)**

- **1850** – The North Sewickley Church Academy was established from a parochial school started in 1847. At the close of the Civil War, Reverend Weber turned the academy into a soldier's orphanage which closed after 1871 and the children were transferred to Phillipsburg (now Monaca). **49("North Sewickley Church Academy," Vol. 38 No. 1, Winter, 2013)**

- **April, 1850** – A meeting of Beaver County teachers was held in Rochester to organize a county teachers' association. **50(145)**

- **Summer, 1850** – President Zachary Taylor stopped at the Metheny Tavern at Rock Point near Ellwood City while traveling to New Castle on the Beaver Division Canal. **36(13)**

- **1850** – The U. S. Census reported county population totals of 26,689. **2(275), 3(50)**

- **December 5, 1850** – A large anti-slavery convention was held in New Brighton and adopted a resolution against the Fugitive Slave Law of 1850. **2(1143).**

- **March 13, 1851** – Richard Woodson (Also known as Richard Gardiner) was seized by slave catchers in Bridgewater and taken to Pittsburgh for trial where he was declared a runaway slave and returned to slavery in Kentucky. Local citizens collected money and on April 16, 1851, he was returned to Bridgewater after his freedom had been purchased. **49(Vol. 36 No. 2, Spring 2011, "Richard Gardiner and the 1850 Fugitive Slave Law", Pgs. 7-10)**

- **March 27, 1851** – The cornerstone of Christ Episcopal Church was laid in New Brighton. Today, it is considered the oldest church building in the town. **57(97)**

- **April 3, 1851** – Harmony Township was formed from a part of Economy Township. **21(104)**

- **May, 1851** – Trinity Episcopal Church was organized in Rochester by Rev. W.H. Paddock. **9(491)**

- **July 30, 1851** – The first Ohio & Pennsylvania railroad train from Allegheny City (now the north side of Pittsburgh) traveled up the Beaver River as far as Block House Run. **2(254), 7(201ff)**

- **August 11, 1851** – The Pittsburgh & Ohio Railroad established a passenger station at the the east end of Beaver Bridge near the diamond in Rochester and named it "Beaver Station." **104(No Title, August 12, 1851)**

- **January 9, 1852** – A meeting was held at the courthouse to condemn Austrian aggression against Hungary and raise funds which were presented to Hungarian patriot, Louis Kossuth who was visiting Pittsburgh at the time. **9(255)**

March 3, 1852 – The Darlington Cannel Coal Railway Company was formed to build a railroad from the James Nicholson farm (New Galilee) to the north fork of the Little Beaver to the cannel mines. At first the coal cars were pulled by horses until a steam engine was purchased. **2(943), 19(137),** *See entry for May 6, 1819*

1852 – Sarah Jane Lippincott of New Brighton, who wrote numerous articles, poetry and books under the pseudonym "Grace Greenwood," became the first woman reporter to work for *The New York Times*. **5(591), (http://www.womenhistoryblog.com/2014/05/grace-greenwood.html),** *See entries for 1842 and October 17, 1853*

1852 – Baden established its first post office. **2(846)**

1852 – A severe flood of the Ohio River reached a depth of thirty-one feet and nine inches. **9(153)**

Ca. 1852 – Thomas Elverson established what was, perhaps, the first pottery business in the county about a quarter of a mile above Smith's Ferry, near a steamboat landing known as Rock Port. They made Rockingham and yellow ware until around 1862. **2(933)**

County poor farm – BCHRLF Collection

January 26, 1853 – The Beaver County Agricultural Society adopted its formal organization. The first agricultural fair was held on September 20 and 21, 1853 and continued thereafter until 1899. **2(280-281)**

1853 – The county poor farm was established in Potter Township. It was originally a small one-story frame structure and grew steadily over the years. When the facility proved inadequate in 1931 an annex was built onto the Beaver County Tuberculosis Sanitoruim in Center Township. In 1959, a new 380 bed home was built in Brighton Township called the Beaver County Home and Hospital. Additions were added in 1965 and again in 1976 and became known as the Beaver Valley Geriatric Center. The original poor farm building was torn down in 2015. **5(324, 05)**

1853 – The Beaver Fair was held on the old Beaver Fair Grounds on the east end of Beaver, featuring a racetrack, tents and buildings The fair was discontinued in 1898 and the land sold to a private owner. The Beaver County Times currently occupies part of this land. **46(68)**

1853 – The United Presbyterian Church of Beaver was organized. **9(402)**

- **July 25, 1853** – Revolutionary War veteran William Hall of Beaver County, aged 104 years, continued to ride from his home to Washington, Pennsylvania, twice a year to collect his war pension. The ride was a distance of nearly twenty eight miles. **120("An Old Soldier," July 25, 1853)**

- **October 17, 1853** – Grace Greenwood (Sarah Jane Lippincott) was married at eight o'clock in the church adjoining her parents' home in New Brighton to Leander K. Lippincott of Philadelphia. The couple would live in Philadelphia and Grace Greenwood would edit "The Little Pilgrim," a paper for children. **119("Grace Greenwood," October 21, 1853),** *See entries for 1842 and 1852*

Beaver College - Courtesy of Beaver Area Historical Museum

- **December 28, 1853** – The Beaver Female Seminary was chartered in the town of Beaver. In 1872, the seminary became the Beaver College & Musical Institute. In 1895, the college was destroyed by fire and subsequently rebuilt. **2(643), 133(2, 10, 34)**

- **1854** – Glasgow was incorporated and was a canal town on the Sandy and Beaver Canal. It was built on the site of land on the north side of the Ohio River owned by George Dawson. **21(99)**

- **1854** – The Hookstown Presbyterian Church was organized by members of the Mill Creek congregation. **9(565)**

- **1854** – Dr. T. Clarke, the father of "Grace Greenwood" passed away. **118("Obituary," February 24, 1854)**

- **1854** – Pulaski Township was formed from New Sewickley Township. It was named after Revolutionary War General Casimir Pulaski. **21(143)**

- **1854** – Grace Evangelical Lutheran Church was organized by Rev. W.A. Passavant in Rochester. **9(488)**

- **1854** – St. Cecelia's Roman Catholic Church was established in Rochester as the second Catholic Church in the county. **2(753)**

- **August 27, 1854** – Rochester Manufacturing Company was organized. **2(740)**

- **1855** – Kenwood School for Boys was built in New Brighton by Henry Fetter on Oak Hill. Many years later, this building would become the Beaver Valley General Hospital. **57(83)**

1856 – A group called the "Wide Awakes" was organized in New Brighton and entertained parade crowds with music, political banners and torchlight processions. The club was affiliated with the Republican Party and later changed their name to the "Lincoln Club" in 1880. They became the oldest Republican marching club in the United States. **57(104)**

1856 – Captain Gilbert and Joseph Pendleton established a firebrick works which was one of the earliest industries in Rochester. **2(740)**

1856 – Phillipsburg's (now Monaca) first post office was opened and was called "Water Cure" after the sanatorium located there, the name of Phillipsburg not being used, to avoid confusion with another town of the same name in Pennsylvania. **2(809)**

1857 – The Evangelical Association of Rochester was organized by Rev. Jacob Rank. **9(491)**

1857 – Merrick, Hanna and Company made wrought iron railroad passenger cars in New Brighton. They were thought to be the first metal rail cars made in the United States. **57(48)**

1857 – The Church of God was organized in Fallston with nine members. **9(466)**

1857 – David Gibb and Jacob Van Reed erected a still-house one mile below Hookstown. It along with several others in the area went out of business with the passage of the Revenue Act during the Civil War which imposed excise taxes on liquor among other things. **2(827)**

First National Bank of Beaver County – BCHRLF Collection

November 25, 1857 – The first state bank chartered to do business in Beaver County opened in New Brighton as the Bank of Beaver County. It was reorganized as the National Bank of New Brighton in 1864. **2(272-273)**

October, 1857 – The first graded public school in the county was established in New Brighton. **2(706)**

Ca. 1857 - 1860 – Famed abolitionist and female rights activist, Anna Dickinson at age fifteen obtained a job at the Greenwood Institute in New Brighton as an assistant teacher (Note: Dr. Bausman states that she was a student, but an 1863 news source places her here as a teacher). Precocious and mature for her age, Anna left school in Philadelphia to find a job to make money to support herself. After a few months, she applied for a teaching position in a nearby school that was vacated by a man. She was offered less than half of his former salary which she declined and eventually went back home to Philadelphia. **2(723), 74(38), 117("Anna E. Dickinson," September 11, 1863)**

- **1858** – The Methodist Episcopal congregation was established in 1858 in Baden. **9(532)**

- **1859** – Joseph M. Smith laid out the village of Homewood. It was named after James Wood who had built an iron furnace along the Beaver River about two miles away. The junction of the Pittsburgh, Fort Wayne and Chicago Railroad with the Erie and Pittsburgh line was located here in 1852 and contributed to the location and growth of the new borough. **21(107)**

- **1859** – The Beaver County Jail and Warden's residence was built in Beaver by Timothy B. White for a cost of $28,853. They were abandoned in 2000 and eventually torn down when the new jailhouse was built in West Aliquippa. **46(75)**

Old Beaver County Jail & Warden House – BCHRLF Collection

- **1859** – Cook's Ferry was established connecting what is now Shippingport with Industry by George Washington Cook. It was operated by the Cook family until 1918, sold to the Flemings, bought by Christy and Morrow in 1919 and renamed Shippingport Ferry. The last ferry trip was in April, 1964. **(BCHRLF Historical Marker)**

- **1859** – Christ Evangelical Lutheran Church was organized in Baden. **9(533)**

September 14, 1859 – The Brighton District of Patterson Township (Beaver Falls), formerly owned by James Patterson, was bought at sheriff's sale by the Harmony Society for $34,500. **2(669)**

October 13, 1859 – Grove Cemetery was dedicated in New Brighton. **57(116) 2(721)**

September 21, 1860 – S.M. Kier of Pittsburgh bought the bankrupt Hunter & Code refinery in Freedom which failed after attempting to refine oil from coal. Kier began to refine petroleum from crude oil. He was perhaps the first in the county and one of the first in the United States to do so. **2(302)**

October 19, 1860 – Marcus T.C. Gould passed away at his home in Rochester. Gould was at one time the only short hand reporter in the country, and invented a system of stenography. A heavy speculator, Gould won and lost several fortunes, the latest being the import of the *Morus Multicaulis* to raise silkworms which failed miserably as did the design to build a manufacturing city at the mouth of the Little Beaver Creek. **104("A Veteran Stenographer Dead," October 27, 1860),** *See also entries for July 4, 1833 and 1836*

November 23, 1860 – Beaver County cast 2,824 votes for Abraham Lincoln compared to 1,624 for other candidates. **121("The Election in Pennsylvania," November 23, 1860)**

December, 1860 – Oil was discovered in the areas of Upper Dry Run and Island Run near Smith's Ferry by Pattens, Finlens, Swan & Company at a depth of 180 feet. Beaver County's first oil well. **1(77), 19(140), 2(934)**

1860 – St. Mary's Catholic Church was formed in Beaver Falls. **5(493)**

1860 - William Patrick Ormes was born a slave in Maryland in 1806. He escaped to Pennsylvania in 1835 and in 1845 moved to Beaver County. Ormes and his sons drilled one of the first producing oil wells in the county on the Thompson farm near Smith's Ferry. The Ormes - Thompson well produced about 20 barrels per day for nearly a century. **108("Famed District Well Calls it Quits," August 25, 1959)**

1860 – County population was 29,140. **2(275), 3(50)**

V. Civil War & its Aftermath: 1861 to 1889

Patriotism has always been a Beaver County trait, and it was no different when the Civil War exploded on the scene in April of 1861 with the attack on Fort Sumter. Beaver County men answered the call to arms by providing soldiers for regiments that the State of Pennsylvania raised during the war. Each of these regiments contained one or more companies composed of Beaver County men, many of whom would suffer serious wounds and others who would pay the ultimate price. The idealistic young men who had marched away to war just a few short years before had been transformed into battle-hardened veterans who would return home only to discover that the old world that they had dreamed about had changed also.

Both during and after the war, new industries grew here. Beaver County became well known for industries like oil, pottery, cutlery, nails, and glass, thanks to our ready supply of natural resources and the power and transportation supplied by the rivers and railroads. In fact, Beaver County became so important that the Pennsylvania Railroad Company built Conway Yards — once the largest rail yard in the world — here to handle the demand. In addition horse drawn street railway cars were coming into existence as an early forerunner to the electric trolley cars making public transportation more convenient in our growing communities. On the political front, Beaver's Matthew Stanley Quay was elected to the United States Senate, and would become known as "Boss Quay" for his political prowess and influence.

- **1861** – P.M. Wallover established an oil refinery in Smith's Ferry to manufacture lubricating oil from the crude produced in the nearby Smith's Ferry oil fields. It was known as Wallover Oil Company. **2(303)**

- **1861** – St. Rose of Lima Catholic Church was formed in Darlington. **5(493)**

- **February 14, 1861** – President Abraham Lincoln's inaugural train stopped in Rochester. He compared heights with Henry Dillon, a "coal heaver" from Freedom who stood just a bit shorter than the President-elect. **19(207)**

- **April 12, 1861** – The Civil War began with the attack on Fort Sumter. Eleven of the 270 regiments which the Commonwealth of Pennsylvania sent to the battlefields of the Civil War had one or more companies recruited in Beaver County. Seven Beaver County soldiers were awarded the Medal of Honor for their heroics. **2(502-504)**, http://pamoh.homestead.com/files/PAMOHA.htm

- **May 9, 1861** – New Brighton native, Robert Roland Glass was drafted into Confederate service while visiting New Orleans and served in the 1st Louisiana Heavy Artillery. Glass deserted during their march to reinforce Vicksburg and joined the

13th Connecticut under the alias of "Robert Johnson." He served until the end of the war and was honorably discharged in 1865 when he returned home. **49("Between Two Countries: Robert Glass's Civil War" Vol. 27 No. 4, Fall, 2002)**

- **June 28, 1861** – Company H recruited in Beaver County was organized with the 38th regiment, 9th Regiment Reserve Pennsylvania Volunteer Infantry, becoming the first unit to leave Beaver County and the first to be mustered into federal service. **2(502-504)**

- **June 29, 1861** – Companies F and K of the 10th Pennsylvania Reserves were recruited in Rochester. **2(505)**

- **August 1, 1861** – Company C of the 63rd Pennsylvania Regiment was recruited mainly in Rochester and New Brighton. **2(506)**

- **August 12, 1861** – Another major flood hit the county doing widespread damage. This one washed away the old Cleveland and Pittsburgh Railway bridge between Bridgewater and Rochester. The loss of property at New Brighton and Fallston was over $10,000. **9(153), 58(67)**

- **August, 1861** – Company K of the 76th Regiment Pennsylvania Volunteer Infantry, known as the "Keystone Zouaves" was raised. **2(508)**

- **September 2, 1861** – Company D, composed of Beaver County men was organized with the 100th Regiment Pennsylvania Volunteer Infantry also called "Round Heads." Company Captain was William C. Shurlock. **2(510)**

- **1862** – Thomas Elverson established a pottery manufactory in New Brighton. **1(52), 9(454)**

Elverson Pottery – BCHRLF Collection

- **1862** – The United States Government attempted to purchase land where (Brighton) Beaver Falls is now situated in order to build a national armory. The effort failed in 1862 and 1863. The original idea was explored in 1822 when engineers were sent to examine the area and reported favorably. All attempts failed due to circumstances elsewhere. **33("Beaver Falls is Century Old Town Under two Names," September 7, 1919)**

- **1862** – Homewood established its first post office with William H. Foster as its postmaster. **2(927-928), 9(589)**

Strolling Through Time: A Chonology of Beaver County, PA History to 2016

- **July, 1862** – Companies E & I both raised in the county, joined the 134th Regiment Pennsylvania Volunteer Infantry and were commanded by Captains J. Adams Vera and John W. Hague respectively. **2(514)**

- **September 3, 1862** – Company H, recruited partly in the county, under Captain John A. Donald was added to the 139th Regiment Pennsylvania Volunteer Infantry and ordered to Washington, D.C. **2(516)**

- **October, 1862** – Companies F and H raised in Beaver County, were organized into the 101st Regiment Pennsylvania Volunteer Infantry. Captains Charles W. May and Alex W. Taylor commanded. Company C which was raised in both Beaver and Lawrence Counties was added also. **2(513)**

- **October 18, 1862** – Company A, recruited in the county, was added to the 162nd Regiment, 17th Cavalry. Originally raised as an independent company of cavalry, it was named the "Irwin Cavalry" in honor of W.W. Irwin of Beaver County, who was at this time Commissary-General of the State of Pennsylvania. **2(519)**

- **December 13, 1862** – Colonel Matthew Stanley Quay, commanding the 134th Pennsylvania regiment earned a Congressional Medal of Honor at the battle of Fredericksburg despite suffering from typhoid. The medal was not awarded until July 9, 1888. **5(800), 19(77)**

- **1863** – The first water-works of Beaver Falls was built. It consisted of a small impounding dam built in a ravine a short distance north of the old Pittsburgh, Fort Wayne & Chicago Railway station. **2(268)**

- **1863** – Lacock's Cemetery was established and was the oldest of the two Rochester cemeteries.
2(765)

- **1863** – Passavant Memorial Home was founded by Dr. William Passavant in Rochester Township and was originally a home for orphan girls. On June 6, 1895, the children were moved to a facility in Zelienople which housed epileptics. Today it works with individuals with intellectual disabilities and behavioral health needs. **5(491, 505), 2(762)**

- **March 14, 1863** – Oak Grove Cemetery in Freedom was incorporated. **2(794)**

- **April 10, 1863** – Eli Sheets was the first judicial hanging in the county. **2(358-360), 49("Murder Mystery," Vol. 24 No. 4, Autumn, 1999), 9(187)**

- **June 22, 1863** – A Confederate prisoner who escaped from a train in Allegheny City was re-captured there. Thomas S. Dannals was a native of Beaver County who had been living in the south and rather than being drafted, he had volunteered for service with the 12th Louisiana Regiment and was taken prisoner at the battle of Champion Hill in Mississippi. **121("Rebel Prisoner Arrested," June 22, 1863)**

July 2, 1863 – Colonel Richard P. Roberts of Beaver was killed leading his 140th Pennsylvania Volunteer Infantry during the battle of Gettysburg. **46(58)**

July 26, 1863 – Confederate cavalry under John Hunt Morgan was captured in nearby Salineville, Columbiana County, Ohio, after conducting a 25 day raid through that state that also caused a great deal of alarm in nearby Beaver County communities. **33("Monument to Storied Raid into Ohio Faces Uncertain Future," October 19, 2015), 94(34)**

1864 – The Keystone Bakery was established in Beaver and later moved to Bridgewater. It went out of business permanently in 1985. **2(775), 58(42)**

1864 – The Homewood railroad station on the Ohio & Pennsylvania Railroad was built. **9(589)**

May 6, 1864 – Former New Brighton native Colonel Charles Read Collins was killed near Todd's Tavern at the battle of Spotsylvania while leading the Confederate 15th Virginia Cavalry. **49("Turncoat: The Story of Colonel Charles Read Collins CSA", Vol. 35 No. 2 Spring 2010)**

June 14, 1864 – The Cleveland & Pittsburgh station in Beaver was completely destroyed by a fire which was started from sparks from the express train, but the freight was saved. **117("Fire," June 18, 1864)**

August, 1864 – Workmen excavating for the track of the new Pittsburgh, Fort Wayne and Chicago Railroad uncovered human remains in the vicinity of Legion Ville which were thought to be Native American. The body had a solid silver ring around the head, with heavy gold rings in the nose and ears. On the chest was a crescent beneath which was a Maltese cross. Gold rings, bracelets, buckles and other items were found. **120(Interesting Indian Relics Discovered," August 23, 1864)**

November 8, 1864 – In the presidential election, Beaver County had a 900 vote majority in favor of President Abraham Lincoln. **120("The Latest News by Telegraph," November 9, 1864)**

1865 – Company H, raised mainly in Beaver and Lawrence Counties was assigned to the 77th Regiment of Pennsylvania Volunteer Infantry. **2(510)**

1865 – Alice Woodby McKane was born in Bridgewater and at the age of seven her parents passed away. Suffering blindness for three years afterward, she re-gained her sight, grew up and went on to graduate with a medical degree from the Women's Medical College of Pennsylvania in 1892. Moving to Augusta, Georgia, she married Dr.

Cornelius McKane, the grandson of a Liberian King and went on to become the first African – American female physician in Georgia at that time. Moving to Monrovia, Liberia for a short time, she and her husband founded the first hospital there. **(http://georgiawomen.org/2010/10/mckane-alice-woodby/)**

- **March, 1865** – Company G, recruited in Beaver County, was added to the 78th Regiment Pennsylvania Volunteer Infantry. The captain was David S. Cook. **2(510)**

- **March 18, 1865** – The Ohio River flooded to a depth of thirty-one feet and nine inches, matching the depth of the flood of 1852. It was caused by rain and melted snow. **9(153)**

Sergeant Joseph McCabe - Courtesy of Beaver Falls Museum

- **April 8, 1865** – Sergeant Joseph E. McCabe, a Beaver County native and one of General Sheridan's most famous scouts located the supply train for General Lee's starving Confederate army, thus forcing Lee's surrender at Appomattox Court House and effectively ending the Civil War. **49("Sergeant Joseph Everson McCabe: The Last Sheridan Scout," Vol. 39 No. 2, Spring, 2014)**

- **April 9, 1865** – Confederate General Robert E. Lee surrendered at Appomattox.

- **April 14, 1865** – President Abraham Lincoln was assassinated by John Wilkes Booth while attending a play at Ford's theater in Washington, D.C.

- **May, 1865** – Soldier's Orphan School of North Sewickley opened in the North Sewickley Academy building under Rev. Henry Webber. Due to monetary losses, the school closed on June 1, 1867 and transferred students to Phillipsburg Soldier's Orphan School. **2(800)**

- **June 19, 1865** – New Bethlehem United Presbyterian Church was organized at the Rarden Run School House in Hopewell Township by Rev. J.M. Witherspoon. **9(576)**

- **September 11, 1865** – Mrs. Burger of Hanover Township was charged with assault and battery on another lady, Mrs. White. Despite being nearly eighty years old and having to lean heavily on a cane to walk, Mrs. Burger walked over 20 miles to her hearing in the Beaver Courthouse. The charges were dismissed. **121("Mrs. Burger, of Beaver County," September 11, 1865)**

- **October 14, 1865** – Ira Mansfield, a Civil War veteran, organized the Robin Hood Club, a hunting and fishing group in Cannelton. He leased and then purchased the Cannel Coal Mines in Cannelton, Beaver County, PA, where he erected a general store and opera house. He served five terms as a member of the state legislature from Beaver County. Mansfield's interest in nature and mining helped him to write several books that were considered authorities in their respective areas. **98(211-212)**

🔔 **October 16, 1865** – The Industry Presbyterian Church began in an old brick building in Industry. It was the daughter church of the Bethlehem Church across the Ohio River and had seventeen members. **9(583)**

🔔 **1866** – Thiel College was founded in Phillipsburg (Monaca) and was the first college in the county. On September 1, 1871 Thiel moved to Greenville, Mercer County. **2(808-809), 5(491, 504)**

🔔 **1866** – The Harmony Society made a new survey of the Brighton District of Patterson Township (Beaver Falls) and appointed H.T. & J. Reeves as real estate agents to offer lots for sale. **2(292), 9(407)**

🔔 **1866** – The Pioneer Pottery Company was started by C.W. Taylor and D.C. Schofield in New Brighton. **9(455)**

Pittsburgh, Fort Wayne & Chicago Railroad – BCHRLF Collection

🔔 **1866** – St. John the Baptist Catholic Church was formed in Baden. **5(493)**

🔔 **1866** – The Phillipsburg M.E. Church was formed and erected a new frame house of worship at a cost of $2,400. **9(524)**

🔔 **1866** – A steel bridge for the Pittsburgh, Fort Wayne & Chicago Railroad (PFW&C) replaced the original wooden structure over the Beaver River between Beaver Falls and New Brighton. **7(21)**

🔔 **March, 1866** – Civil War veteran Joseph Hoopes while serving on the U.S.S. Kearsarge which was sailing off the coast of Liberia, Africa, contracted yellow fever and was buried at sea. A monument was erected in his memory in Grove Cemetery in New Brighton. **34("Historic Cemetery Falls into Disrepair", August 12, 2007)**

🔔 **March, 1866** – Soldier's Orphan School in Phillipsburg opened in the former Water Cure buildings under Rev. W.G. Taylor. It was destroyed by fire on August 22, 1876. **2(800)**

🔔 **August 15, 1866** – The present Beaver Cemetery was established. **2(659-660)**

Strolling Through Time: A Chonology of Beaver County, PA History to 2016

- **November 15, 1866** – The County treasury was robbed of $8,000 by blowing open the safe with gunpowder during the administration of M.R. Adams. Despite the loud noise from the blast, the thieves were able to escape. **9(132), 104("Robbery of the Beaver County Treasury," November 16, 1866)**

- **March 25, 1867** – St. Clair Borough was incorporated by court decree. In 1896 it merged into the town of Freedom. It was initially laid out by Captain William Vicary in 1837 on his land and was variously called "Vicary Extension" or "Vicary." **2(795), 9(531)**

- **March, 1867** – The Methodist Episcopal Church in Rochester was organized by the Pittsburgh Conference held in Massillon, Ohio. **9(494)**

- **May 2, 1867** – The First Sunday School Association was formed in the county. **9(256), 49("Beaver County History: An overview from 1931," Vol. 36 No. 1, Winter, 2011)**

- **1867** – The Beaver Falls Cutlery Company was formed in Rochester and moved shortly afterwards to Beaver Falls. In 1870 the company stock was largely owned by the Harmony Society. *See entries for 1872 & 1877.* **2(670), 9(483)**

- **1867** – The First Baptist Church was organized in New Brighton with sixteen members. **9(466)**

- **1867** – The Methodist Episcopal Church of Glasgow was organized. **9(547)**

- **1867/1868** – St. Paul's Evangelical Lutheran Church was established in Rochester. **9(495)**

- **1868** – The Howard Stove Company was formed in Beaver Falls for the manufacture of all types of stoves and ranges. After several fires, it was sold in 1883. **2(677)**

- **1868** – The name of the town of "Old Brighton" was changed to Beaver Falls. **44(16)**

- **1868** – H.J. Heinz and Thomas Noble purchased a brickyard in Beaver Falls which they sold in 1872. Noble went west and H.J. Heinz relocated to Sharpsburg where he began building his food empire. **44(156)**

- **1868** – New Galilee Borough was incorporated. It began as a village on the Pittsburgh, Fort Wayne and Chicago Railroad. Most of the land in the borough was originally part of the James Nicholson farm, located on the Little Beaver Creek in the western part of Big Beaver Township. *See Entry for May 6, 1819.* **21(130)**

- **1868** – The Penn Bridge Works, specializing in railroad and highway bridges, began operations in New Brighton and moved to Beaver Falls in 1878. **7(21), 9(432)**

Strolling Through Time: A Chonology of Beaver County, PA History to 2016

- **March, 1868** – The Economy Savings Institution was established in Beaver Falls with the Board of Directors consisting of officers of the Harmony Society who backed the institution. It closed its business on May 1, 1893, and was succeeded by John T. Reeves & Company. **2(684)**

- **March 19, 1868** – The towns of Sharon and Bridgewater were consolidated to become Bridgewater. **9(503)**

- **April 1, 1868** – The Borough of Baden was incorporated. The original village was surveyed in 1838. *Refer to the entry for 1838.* **21(54)**

- **November 9, 1868** – Beaver Falls was incorporated as a borough. **2(669), 9(411)**

- **1869** – The Economy Works were established in Beaver Falls to make shovels, spades and scoops of all kinds. In 1875 the Works became H.M. Myers & Company, Limited and in 1902 was absorbed by the Ames Tool & Shovel Company. **2(676-677)**

- **1869** – The Great Western File Works was built in Beaver Falls by David Blake and James Fessenden. In April, 1880 the works was destroyed by fire and rebuilt. In 1899, the works was absorbed by the Nicholson File Works and was out of operation by 1904. **2(675)**

- **1869** – The Methodist Episcopal Church was organized in Homewood by Rev. J.W. Clabaugh. **9(589)**

- **1869** – The Spring Water Brewery was founded in Beaver Falls by James Anderton, and in 1891 became incorporated as the Anderton Brewing Company. **2(672)**

- **1869** – The Trinity Evangelical Lutheran Church was established in St. Clair and consisted of people unhappy with the Freedom church. **9(531)**

- **1869** – The Baker Brothers opened a flour mill in Industry Township. **9(583)**

- **1869** – The firm of Miller, Dobson & Trax opened a lumber yard in Rochester and ran their contracting business from an office in Pittsburgh. In 1884, the business became William Miller & Sons. Some notable buildings which they erected were the Montgomery County, Washington County and York County courthouses. **2(742-743)**

- **April 1, 1869** – Former Beaver County state and U.S. Representative John Allison of Beaver was appointed Register of the Treasury by President Grant, a position which he held until his death in 1878. There exists in the Bureau of Fiscal Services History Center in Parkersburg, West Virginia, a photograph of Allison and staff taken by famous Civil War and Wild West photographer Alexander Gardner. **132(1-2), 2(346-347)**

🍁 **May 23, 1869** – The First Methodist Protestant Church was founded in Beaver Falls. **9(414)**

🍁 **July 26, 1869** – The First United Presbyterian Congregation of Beaver Falls was organized by the Presbytery of Allegheny with a membership of fifty-one. **9(413)**

Andriessen Drug Store on right- Courtesy of Beaver Area Historical Museum

🍁 **October, 1869** – Pharmacist and political radical Hugo Andriessen moved to Beaver and opened his "Beaver Drugstore" on Third Street in Beaver. His store was to become locally famous, not only for its pharmaceutical inventory, but also because it contained a large natural history collection. In 1906, Andriessen sold his store to Edwin Rowse and the natural history collection to a gentleman in Pittsburgh. **49("Hugo Andriessen," Vol. 34 No. 4, Fall, 2009)**

🍁 **November 3, 1869** – Speyerer & McDonald Bank was the first banking institution established in Rochester. **2(748)**

🍁 **1870** – The Empire Axe & Hoe Works was established in Beaver Falls by Joseph Graff and Company. In 1879, it became Hubbard, Bakewell & Company, and in 1893 became the American Axe & Tool Company. Its axes were sold all throughout the United States, Canada and South America. **2(676)**

🍁 **1870** – According to legend, a group of Civil War veterans while picnicking at a waterfall near Homewood gave a toast with buttermilk and the falls were thereafter named "Buttermilk Falls." Today the site is a part of the Beaver County park system.
(http://www.beavercountypa.gov/parks-recreation-buttermilk-falls-park), (Sign at Buttermilk Falls)

🍁 **1870** – The U.S. Census reported that county population was 36,148. **2(275), 3(50)**

🍁 **May 2, 1870** – African-American citizens of Beaver County held a grand procession beginning in New Brighton and ending in Fallston where they were met by delegations from Beaver, Rochester and Bridgewater to celebrate the earlier passage of the 15th Amendment to the Constitution which gave black men the right to vote. **117("Celebration of the Colored People of Beaver County," May 5, 1870)**

🍁 **1871** – The Beaver Division of the Pennsylvania Canal System ceased operations. **4(90)**

1871 – Beaver Falls Gas Co. was organized. It manufactured illuminating gas and supplied the towns of New Brighton and Beaver Falls. Due to competition in the gas industry, it ceased operations in 1902. **2(673)**

1871 – John Conway's Bank was established and was the second banking institution in Rochester. **2(749)**

1871 – St. Theresa's Catholic Church was formed in what is present day Koppel. **5(493)**

McKinley School – BCHRLF Collection

1871 – Jewish residents of the New Brighton area rented the Methodist Church and brought in a rabbi as a guest speaker. **5(497)**

January 1, 1872 – The Cooperative Foundry Association was founded in Beaver Falls to produce stoves, hollow ware and ranges. Later known as the Paisley Foundry, it was out of business by 1904. **2(671)**

Spring, 1872 – The Rochester Tumbler Co. began glass making operations in Rochester. At a later point, the plant was lit throughout by electricity generated by the company's own motors. In 1899, the National Glass Company took control of the plant following a devastating fire. **2(740 -741, 744ff)**

1872 – William McCool patented machinery for drawing cold steel tubes; he is associated with William Hartman of Beaver Falls and Andrew Carnegie of United States Steel. It was the beginning of the Cold Draw process in the United States. **79(59)**

Olive Stove works abandoned picture taken Ca. 1940 –Courtesy Library of Congress

1872 – McKinley School, a one room schoolhouse was built on land owned by John McKinley in present day Chippewa. It was closed in 1930 and today is a museum located at McKinley Road and 37th Street Extension. **1(27), 19(176)**

1872 – Standard Horse Nail Works opened in Fallston by Job Whysall and Charles Merrick. Following a fire in 1884 (**NOTE: Jordan puts this date as 1886**), the Works moved to New Brighton and was still in business as of 2015. **1(53), 4(100), 9(457), 2(710)**

1872 – The Olive Stove Works was established in Rochester for the manufacture of cooking and heating stoves and ranges. **2(747)**

1872 – The Doncaster House Hotel was erected in Rochester. It was a four story frame structure 60 by 100 feet with thirty seven sleeping rooms and three parlors built by Richard Doncaster. **9(485)**

1872 – Self-styled Captain Samuel Adams of Beaver Falls, the son of Dr. Milo Adams, announced that he had explored the Colorado River and its tributaries and claimed fantastic discoveries that included: "ancient ruins, cities, canals, abandoned mines, etc. – Valleys of wild wheat, oats, barley, rye, and clover the latter growing over seven feet in height an extent of country sufficient for three states......" He further claimed that the Colorado River was freely navigable for nearly six hundred miles from its mouth and that the walls of the canyon held large veins of gold, silver, copper and lead with great patches of oil floating on some of the streams that entered the river. None of these proved to be true. **135(x), 136(183)**

July 1, 1872 – When a labor strike threatened, a group of seventy five Chinese workers arrived in Beaver Falls from San Francisco to work at the Beaver Falls Cutlery Company, and within a year, another hundred had arrived and monopolized the work of the factory. At this point, all white workers were dismissed. Due to poor profitability, the Cutlery ceased business in 1886. **49(Vol. 25, No. 2), 91(414-415),** *See entry for 1877*

July 4, 1872 – The cornerstone was laid for St. Mary's Immaculate Conception Catholic Church in Beaver Falls. It was slowly demolished through the fall of 2014 and into the winter of 2015. **9(416), 49("St. Mary's Catholic Church Demolition," Vol. 40, No. 1, Winter, 2015)**

1873 – Judge Daniel Agnew of Beaver became Chief Justice of the State Supreme Court. **2(315)**

1873 – William Ziegler, born in Beaver County in 1843, along with two partners formed the Royal Chemical Company which later became the Royal Baking Powder Company. With his new fortune, he later outfitted three separate polar expeditions, none of which were successful in reaching the North Pole. Ziegler passed away in 1905. In 1929 the Royal Baking Powder Company along with four other companies including the Fleischmann's Yeast Company merged to form Standard Brands, the number two brand of packaged foods in the United States after General Foods. **(http://whatscookingamerica.net/History/BakingPowderHistory.htm)**

October 3, 1873 – The First Baptist Church of Rochester was established. **9(492)**

1874 – The A.S. & R.W. Hall Carriage Works was founded in Beaver Falls to make buggies, phaetons, barouches, buck and spring wagons and other general carriage goods. **2(680)**

April 3, 1874 – *The Beaver Times* was first published by Michael Weyand. The name was changed to and remained the *Beaver Argus* until 1909. It was changed again to *The Daily Times*, which was published from 1909 to 1946. The paper was sold in 1946 to the father of the present-day *Times* owner, S.W. Calkins. The paper was known as *The Beaver Valley Times* until 1956, when it became *The Beaver County Times* after its acquisition of the *Ambridge Daily Citizen*. **2(460), 5(353)**

April 14, 1874 – The First Presbyterian Church was organized in Rochester by a committee of the Presbytery of Allegheny. **9(496)**

September 19, 1874 – The First Methodist Episcopal Church of Beaver Falls was incorporated. **9(416)**

November 24, 1874 – The Reformed Presbyterian Congregation of Beaver Falls was organized with a membership of twenty four. **9(414)**

1875 – Beaver Falls Steel Works was absorbed by Crucible Steel. Three years later it was purchased and run by the Harmony Society. In 1893, it was bought from the Harmonists, and in July, 1900, the company was absorbed by the Crucible Steel Company of America. **2(675ff)**

1875 – The Peirsol Academy was established in Bridgewater by Scudder Peirsol who was also the principal. **2(776)**

1876 – The Philadelphia Centennial displayed the largest knife and fork in the world made by the Beaver Falls Cutlery Company. The knife and fork cost $1,500 and the handles were made of solid ivory – each one elephant's tusk – and intricately carved with flowers and vines. **44(149)**

June 25, 1876 – Former Phillipsburg resident, Captain Grant Marsh who was in command of the steamer "Far West" arrived with supplies at the mouth of the Big Horn River in the Montana Territory at nearly the same time as General Custer began his ill-fated attack on a large Indian village on the Little Big Horn River eleven miles away. Tasked with carrying the wounded from Major Reno's command, Marsh made a perilous 710 mile journey to Fort Lincoln (Today's Bismarck, North Dakota) in a record 54 hours without incident. It was hailed as a navigational feat never equaled again on western waters and one of the most remarkable exploits in the annals of Missouri River steamboating. **49("Grant Prince Marsh: Legendary Missouri Riverboat Captain," Vol. 34 No. 1, Winter, 2009)**

August 22, 1876 – The Soldier's Orphan School in Phillipsburg (Monaca) was destroyed by fire. **2(800)**

- **December 21, 1876** – Nearly one hundred people witnessed a series of fifty fireballs, about the size of a man's fist and trailing two foot flames, floating past at the close of services at Zion Church in Raccoon Township. The phenomenon was unexplained. **19(238)**

- **1877** – Beaver Falls established a high school. **5(257)**

- **1877** – The Pittsburgh & Lake Erie Railroad was laying track through Logstown Botttom. A post office was established and given the name Woodlawn. An amusement park was built in the area north of Woodlawn and named Aliquippa Park and an adjacent village was established with its own passenger station and named Aliquippa. Contrary to popular belief, the name Aliquippa was assigned by the railroad as they were giving Indian names arbitrarily to stations along the route. There is no historical evidence that Queen Aliquippa ever lived there. **56(16)**

- **1877** – The Greersburg Academy in Darlington no longer functioned as a school house. **77(11)**

- **1877** – The last of the Chinese workers at Beaver Falls Cutlery leave Beaver Falls. About 225 worked here at its height, but many had left earlier. When it was over, the experiment of replacing American workers with Chinese workers had failed and eventually ended up costing the Cutlery Company approximately $42,000. **49(Vol. 25, No. 2), 92(414-415)**

Third County Courthouse - BCHRLF Collection

- **May 1, 1877** – The third county courthouse was built. The building was designed by Thomas Boyd of Pittsburgh and built by William M. Keyser of New Brighton for $115,000. It was later destroyed in 1932 by a fire caused by a painter's blowtorch. **5(194), 46(73)**

- **September 21, 1878** – The first locomotive crossed the Pittsburgh & Lake Erie bridge from Monaca toward Beaver, and this was the first rail bridge over the Ohio in the county. This bridge was replaced around 1910, when it became too small for additional tracks. **2(261)**

Old and new P&LE Railroad Bridges - BCHRLF Collection

Strolling Through Time: A Chonology of Beaver County, PA History to 2016

- **1878** – The Beaver Falls Planing Mill Company was organized in Beaver Falls. **2(678)**

- **1878** – Robert Magee Downie invented the first well drilling rig to be mounted on wheels under a locust tree in his father's yard in Valencia, Pa. Although he drilled many wells throughout Pennsylvania, the first well drilled by Downie in Beaver County was for the Harmony Society in 1879. The Keystone Steam Driller Company was formed on February 2, 1882. *Refer to entry on February 2, 1882.* **93(6)**

- **1878** – Pittsburgh & Lake Erie Railroad completed the line from Youngstown, Ohio, through Beaver County to Pittsburgh. Passenger service began in 1879. **2(259ff), 13(65), 22(31ff)**

- **1878** – The Beaver Falls Car Works was founded and manufactured all grades of rail cars and did general repair and foundry work. The business closed in 1897. **2(671)**

- **1879** – Algeo & Sons Coffin Works relocated to Beaver Falls from Rochester, New York. **2(674)**

- **1879** – The Rochester Flint Vial and Bottle Works was organized to manufacture flasks and fruit jars. Later they expanded to prescription and liquor bottles. **2(743-744)**

- **1879** – The Beaver Falls Bridge Company was organized to erect the Fetterman Bridge, connecting Beaver Falls and Eastvale, (formerly known as Fetterman). Construction was begun in May, 1880, by the Penn Bridge Company. It was a toll bridge most of the years of its existence, and this bridge was replaced by the Eastvale Bridge in 1964. **107("Fetterman Bridge Named After Nathanial Fetterman," July 5, 1982)**

PFW&C Station New Brighton Now Merrick Art Gallery – BCHRLF Collection.

- **1879** – Sherwood Brothers Pottery opened in New Brighton and was owned by G.W. and W.D. Sherwood. It absorbed the Elverson, Sherwood & Barker Pottery Works. The pottery closed in 1948. **57(14), 9(456)**

- **1879** – Freedom Oil Works was founded in present Conway and moved to

Freedom around 1883. Freedom Oil and Valvoline Oil merged in 1944. **2(793)**

1879 – The Bethel Methodist Episcopal Church was organized in New Sewickley Township. **9(604)**

1879 – Leasing Western Union Company wires that followed the Ohio River west from Pittsburgh, the Central District and Telegraph Printing Company brought the earliest telephone service to the Beaver Valley. **(Note: it is not stated who used this service).** **5(355)**

February 7, 1879 – The Beaver Falls Cooperative Glass Company, Limited, was formed and manufactured general glass tableware. The company was succeeded by the Co-operative Flint Glass Company, Limited, in 1889. **2(677)**

April 7, 1879 – The Woodlawn Academy in Woodlawn (present day Aliquippa) was chartered and a two story frame building was erected for $2,500. **9(577)**

May 20, 1879 – The first commencement exercise for Beaver Falls High School was held on this date. Beaver Falls High School was the first high school established in the county and was in the Eleventh Street or Central school building. **2(694-695)**

1880 – Edward Dempster Merrick established the Merrick Art Gallery in New Brighton. **(Cynthia Kundar, Director 7/18/2015)**

1880 – Presidential nominee (later President) James Garfield's train stopped at Beaver Falls where no plans had been made to receive him. He stood gazing at the audience in embarrassed silence until three cheers were raised by the crowd. Upon his death in 1881, his funeral train would pass through the county. **9(243)**, *See entry for September 24, 1881*

Geneva College Old Main - BCHRLF Collection

1880 – The Acme Oil Company established itself in Industry Township and refined the crude oil from Smith's Ferry. **9(583)**

1880 – Henry Wagner established Wagner's Brewery in Beaver Falls. The plant had a yearly capacity of nearly five thousand barrels of beer and was out of business by 1904. **2(672)**

April, 1880 – New

Brighton became an independent school district. **57(84)**

June 8, 1880 – The United Presbyterian Congregation of Camp Run was incorporated in Franklin Township. **9(608)**

July 1, 1880 – Aliquippa Park, built by the Pittsburgh & Lake Erie Railroad, opened to the public on a 100 acre plot of land known as Jones Woods. It closed down on January 7, 1907, and the land was sold to Jones & Laughlin Steel Company for their plant (now West Aliquippa). **56(9)**

August, 1880 – Phoenix Glass began operations in Phillipsburg (Monaca) and made lamp chimneys and reflectors. **1(97), 13(77), 55(77), 2(802)**

September, 1880 – Geneva College relocated from Northwood, Ohio, to what was then Chippewa Township (Now Beaver Falls). **1(29), 19(18)**

1880 – County population was 39,605 **2(275)**

1881 – J.&E. Mayer & Co. opened in Beaver Falls, and following a devastating fire in 1896, it re-opened as Mayer China. In 1946, Mayer was the only company in America that could boast of having a woman, Miss Sadie Megown, a worker of sixty years, still active and working. In 1964, ownership of the company was assumed by the Shenango China Company which later became a division of Syracuse China Corp. in 1984. **1(26), 2(679), 5(110-111)**

Mayer China plant – BCHRLF Collection

1881 – The county treasury was robbed of $17,000 during the administration of W.F. Dawson. **9(132)**

March 30, 1881 – Conway, formerly known as "Agnew," established its first post office with Charles Cheney as postmaster. **2(852)**

September 24, 1881 – A fast train carrying reporters covering President Garfield's funeral who were running ahead of the funeral train, struck a hand car carrying nine carpenters who had just left Beaver Station on the bridge across Brady's Run killing six. The railroad paid the families of the victims $1,000 each. **9(243)**

🍂 **November, 1881** – The Women's Christian Temperance Union was established in Beaver to remonstrate against the granting of a liquor license to a hotel in a neighboring borough. Membership was 67. **9(395)**

🍂 **February 2, 1882** – Keystone Steam Driller Company was organized in the back room of Mr. McAnlis's Jewelry Shop in Beaver Falls. The actual manufacturing was done in the old Thornily Foundry and Machine Shop at Fallston. The company was moved to Beaver Falls in 1887, and the company was out of business by July of 1959. **2(678), 9(434), 93(7, 90)**

🍂 **1882** – J. H. Knott & Company built a flour mill on the site of the old Patterson mill in Beaver Falls, which burned down the year before. The company sold out in 1896. **2(672)**

🍂 **1882** – The Beaver Valley Glass Manufacturing Company, also called the "Dinkey Glass Works," was established in Rochester to manufacture flasks, brandy bottles, and prescription vials. The plant was destroyed by fire in July of 1890 and not rebuilt. **2(745)**

🍂 **1882** – The Rochester Flouring Mills Company was established in Rochester opposite the Fort Wayne freight depot. **2(747)**

🍂 **1882** – The Baptist Church of Beaver Falls was organized with a congregation of thirty people. **9(415)**

🍂 **March 23, 1882** – The Women's Christian Temperance Union of Rochester was organized by Mrs. J. S. Rutan and Mrs. Rev. Satterfield. **9(502)**

1883 survey stone near Georgetown - Applegate Collection

🍂 **1883** – Pennsylvania's western boundary with West Virginia was re-surveyed and re-marked. The survey was begun at the Ohio River and run south to the southwest corner of Pennsylvania, a distance of about 63 ½ miles. Twenty three of the original 1785 markers were found and 48 more were established, including one by the original 1785 marker at Georgetown. **95(128-129)**

🍂 **1883** – The Beaver Falls Paper Company was organized as a branch of the New Castle Company and was owned by the Dilworth Brothers of Pittsburgh. It was out of operation by 1904. **2(672)**

- **1883** – The Hartman Steel Company, Limited, was organized to manufacture wire in Beaver Falls. **2(674)**

- **1883** – Greersburg Academy was sold to the New York, Pittsburgh & Chicago Railroad for $300. The money was used to build the larger red brick building three blocks away that would serve as Greersburg Academy until 1908 when it was converted to a public school. The old Greersburg Academy building was converted to a railroad passenger station and served until 1944. The former Academy is now a part of the Little Beaver Historical Society Complex. **77(13)**

- **1883** – The county school superintendent reported that 53 of the schoolhouses in Beaver County were without "suitable privies." **49("Teaching in Beaver County in the "Good" Old Days was no Picnic," Vol. 35 No. 2, Spring 2009)**

- **January 2, 1883** – John Ubalto of Beaver passed away and was buried in the present Beaver Cemetery. His real name was John Specht, and before coming to Beaver, he had served in the British Army during the Crimean War and was one of the members of the famous Light Brigade whose charge against hopeless odds during the Battle of Balaklava became immortalized by a poem written by Alfred, Lord Tennyson. **2(660, Note 2)**

- **February 4, 1883** – The *Beaver Valley News* became the first daily newspaper in the county. **57(21)**

- **November 19, 1883** – Bridgewater Gas Co. became the county's first supplier of natural gas for fuel and lighting. **2(270)**

- **Before 1884** – James I. Park established the Park Stone Quarry and a brickyard in Crows Run Valley (New Sewickley Township). **1(50ff)**

- **February 8, 1884** – Flooding on the Ohio and Beaver Rivers inflicted extensive damage in low-lying areas. Bridges at Fallston and at Wolf Lane in Rochester were swept downstream taking out sections of the Cleveland & Pittsburgh Railroad bridge (Beaver River) at Rochester as well as the Pittsburgh & Lake Erie Railroad bridge (Ohio River) between Monaca and Beaver. **2(8, 240ff), 9(153)**

- **March 15, 1884** – A group of ladies from Beaver Falls started their own Woman's Christian Temperance Union. As a result of their work, a school for boys was established to teach boys from the street good moral and Christian values. **9(427)**

- **1884** – The Phoenix Glass factory in Phillipsburg (Monaca) was destroyed by fire and steps were taken to rebuild. **55(77).**

- **1884** – Beaver Falls ladies began a Young Ladies' Christian Temperance Union. This group started and maintained an industrial school for girls in 1887 to teach them a vocation as well as sewing, singing, gymnastics and light literary work. **9(427)**

- **1884** – The First Christian Church was established in Beaver Falls. **9(415)**

- **1884** – The Salvation Army established itself in Beaver Falls, and within a year a branch was also established in Rochester. **5(498)**

- **1884** – Lieutenant Emory Taunt, a former student educated at the Kenwood School for Boys in New Brighton was a member of the relief expedition which rescued the Greely party. The Greely party was trapped on the Arctic ice, and its remaining members were near death from starvation and exposure. Nineteen of Greely's original twenty-five men perished. **33("He is a Pittsburger," July 30, 1884)**

- **1884** – The Fallston Bridge was re-built to replace the 1836 wooden covered bridge that was swept away by the February flood. It was a Pratt Whipple truss design. **5(77), 49(Vol. 37 No. 3, pages 1-4)**

- **1884** – Knott, Harker & Company operated for a few months in New Brighton before moving to Beaver Falls and purchasing the American Grate & Fender Company. The company manufactured mantels, grates and all kinds of fireplace goods. **2(677)**

- **1884** – The Beaver Falls Chemical Company was organized to manufacture general chemical products by a group of men in Cleveland, Ohio. **2(679)**

- **1884** – John H. Park built the North Shore Railroad connecting the Park Quarry in Crow's Run to the Pennsylvania Railroad at Conway. **49("History of Crow's Run, New Sewickley Twp.," Vol. 29, No. 4, Fall, 2004)**

- **1884** – The New Brighton and New Castle Railroad Company bought the Metheny Tavern, opened Felician Park (Happy Park) just outside of Ellwood City on a triangle of land where the Connequenessing Creek flows into the Beaver River, and made it into one of the finest Victorian amusement resorts in western Pennsylvania. In 1905 Rock Point Amusement Co. leased Felician Park and renamed it "Rock Point Park." Due to a steady decline in business, the park closed after the 1911 season. A fire in 1915 destroyed most of the vacant buildings. **36(16-17)**

- **1884** – The first South Heights school opened at Third Street and Cherry Avenue. The second building opened in 1930 and continued until South Heights (at that time known as Shannopin) merged with the Ambridge School District. **49("First South Heights School," Vol. 35 No. 4, Fall, 2010)**

- **August, 1884** – The Young Woman's Christian Temperance Union was organized in Beaver with Mrs. William Patten, state superintendent. **9(395-396)**

Strolling Through Time: A Chonology of Beaver County, PA History to 2016

- **September 23, 1884** – Beaver Valley Street Railway Company obtained its charter. **2(265)**

- **September 24, 1884** – Excavations began for the foundations of the new courthouse and jail by the Norcross Brothers. A contract was made for all of the stone to be quarried at the A. J. Jolly & Sons quarry in Homewood. **33("Commence Work To-Day," September 24, 1884)**

- **October 29, 1884** – The National Bank of New Brighton was opened and was the first, and for years, the only national bank in Beaver County. This bank succeeded the Bank of Beaver County, a state bank organized in 1857. **2(719)**

- **November 1, 1884** – The Providence Baptist Church of North Sewickley was incorporated. **9(607)**

- **1885** – The Mill Creek Valley Fair began. In 1905, the fair was reorganized and renamed the Hookstown Fair. **49(Vol. 32, No. 1, pg 4)**

- **July 4, 1885** – Beaver Valley Street Railway Co., the first street railway in the county, began operating horse-drawn cars from the Pittsburgh Fort Wayne & Chicago Railroad Station at New Brighton to the foot of College Hill (Beaver Falls). **2(265)**

- **November 2, 1885** – The Concord Presbyterian Church was incorporated in Economy Township. **9(593)**

- **October, 1885** – The Beaver Falls Iron Company was founded and produced sheet metal until November 19, 1888, when the plant burned down and was not rebuilt. **2(671)**

- **October 25, 1885** – Pittsburgh Hinge & Chain Factory in Beaver Falls was destroyed by fire. The company was founded in 1870. **2(673)**

- **December 4, 1885** – At approximately 4:00 in the morning, a group of daring professional burglars inserted a dynamite charge into a hole drilled in the safe of Bentel & Co. Bank in Freedom and blew it open. The loss amounted to about $8,000. No suspects were apprehended. **112("Burglars Blow Open a Safe," December 5, 1885)**

- **1886** – The First National Bank of Beaver Falls was organized. **2(273)**

- **1886** – Beaver Falls Cutlery went out of business due to poor profitability. **2(670)**

- **1886** – St. Cecilia Parish in Rochester formed its first parochial school in a vacant carpentry shop on Adams Street. **5(297)**

- **March 15, 1886** – The Mill Creek Valley Fair was formally chartered. On August 7, 1900, the association changed its name to the Mill Creek Valley Agricultural Association and was incorporated as a farmer's association. **2(282),** *See entry for August 7, 1900*

- **May 11, 1886** – The Young Men's Christian Association of Rochester was established. **9(496-497)**

- **September 22, 1886** – A slight earthquake shook Beaver County, but no damage was reported. **19(222)**

- **October 21, 1886** – Standard Oil Company purchased 7,000 acres of promising oil and gas territory belonging to the Raccoon Oil Company at Shannopin (present day South Heights) for $750,000. **105("Negotiations," October 21, 1886)**

- **1887** – James Madison Toy of Beaver Falls became the first Beaver Countian to join a major league baseball team; the Cleveland Blues. Although surrounded by controversy, he is thought by some to be the first American Indian major league player. **(Beaver County Sports Hall of Fame)**

- **1887** – Matthew Stanley Quay of Beaver was elected to the Senate. He became known throughout his political career as "The Napoleon of Politics" and "King-Maker." He was also popularly known as "Boss Quay." **2(221-222), 1(67),** *Refer to entry for July 19, 1888*

- **1887** – Whitla Glass Company, Limited was organized in Beaver Falls to produce a general line of glassware. On April 25, 1890, it was incorporated as The Valley Glass Company and burned down and not rebuilt until April 9, 1892. **2(673)**

- **1887** – White Township was created from a part of Chippewa Township and was named for early settler John White. It was considerably reduced in size when College Hill Borough was incorporated in 1892 and West Mayfield separated from White taking a large portion of the northern section. This left White Township with only .72 square miles and making it one of the smallest townships in Pennsylvania. **21(160)**

- **1887** – The Beaver Falls Glass Company, Limited, was organized to manufacture all varieties of pressed glassware which shipped throughout the country and abroad. It went out of business by 1904. **2(674)**

Conway Rail Yards – BCHRLF Collection

- **1887** – Conway Rail Yards was established by the Pennsylvania Railroad. A major expansion was done in 1905, and by 1956 it was the largest push button railroad yard in the world until around 1980. **48(57). The Conrail Historical Society, BCHRLF Historical Marker**

- **February, 1887** – The Keystone Chemical Works was started in Beaver Falls to manufacture silicate of soda for making soap, stiffening prints, etc. in the rear of the Mayer Pottery building. The Works were out of operation by 1904. **2(673)**

- **February 1, 1887** – The Beaver Falls Art Tile Company, Limited, was organized to produce artistic decorative tile including stove, fireplace, and mantel tiles. **2(679)**

- **May 1, 1888** – The first oil well was drilled in the Hanover Oil Fields. **50(139)**

- **July 19, 1888** – Senator Matthew Stanley Quay was belatedly awarded the Medal of Honor for his actions at the Civil War Battle of Fredericksburg on December 13, 1862. **2(221-222), 1(67)**

- **November 5, 1888** – Over a ton of nitroglycerine exploded at 4:20 in the morning near Shannopin (present South Heights) sending a shockwave nearly forty miles away, breaking windows and rolling people out of their beds. The nitro was owned by the Torpedo Company of Delaware for use in the Shannopin (now South Heights) oil fields. **45("The Earth Shook," November 5, 1888)**

- **November 19, 1888** – Beaver Valley Electric Light & Power Co., received a charter to build a power plant on the bank of the Beaver River and became the first commercial supplier of electric power in the county. The first plant was installed in the works of Mr. Hartman. **2(271)**

- **1888** – New Brighton telephone service began. By 1907, the 538 telephone subscribers found their service connected with the Beaver Falls exchange. **5(355)**

- **1888** – The Metric Metal Works for the production of gas meters, opened in Beaver Falls in the former cutlery company plant. The company was moved to Erie around 1892. **2(670)**

- **May 6, 1889** – The Union Drawn Steel Co. was organized in Beaver Falls to produce cold drawn steel shafting, pump-rods, piston-rods, and special shapes of cold-finished steel on a large scale. It became Republic Steel in 1960 and is still in operation today (2015) as the cold draw facility, Pennsylvania Cold Draw. **2(680), 79(59)**

Rudyard Kipling - Courtesy Beaver Area Historical Museum

🦫 **July/August, 1889** – World-renowned author and journalist Rudyard Kipling made a prolonged visit to Beaver. He stayed with Dr. R. T. Taylor, the President of Beaver College and was great friends with his daughter Edmonia whom he had met in India. During his stay, Kipling and Edmonia's younger sister Caroline Taylor would develop a short romantic attachment that would end in 1890 after his journey to England. Kipling was awarded the Nobel Prize for Literature in 1907. **67(141-143), 129(106)**

Caroline Taylor - Courtesy Beaver Area Historical Museum

🦫 **1889** – St. Mary's Catholic School in Beaver Falls was founded. **5(297)**

🦫 **1889** – Henry Hartman, a Pittsburgh steel manufacturer, purchased the Marginal Beaver Falls Railroad from the Economites along with all of their franchises, real estate, etc. belonging to it. **101("Has Bought a Railroad," May 13, 1889)**

🦫 **1889** – The Craig Manufacturing Company was founded in Freedom to produce caskets, linings, and robes along with a full line of goods adapted to the undertaking trade. It was reorganized as the Freedom Casket Company on June 28, 1901. **2(793-794)**

🦫 **1889** – A bridge was built over the Beaver River at Sharon (upper Bridgewater). **2(243)**

Sharon Bridge - Courtesy James Camp III

VI. Small Business & Big Dreams: 1890 to 1904

During this era, small steel companies were established along with smaller industries of many different types. Oil was discovered in the county and proved to be a short lived industry as it would peak around 1910 and decline rapidly from there. The rise of these industries created a demand for a rapid increase in transportation, which was partially answered with the establishment of the first highway bridge linking the north and south sides of the Ohio River between Monaca and Rochester. With more workers needing a convenient way to get to work, a new mode of transportation grew as the earlier horse-drawn street railway systems gave way to electric street cars within and between county towns. In order to help make river navigation more reliable and to control the disastrous floods that plagued the river communities, the U.S. government built the Merrill Lock and Dam in nearby Industry.

New innovations during this time included hospitals, electric power stations, trolley parks, and more and more companies to supply natural gas to the general public for fuel and lighting. With all of these advantages in place, Beaver County was poised to take a major leap forward.

- **1890's** – With oil discovered in the Economy Oil Field, Wallace City became the center of the booming oil industry which would peak around 1910 and decline rapidly after that. **1(55)**

- **1890** – The Tenth Street Bridge over the Beaver River at Beaver Falls opened as a toll bridge for highway traffic. The bridge was dismantled in 2001. **4(169)**

- **1890** – The U.S. Census reported that the county population totaled 50,077, and the largest town was New Brighton which totaled 5,616. **2(275, 723)**

- **1890** – Miss Agnes I. Schade of Phillipsburg (Monaca) became the first single female missionary of the Lutheran Church of America when she was sent to India. **55(98)**

- **1890** – Freedom native, Reverend Isaac Taylor Headland joined the Methodist mission in China. Upon the death of his first wife, Rev. Taylor married Dr. Mariam Sinclair who was the head of the Presbyterian Women's Hospital in Peking and was also the physician to the Imperial Chinese Court. In 1907, the Headlands returned home and brought with them a collection of nearly 500 paintings, including some by the Empress Dowager herself and many of which now are in the Boston Museum of Fine Art. **49("Rev. Isaac Taylor Headland Missionary to China", Vol. 34 No. 3 Summer, 2009)**

- **March 10, 1890** – The Rochester Electric Company was chartered. The plant was installed on Delaware Avenue, near Madison Street in Rochester. **2(272)**

- **July 29, 1890** – A mob of unruly passengers took over a picnic excursion train in Shannopin (present day South Heights), insulting female passengers and refusing to heed the conductor's instructions to get off. The crew was badly beaten in an attempt to restore order. When another train crew tried to intervene, the badly outnumbered railroad men were also beaten and threatened with revolvers. Police arrived after a three and a half hour battle and the mob scattered, all but three escaped. **105("Captured a Train," July 29, 1890)**

- **February 2, 1891** – A charter was granted for a YMCA in New Brighton. **5(370).**

- **1891** – The Hotel Oliver was opened in Ellwood City, and was the first major building project in Ellwood City by the Pittsburgh Company. Lawrence High School (later Lincoln High School) was later built on this site. **63(10, 119)**

- **October 15, 1891** – The J.C. Russell Shovel Company was started in Aliquippa. **2(851)**

Beaver Valley Traction Company – BCHRLF Collection

- **December 5, 1891** – Beaver Valley Street Railway. Co. was absorbed by the Beaver Valley Traction Co., which converted to the first electric power streetcars and extended service to Beaver. **2(265), 66(10)**

- **June 13, 1891** – Pittsburgh and Western Railroad ran the first train on the Ellwood Short Line through Ellwood City.

- **1892** – Phillipsburg was renamed "Monaca" after Monacatootha, an Oneida Indian chief who was also known as Scaroudy. The shortened version of the name was first used by the Pittsburgh & Lake Erie Railroad on a station at the east end of town. **13(15)**

- **1892** – The Eclipse Bicycle Company of Indianapolis, Indiana, moved into the former Beaver Falls Cutlery Company building and manufactured the Eclipse Bicycle, and in 1893, the first with pneumatic tires. The plant was moved to Elmira, New York, in 1896 and is still in business today. **2(670)**

- **1892** – The Standard Gauge Steel Company was incorporated in Beaver Falls to manufacture finished machine keys, machine racks, square, flat, round, and special shapes in finished steel. **2(680-681)**

Strolling Through Time: A Chonology of Beaver County, PA History to 2016

🦫 **1892** – H.W. Hartman established the Hartman Manufacturing Company in Ellwood City to manufacture tree guards, flexible wire mats, panel and wrought iron fencing known as Hartman Diamond Point fence. **63(52)**

🦫 **May 2, 1892** – College Hill Borough was incorporated from a part of White Township, and grew up around Geneva College. In 1932, it merged with the city of Beaver Falls. **2(847)**

🦫 **July, 1892** – Eastvale, formerly named "Fetterman," was incorporated as a borough, and was once a part of Pulaski and North Sewickley Townships. It lies on the east bank of the Beaver River opposite Beaver Falls, and was considered the smallest municipality in Beaver County. **21(84)**

🦫 **August 13, 1892** – Peoples Electric Street Railway Company completed a line from Junction Park to St. Clair (Freedom) Borough. Regular service began on this date. **2(265ff), 66(11)**

🦫 **August 18, 1892** – Nearly 12,000 to 15,000 Civil War veterans and their families attended "Grand Army Day" in the Rock Point Park picnic grounds. A Grand Army dress parade was held and reviewed by the department commander. **45("Grand Army Day," August 18, 1892)**

🦫 **October 12, 1892** – Aliquippa established its post office, and its first postmaster was Joseph Stubert. **2(851)**

🦫 **November 29, 1892** – Hookstown native, the Rev. John Witherspoon Scott passed away in Washington, D.C. where he was living at the White House with his daughter, Caroline Lavinia Harrison who was the First Lady of the United States, having married future President Benjamin Harrison in 1853. Caroline was also the First President General of the D.A.R. and passed away at the White House one month before her father. **(https://www.whitehouse.gov/1600/first-ladies/carolineharrison), (http://www.findagrave.com/cgi-bin/fg.cgi?page=gr&GRid=26021118), 94(46)**

🦫 **April 18, 1893** – The Geneva College basketball team played the first college basketball game in the world defeating the New Brighton YMCA 3 – 0. Peach baskets were used as goals. However, recent evidence suggests that Vanderbilt may have beaten Geneva to the punch by playing its first game on February 7, 1893. **35("Vanderbilt lays claim as the true 'birthplace of college basketball'", November 29, 2014)**

🦫 **1893** – The Union Water Co. built a pumping station on the east bank of the Beaver River near Eastvale to supply water to the borough of Beaver Falls through cast iron pipe previously laid in the 1870s. **2(269)**

Strolling Through Time: A Chonology of Beaver County, PA History to 2016

1894 – The Borough of Aliquippa was incorporated. *See entry for Woodlawn in 1877.* **21(50)**

1894 – Rochester native Oliver Shallenberger was credited with the invention of the "Watthour meter" (electric meter), while working for the Westinghouse Corporation. The meter would measure current usage and allow the public to use alternating current. **19(34),** *See entry for 1932*

1894 – Baker Forge Company was established in Ellwood City to manufacture wagon hardware. It was later named the Steel Car Forge Company. **63(42)**

1894 – Populist leader Jacob Coxey led his "army" of approximately 500 unemployed men through Beaver County. Coxey and his men were travelling from Massillon, Ohio, to Washington, D.C. to protest the high unemployment caused by the depression of 1893. **49(Vol. 30 No. 1 Winter, 2005 "Coxey's Army Marches Through Beaver County")**

January 27, 1894 – Daugherty Township was formed from Pulaski Township and was named after lawyer Edward Black Daugherty. The petition for township status passed by a mere four vote margin. **21(80)**

January 1, 1895 – Beaver Valley General Hospital was originally built on the corners of Ninth and Fifth Streets in Beaver Falls in the former Merchant's Hotel. It relocated to New Brighton on July 1, 1896. **5(311-313), 1(43), 2(391)**

June 25, 1895 – The Keystone Pottery Company in Rochester was destroyed by fire. **2(743)**

1895 – John Reeves built the Patterson Heights Incline. Also known as the Patterson Heights Street Railway, it opened on January 19, 1896 with only one car, and it closed in 1927. **5(61), 66(43-47)**

1896 – The McCool Tube Company next occupied the old cutlery works and manufactured iron and steel material into tubes. **2(670)**

Patterson Heights Incline 1898 BCHRLF Collection

December 17, 1896 – People's Water Co. of Beaver Falls was incorporated. **2(269)**

February, 1897 – The Keystone Tumbler Company was established in Rochester. On November 1, 1899, it was taken over by the National Glass Company. **2(744)**

Strolling Through Time: A Chonology of Beaver County, PA History to 2016

1897 Rochester-Monaca Bridge – BCHRLF Collection

🕮 **1897** – The Rochester – Monaca suspension bridge, the first highway bridge across the Ohio River between Pittsburgh and Wheeling, West Virginia opened, eliminating the need for ferry service by the "Mary C" which had operated since 1873. **1(51, 32), 2(245)**

🕮 **1897** – The Valley Ice Company was established in Beaver Falls and specialized in pure ice as well as coal and coke. **2(680)**

🕮 **1897** – The first factory built in Ellwood City was the Ellwood Shafting and Tube Company. **63(49)**

🕮 **1897** – Dawes & Myler established a factory in New Brighton for the manufacture of enameled ironware and pump cylinders. **2(710ff), 4(100)**

🕮 **1897** – Pittsburgh Architect Elise Mercur, one of the first independent female architects in the country, married Karl Wagner of Economy. She was noted for many of her designs including one of the buildings for the Beaver College & Musical Institute. In 1900 she moved her practice to Economy. **131(137-138)**

🕮 **1897** – The Pittsburgh & Lake Erie Railroad built a passenger station in Beaver, said to be the finest station building in the Beaver Valley at that time. **104("An Ornament to Beaver," November 9, 1897)**

🕮 **January 12, 1897** – Two dynamite explosions rocked Shannopin (now South Heights) with shocks that could be felt sixty miles away. Four people were killed and over $10,000 damage was done, and the cause was unknown. **33("The Earth Rocked," January 13, 1897)**

🕮 **September 13, 1897** – Romigh School, New Sewickley, was opened in a log cabin. **5(249-261)**

🕮 **December 9, 1897** – The Valley Electric Company was chartered and gained control of both the Rochester Electric Company and the Beaver Valley Electric Company to control all electric power generation in the county. **2(272)**

🕮 **1898** – J. S. Mitchell & Sons bought the former Steam Planing Mill Company in Beaver Falls and dealt in rough and planed lumber and in general planing-mill products. **2(678-679)**

Strolling Through Time: A Chonology of Beaver County, PA History to 2016

1898 – The Douglas Whisler Brick Company was incorporated in Beaver Falls. In 1902, they moved their offices to the Masonic building in Beaver Falls and began a factory in Eastvale. **2(681)**

1898 – The Riverview Electric Street Railway operated between the Pennsylvania Railroad depots in Beaver Falls and New Brighton. Service ended in 1904. **66(12-13)**

April, 1898 – The Spanish – American War broke out.

July 21, 1898 – Company B of the 10th Regiment Pennsylvania National Guard stationed at New Brighton arrived in the Philippines to participate in the Spanish-American War. **5(229)**

December 10, 1898 – Spain and the United States signed the Treaty of Paris which officially ended the Spanish-American War. Hostilities had ended earlier on August 12, 1898.

1899 – Rochester Hospital, originally known as the Beaver County General Hospital, was organized as a semi-private institution. It was turned over to the public in 1902. **5(315)**

1899 – The Atlantic Tube Company was organized (ATC was chartered in New Jersey) and built the second seamless piercing mill in the United States at Beaver Falls. **82(4)**

June 19, 1899 – Patterson Heights was incorporated from a part of Patterson Township and was one of the smallest municipalities in the county. **21(137)**

November 1, 1899 – The newly formed National Glass Company took over numerous glass companies including the Rochester Tumbler Works and the Keystone Glass Company. At its height, the company employed nearly 7,000 people in its combined Keystone-Rochester plant. **2(744-745)**

Before 1900 – Beaver Falls' first telephone exchange provided service for 283 telephones. **5(355).**

Junction Park Merry-Go-Round – BCHRLF Collection

Ca. 1900 – Junction Park was built by the Beaver Valley Traction Company along present day Route 65 at the lower end of New Brighton. **1(47), 5(399)**

1900 – Morado Park was built on College Hill,

Beaver Falls by the Beaver Valley Traction Company. **5(398)**

1900 – John Buchanan speaking at the Beaver County Centennial stated that the educational system of "The townships of Hanover, Greene and Raccoon have placed in the Christian Ministry, one hundred thirty of her sons, more than one hundred physicians and many lawyers and teachers." **94(47)**

1900 – James Bruien, a former slave who escaped captivity three times and fought in the Civil War, was honored at the Beaver County Centennial Celebration. Also attending the four day celebration were Major General Nelson Miles, Civil War veteran and hero of the Indian wars and Pennsylvania Governor William Stone. **49(Vol. 30 No. 2, page 20), 33("Beaver County's Centennial," June 13, 1900)**

1900 – The U.S. Census reported county population totaled 56,432, with the largest town being Beaver Falls at 10,054. **2(275, 699)**

1900 – Mount Gallitzin Academy, founded in 1869 as a boarding school for boys in grades 1 through 8, was relocated to Economy from Ebensburg, Pennsylvania. The name was derived from Demetrius Gallitzin, a Russian prince who was instrumental in founding the original school. **5(297)**

1900 – The federal census reported that there were 2,602 farms in the county averaging 95.7 acres with a gross income of $1,604,652. The number of farms had decreased to 512 in 1992 and decreased again to 499 in 1997. **2(283), 19(128)**

1900 – Rochester telephone exchange had 134 telephones. **5(355)**

1900 – Jemuel Woodruff of Rochester passed away. Just prior to his death, he was considered the oldest Freemason in the United States. He was 96 years old having been born in 1804 and became a member of the order in 1825. **2(746), 61(8), 34("Noteworthy Names Contributed to Rochester's Heritage", August 10, 1999)**

1900 – The Pittsburgh Wallpaper Company opened a factory in New Brighton. In 1901, it became the largest factory of its kind in point of capacity in the country at that time. It was devastated by a fire on October 26, 1915, leaving over 650 workers unemployed. **57(15)**

1900 – The Imperial Glass Company was formed in Beaver Falls and occupied the premises of the former Beaver Falls Glass Company. **2(677)**

May 31, 1900 – The Boxer Rebellion broke out in China. The Boxers, whose name means "Fists of Righteous Harmony," began attacking foreign missionaries in and around the capital of Peking. The foreign legations were under siege until relieved by an allied force on June 19th. **129(14-15)**

Strolling Through Time: A Chonology of Beaver County, PA History to 2016

- **June 19-22, 1900** – Beaver County held its Centennial Celebration in Beaver. **2(1039)**

- **June 20, 1900** – The Soldiers and Sailors Memorial was dedicated in McIntosh Square, Beaver to commemorate all who served from the Revolution to the Spanish-American War. **5(247)**

- **August 7, 1900** – The Mill Creek Valley Agricultural Association was incorporated as a farmer's association. **2(282),** *See entry for March 15, 1886*

- **October 1, 1900** – The Traction Company combined with: The Beaver Valley Street Railway, the Central Electric Street Railway, the Peoples Electric Street Railway, the College & Grandview Electric Street Railway, the Rochester & Monaca Electric Street Railway and the Beaver & Vanport Electric Street Railway to form the Beaver Valley Traction Company. **66(15)**

- **November 28, 1900** – A Cleveland and Pittsburgh railroad train wrecked a half mile west of Beaver Station with the express car falling into the Ohio River. No trace of the rail car was found, but a safe containing $100,000 was recovered intact from the river. The operation was kept secret until the safe was removed. **45("Safe Take From the Ohio River," December 1, 1900)**

- **1901** – Beaver County had 253 female teachers earning an average of $36.23 per month and 83 male teachers earning an average of $44.98 per month. The average number of students attending school was 8,422. **2(409)**

- **1901** – Ingram-Richardson Co., a leading manufacturer of porcelain enamel products, was founded in Beaver Falls. **1(25)**

- **1901** – The Ellwood Stone Company began operations as a partnership of David J. Jones, Jr. and his father. **63(19)**

Colonial Steel Company – BCHRLF Collection

- **1901** – McLaughlin's Blacksmith Shop was the first business established in Chippewa Township. **(Note: The Beaver County Industrial Museum has the records of a trading post run in the 1830's by Azariah Inman that disputes this.)** **21(72)**

- **June 5, 1901** – Colonial Steel Company announced that it would begin building a plant in Colonna, which is now a part of present day Monaca, along with employee housing. **45("Site Selected for Big Plant: Colonial Steel to build mills and town at Colonna," June 5, 1901)**

- **June 25, 1901** – Two persons were killed and thirty-nine injured when a Pittsburgh & Lake Erie Railroad express train went off the tracks in South Monaca and fell over a fifteen foot embankment. The Cleveland bound train was travelling at approximately 50 miles per hour when the accident occurred. **104("Two Killed and 39 Injured in P&LE Wreck," June 25, 1901)**

- **1902** – Chief Justice Daniel Agnew of Beaver died at age 94. **46(65)**

- **1902** – The Finished Specialty and Machine Company, controlled by Union Drawn Steel, was set-up in Beaver Falls. **2(680)**

- **1902** – The New York-Pittsburgh Company was organized in Beaver Falls to manufacture typewriters as well as an attachment for sewing-machines for blind stitching. It was located in a portion of the old Beaver Falls Cutlery Works. **2(681)**

- **1902** – The Standard Connecting Rod Company was incorporated in Beaver Falls for the manufacture of connecting-rods, strap-joints and finished crank shafts. **2(681)**

- **1902** – Commercial Sash and Door Company built a large mill in Beaver Falls near the Tenth Street Bridge. **2(680)**

- **1902** – The Pittsburgh Tool & Wire Company was formed in Monaca and was known locally as the "wire mill." **55(80)**

- **1902** – The Atlantic Tube Company in Beaver Falls, consisting of a piercing mill and cold draw facility, was sold to the Pittsburgh Seamless Company for $423,000. **82(5)**

- **1902** – According to former Beaver Falls Councilman Harry Crowl, there were exactly twenty-two automobiles registered in the county. First the driver had to register his car with the county, then he purchased numbers at a hardware store and had a saddler mount the numbers on a leather "license plate" which was then attached to the car. Since there were no gas stations at the time, the driver bought a quart at a time from the local drugstore or dry cleaner (at the time, they used gas to clean clothes). **5(62), 19(118)**

- **1902** – The Kristufek Agency was founded and contracted by the American Bridge Company to construct housing and to provide food for the workers building their plant. **62(pages not numbered)**

- **1902** – Armstrong Industries opened a plant in Beaver Falls to produce clay bounded cork products. It was later renamed Armstrong World Industries as it established plants world-wide. The Beaver Falls plant closed on May 11, 2011. **5(119), 10(117), 49(Vol. 36 No. 4, page 7)**

- **Spring, 1902** – Union Water Company and The People's Water Co. of Beaver Falls, merged into the Beaver Valley Water Company to supply water to most of the towns in the county. **2(269ff)**

- **March 17, 1902** – The Beaver Clay Manufacturing Works was established in New Galilee to make brick for building. **2(844)**

- **April 11, 1902** – Another dynamite explosion rocked Shannopin (present day South Heights) when a half ton of dynamite went off killing two and injuring another. The explosion left a hole nearly thirty feet in diameter where the building housing the dynamite once stood and caused nearly $5,000 in damages. The cause was unknown. **104("Two Victims of Explosion," April 11, 1902)**

- **May, 1902** – The earliest track meet on record was held between Beaver Falls, New Brighton, Beaver and Geneva Prepatory. **5(381)**

- **June 20, 1902** – Conway was incorporated as a borough. **21(74)**

- **June 28, 1902** – H. C. Fry Glass Co. was founded in Rochester by Henry Clay Fry, and became a world renowned producer of glass products. It was considered the finest and best equipped glass factory in the United States at the time. **2(46, 741-742)**

- **July 1, 1902** – The United States Sanitary Manufacturing Co. began the manufacture of cast iron enameled plumbing fixtures in Monaca. **55(85)**

- **October 26, 1902** – One of the pioneers of the women's Rights Movement, Elizabeth Cady Stanton passed away at her home in New York. **129(45)**

- **1903** – American Bridge Company, a division of U.S. Steel Corporation, opened in Ambridge. **1(100), 30(2)**

- **1903** – Beaver County had 44 post-offices. **2(275-276)**

Carnegie Library Beaver Falls - BCHRLF Collection

- **1903** – Carnegie Free Library was built on 7th Avenue in Beaver Falls, becoming the first public library building in the county. **1(21), 44(94)**

- **1903** – The Beaver Valley Brewing Co. opened on Railroad Street, Rochester. **1(43)**

- **1903** – The Sisters of Charity established and began operating Providence Hospital in the former Reeves mansion in Beaver Falls. **1(32)**

1903 – Aliquippa telephone service was established, and was subsequently known as "Woodlawn" during the period from 1911 until 1928. **5(355)**

May 2, 1903 – The Harmony Society sold all of its land in Beaver County amounting to 26,000 acres along with twenty acres in Allegheny County for $4 million to the Liberty Land Company. The Harmonists would retain three blocks of dwellings in the village of Economy, the graveyard and the church. **103("Economites Sell for $4,000,000," May 2, 1903)**

July 10, 1903 – Brady's Run Land Company was formed for the purpose of building houses for workmen at the nearby clay plants. The clay plants were: Brady's Run Brickworks, Fallston Fire Company, Keswick Pottery and Standard Fire Clay. As of this date, seven houses had been built and rented out. The new development was in the Borough of Bridgewater, and around three miles from the center of the population of the borough. **30("A Town Springing Up in Brady's Run", July 10, 1903)**

November 24, 1903 – Beaver Council passed a resolution to name its four public inner squares as Gibson, Harmar, Irvine & McIntosh, and its outer public squares as Brodhead, Wayne, Bouquet & Clark. **2(662-664)**

December 13, 1903 – The Harmony Society officially dissolved with Susie Duss (the trustee) and Franz Gillman the only remaining members. Susie's husband, John Duss was Head Trustee until May 12, 1903, when he left the Society to pursue his music career. He needed the money that he received upon leaving the Society to pay his musicians. Because his wife was still a member, Duss stayed involved with the Harmony Society until the end, and was very active with the land, buildings, and "chattel." Following the dissolution, he died in 1951. **(Sarah Buffington Curator OEV)**

Ca 1904 – Beaver Valley Country Club in Beaver Falls, which has one of the oldest golf courses in Western Pennsylvania, began holding tournaments. **5(383)**

1904 – First known Jewish Synagogue, Agudath Achim, was built in Beaver Falls. **5(497)**

1904 – The public schools of Monaca consisted of eight rooms in a substantial building, with three rooms in other places; and eleven teachers. There was also a high school with a three year course. **2(807)**

May 28, 1904 – Senator Matthew Stanley Quay died in Beaver and was interred in Beaver Cemetery. He was awarded the Medal of Honor for his actions during the Civil War battle of Fredericksburg. **2(221-222), 1(67),** *See listings for December 13, 1862, 1887, July 19, 1888, May 15, 1975*

- **June, 1904** – William Payne became the last prisoner executed inside of Beaver County. He was hung on a scaffold at the rear of the old jailhouse. Since the last hanging had been 41 years earlier, the sheriff was unable to find the scaffold, so he had to get an old condemned one from Allegheny County. **19(215), 45("Had No Scaffold," June 1, 1904)**

- **August, 1904** – Merrill Lock & Dam #6 was opened on the Ohio River west of present Vanport and was named after Colonel William E. Merrill then head of the Army Corps of Engineers. It was flooded by the new Montgomery Dam in 1936 and no longer needed. **5(53), 23**

- **1904** – Babcock and Wilcox, a New York manufacturer of boilers, purchased the Pittsburgh Seamless Tube Company of Beaver Falls, a small manufacturer of bicycle tubing. At its peak in 1979, B&W employed over 6,000 people in the county. **1(19)**

- **1904** – Dr. Joseph Bausman published his definitive "History of Beaver County Pennsylvania." **2(Title Pages)**

- **1904** – Beaver Falls, New Brighton and Geneva Preparatory schools formed the first formal football league. **5(372)**

- **1904** – The Fort McIntosh Chapter of the Daughters of the American Revolution was chartered in Beaver. The original charter is on loan to the Beaver Area Historical Museum. **(http://www.rootsweb.ancestry.com/~fmdarns/index_files/Page541.htm)**

VII. Big Steel Brings Big Changes: 1905 to 1919

J ust after the turn of the century, large industries recognized the advantages of locating within the county, and began moving here. Some, like the steel companies, chose plots of ground along the Ohio River and began building not only their massive plants, but whole communities for their own workers, many of whom were new immigrants. This made Beaver County a melting pot of nationalities. Steel wasn't the only industry; other plants were built that produced things like porcelain enamel license plates, steel tubing and boilers, among other things, which firmly established Beaver County as a manufacturing center of national importance.

Transportation became even more important when the big steel companies turned their eyes toward the Ohio River in order to move large quantities of raw materials and finished products. Also, recognizing the need for handling more freight and passengers, the P&LE Railroad expanded to a four-track system and built the largest cantilever type bridge in the world between Monaca and Beaver. The demand for automobiles increased as they started to become more affordable for the average person, which in turn caused more need for better roads and bridges on which to drive them.

Beaver County industry and life were booming as the country became involved in WWI. Once again, we were well represented as the Fifth Engineers became the first county troops to arrive in France, and Beaver Falls native Colonel Joseph H. Thompson was awarded the Medal of Honor. As the war drew to a close, the deadly Spanish Flu epidemic swept through the county indiscriminately killing hundreds.

- **January 1, 1905** – Judge J. Sharp Wilson eliminated the toll on the Rochester-Monaca Bridge, making it the only free bridge crossing the Ohio River at that time. **5(76)**

- **1905** – The Borough of Ambridge was incorporated, taking its name from the American Bridge Co., the largest steel fabricating company in the world and responsible for the steel used in constructing the Empire State building in New York City. **21(52)**

- **1905** – The United States Steel Ellwood plant merged with the Shelby Steel Tube Company and National Steel Tube Company to form the National Tube Company, a division of the U.S. Steel Corporation in Ellwood City. **63(46)**

- **1905** – Ambridge telephone service was established, at which time there were only 82 telephones in the exchange. **5(355)**

- **1905** – The Mutual Union Brewing Company was established and became one of the larger employers in the community of Aliquippa (West Aliquippa). **56(55)**

- **1905** – Jones & Laughlin Steel purchased Woodlawn Park and several farms for the site of the new Aliquippa Works. **83(277)**

- **April 19, 1905** – The Commonwealth of Pennsylvania passed the Automobile Act that required drivers to have an operator's license from the state highway department, that they be over 18 years of age and carry the license with them. The speed limit in Beaver County was 8 mph. **5(63)**

- **December 17, 1905** – The Shannopin United Methodist Church was dedicated. Shannopin is known today as South Heights. **49("Shannopin United Methodist Church," Vol. 35 No. 4, Fall, 2010)**

- **1905** – The Midland Steel Company, represented by T.K. Miller, purchased land from the Neel, Kane, Brucker and McCoy farms on which to build the new steel plant as well as the town of Midland in Industry Township. **21(120)**

- **1905-1906** – The first blast furnace and other facilities of the Midland Steel Company were being built and the town of Midland was also under construction as employee housing. **1(72)**

- **January 1, 1906** – The French Point Street Railway was organized in Ambridge by J.N. Jarvis. **5(60)**

- **May 5, 1906** – First National Bank of Midland was established. **5(97)**

- **1906** – The Ingraham-Richardson Manufacturing Company produced the first enameled license plates for automobiles, and they were in use in Pennsylvania and other states prior to WWI. **44(128)**

- **1906** – The Koppel Steel Company purchased 558 acres of land above the Beaver River in Big Beaver Township to establish their steel mill. Special types of small push cars were built for such diverse uses as sugar cane and crushed rock. They later began making rail cars for the Pittsburgh & Lake Erie Railroad among others. During WWI, the company and town of Koppel were seized by the Alien Property Custodian and later sold to the Pressed Steel Car Company. **49("Koppel Celebrates 100 Years: 1912-2012," Vol. 37, No. 4, Fall, 2012), 116("Beaver County Town on Block," April 22, 1937),** *See entries for 1912 and April 22, 1937*

- **1906** – One of the earliest automobile dealers in the county, B.O. Fair opened a garage and repair shop in Beaver Falls. It was the first of its kind in Beaver County. **19(117)**

- **1906** – St. Felix Catholic Church was formed in Freedom. **5(493)**

J & L Company Houses in Aliquippa – Courtesy of the Library of Congress

🔹 **1907** – Plan 1 of housing was started and considered a part of Logstown (now Aliquippa) and was completed the same year. It was one of the first plans built by Jones & Laughlin Steel exclusively for employee housing. **56(29)**

🔹 **1907** – Presentation of the Blessed Virgin Mary Catholic Church was formed in Midland. In 1994, this church merged with St. Christine in Industry to become St. Blaise. **5(493)**

🔹 **1907** – The Holy Ghost Russian Orthodox congregation was established in Ambridge. **5(495)**

🔹 **March, 1907** – Flooding on the Ohio and Beaver Rivers invaded over 1,000 homes and businesses, and a number of bridges were closed. The Ohio River crested at 38 feet. **5(568), 58(71)**

Former Aliquippa Dance Hall turned into J&L offices Circa 1930's. Dance hall was top floor with first floor added. Photo courtesy of Don Inman.

🔹 **March 12, 1907** – Renowned politician, famous orator and perennial Presidential candidate William Jennings Bryan, also known as the "Great Commoner," spoke to an overflow crowd at the First Presbyterian Church of Beaver. Bryan is best remembered for his opposition to the theory of evolution and his part in the "Scopes Monkey Trial." **49("The "Great Commoner" Visits Beaver County," Vol. 37, No. 2, Spring, 2012)**

🔹 **February 16, 1908** – Celebrated artist Emil Bott died in the Beaver County Home for Indigent Residents and was buried in the St. Peter's Evangelical Lutheran Church Cemetery. **36(61)**

- **June 8, 1908** – The former Aliquippa Park Dance Hall was moved approximately one mile and became office space for the new Jones & Laughlin Steel plant until 1984. It was razed in 1990. **56(40)**

- **June 28, 1908** – The first trolley car pulled into Ellwood City. **63(27)**

- **September 14, 1908** – Beaver Falls began a week-long celebration known as the Home-Week Fair. The festivities included a high wire performance, aerial and trapeze acts, a death defying slide for life down the tallest building in town, daily balloon ascensions and a band concert. **99("Beaver Falls About Ready for its Home-Week Fair, September 6, 1908)**

- **October 1, 1908** – The Model T Ford hit the market in the United States and was the first car with the steering wheel on the right side. **129(117)**

- **October 15, 1908** – A farm hand employed by H. K. Reed discovered a freshly dug mound in Hopewell Township and proceeded to investigate. He dug up a box-like wooden vault about four feet deep fitted with a trap door. Inside, he pulled out a rough box such as is employed to encase a casket. Being unable to open the heavily nailed box, he walked back to the Reed farm to get help, and returned to find the mysterious sealed box missing. Three unknown men had been reported in the vicinity. **33("Beaver County Has Mystery," October 16, 1908)**

- **October 23, 1908** – Forest fires reached a nitroglycerin magazine near Shannopin (present South Heights) causing two explosions at the John H. Hamel Company. The blasts sent shockwaves as far as Pittsburgh shattering windows and causing nearly $15,000 in property damage. **104("Terrific Explosions Caused by Forest Fire," October 23, 1908)**

- **1908** – East Rochester Borough was incorporated from Rochester Township. It was once known as "Seldom Seen." **5(82)**

- **1908** – East Liverpool, Ohio, historian Harold Barth began the first major study of the Indian petroglyphs located at Smith's Ferry along the Ohio River. He and a crew of potters made molds and detailed drawings of the rock carvings that were visible that year. The last time that the carvings were observable was during the 1930's when the river was exceptionally low. Barth's work is featured in the 1973 book "Rock Art of the Upper Ohio Valley" by James L. Swauger while his originals were stored by the East Liverpool Historical Society. **108("Italian Students See Slides of Barth's Work From 1908," November 4, 1908)**

- **1908** – Frankfort Springs organized its own telephone company. **5(355)**

- **1909** – Providence Hospital in Beaver Falls was founded by Father Wertz, pastor of St. Mary's Church. **5(313)**

1909 – Aliquippa's Plan 1 was already laid out and mostly built by the time Woodlawn borough was incorporated. It had a large Serbian and Croatian population. **64(23)**

1909 – South Heights was incorporated as a borough from the southeast corner of Hopewell Township. It was originally known as "Shannopin" from the name of the railroad station located there. Around 1904, present South Heights was also known as "Ethel Landing" but the name became South Heights permanently with its incorporation in 1909. **5(155)**

January 3, 1909 – As of this date the United States had 10,000 movie theaters which were attended by nearly 1 out of every 2 Americans. The cost per attendance was upwards of ten cents. **129(120)**

April 6, 1909 – Following a 36 day trek across the Arctic, Commander Robert Peary and his assistant Matthew Hensen planted the American flag at the North Pole. **129(123)**

July 4, 1909 – The Ringling Brothers Barnum and Bailey Circus arrived by train in New Brighton and paraded down Third Avenue on their way to Junction Park for a performance. **57(75)**

July 20, 1909 – Beaver Valley Motor Club was established to protect driver's rights. Fifty-two of the sixty car owners in the county joined. **5(63)**

One of the first cars in Ambridge the "Steam Roller" – BCHRLF Collection

Fall, 1909 – Aliquippa public school system was established. **56(63)**

September, 1909 – Plan 8 in Aliquippa was finished with additions in September, 1912 and February, 1914. The residents were skilled laborers of mixed northern European ethnicity. **64(23)**

December 1, 1909 – Jones & Laughlin Steel Corporation's Aliquippa Works produced its first batch of iron. **1(94), 83(277)**

1910 – County population climbed to 78,353. **21(47), 33**

- **1910** – The most costly fire in Beaver Falls history occurred causing a million dollars worth of damages and totally destroying the Union Drawn Steel Works and the Acme-Keystone plant. Fortunately, no lives were lost. **5(331)**

- **1910** – Shippingport Borough was incorporated from the village of Shippingport and the east district of Greene Township along with a part of Raccoon Township. It was originally known as "Christler's Landing." **21(152)**

- **1910** – The peak production of the Economy Oil Field was reached. In that year, the North Shore Railroad abandoned its spur line to Wallace City as unprofitable because of the decline in oil speculation. **19(141)**

- **1910** – Beaver Falls Pittsburgh & Lake Erie Railroad station was built on College Hill by Anderson and Cook Construction for $9,933. On July 12, 1985 it was the final stop for the last passenger train to service the Beaver Valley. **36(36)**

- **1910** – Construction of Highland School of the Woodlawn School District was complete. The building was considered the first fireproof building in the county. **56(66)**

Pittsburgh Mercantile Company Aliquippa – Courtesy of the Library of Congress

- **1910** – Dr. N. Bell Drake established the first hospital in Ellwood City in the former H.S. Blatt house. **63(120)**

- **1910** – Ellwood City Forge Company began the manufacture of connecting rods and crankshafts for gas, steam and diesel engines. It remained one of the original steel manufacturing companies remaining in Ellwood City. **63(51)**

- **January 6, 1910** – Former heavy-weight boxing champion John L. Sullivan and his sparring partner held exhibition matches at the Majestic Theater in Rochester. **60("Sullivan Arrives and is Interviewed," January 6, 1910)**

February 1, 1910 – James Stuart was awarded a contract from Jones & Laughlin Steel to build a five story department store building on Franklin Street, Woodlawn (now Aliquippa) which would house the Pittsburgh Mercantile Company. Pittsburgh Mercantile was owned by J&L Steel. **33("Contract is Let for Large Store," February 11, 1910)**

March 14, 1910 – Beaver freight station was built by Anderson and Cook Construction at a cost of $5,229. **36(35)**

May 13, 1910 – The Pittsburgh & Lake Erie Railroad expanded to a 4-track system and built a new double-stack bridge over the Ohio River between Monaca and Beaver at a cost of two million dollars. It was the largest cantilever type bridge in the world at that time and replaced the earlier 1878 railroad bridge. The engineer who drove the first train over the new bridge was J.L. Whitla of Beaver Falls. In 1878 Whitla was the same engineer who drove the first engine over the original Beaver railroad bridge. **5(56), 13(73), 46(88)**

May 23, 1910 – Pittsburgh & Lake Erie Railroad contracted with Kress House Moving Co. to move the 1897 Beaver railroad station about 100 feet to a new location and slightly turn the building to face the tracks. **Note: one source claims the building was moved 120 feet and the contemporary news article claims 100 feet. 36(34). 104("$1,000,000 Contract to Local Firm," May 27, 1908)**

Aliquippa Railroad Station 1910 – BCHRLF Collection

May 25, 1910 – Pittsburgh & Lake Erie Railroad built the freight and passenger station in Aliquippa. The last passenger ticket bought at the station was on July 15, 1968, and it was placed on the National Register of Historic Places on April 26, 1990. **36(31-32), 56(26)**

September, 1910 – Aliquippa's Plan 2 was finished. It was composed of Serbians, Italians, Croatians, Ukrainians, and Hungarians. **64(23)**

September 10, 1910 – Homewood Borough was formed. *See Homewood entry 1859.* **21(107)**

September 28, 1910 – Construction was begun on the Fallston Pittsburgh & Lake Erie Railroad station by Anderson and Cook Construction at a cost of $9,297. **36 (36)**

1911 – The Colonial Theater was built in Beaver Falls by William E. White. It was closed in 1919 and re-opened as the "New Colonial." The theater was sold in 1925 and renamed the Granada. The Granada closed permanently in the 1960's. **1(23)**

1911 – The Midland Steel Company was acquired by the Pittsburgh Crucible Steel Company, a subsidiary of the Crucible Steel Company of America. The unsold portion of the Midland town site was purchased by the Midland Improvement Company which built employee housing which also included both the "Toyland" section of stucco houses and several Edison cement homes. **5(145), 7(296)**

April, 1911 – Aliquippa's Plan 7 was finished and consisted of Slovaks, Poles, Ukrainians and some Serbians. **64(23)**

April 29, 1911 – The first porcelain enamel kitchen range in the U.S. was produced at Ingram-Richardson Manufacturing in Beaver Falls. At this time, they also made a few porcelain panel houses, a sample of which is in the McCarl Industrial Museum. **5(124), (McCarl Industrial Museum)**

July 18, 1911 – Charles Hickman, convicted of murdering his estranged wife in Beaver Falls, was scheduled to be hanged, but managed to cheat the gallows when he died of poisoning hours before his scheduled execution. Hickman, who had escaped twice from the Beaver County Jail, bragged that "they will never hang me." **5(590-591)**

September 1, 1911 – Beaver Falls High School was opened. **5(257)**

January 1, 1912 – The Woodlawn & Southern Street Railway Company was organized by Jones & Laughlin Steel to provide transportation for employees of the Aliquippa Works, and it ran from the mill through Aliquippa to Woodlawn. Operations were terminated on March 27, 1937, due to low ridership. **66(69-75)**

1912 – Edward J. Spratt of Beaver Falls designed, built and drove the first motor driven ambulance in Pennsylvania. It was a converted Maxwell purchased from the B.O. Fair Garage. **44(128)**

1912 – Paul Moore established the P.M. Moore Company in Aliquippa to build company houses for Jones & Laughlin Steel Co. employees. **5(41)**

1912 – Koppel Borough was incorporated and named for Arthur Koppel of the Orenstein-Koppel Company. In 1906, the Orenstein-Koppel Company purchased 558 acres of land above the Beaver River in Big Beaver Township and houses were built in the same year, while the plant had been constructed in 1907. **21(116),** *See entries for 1906 and April 22, 1937*

1912 – Alice Phillips, a young English girl, survived the Titanic disaster and following her rescue, came to live with her uncle William Phillips in New Brighton. She shortly returned to England and died in the Spanish Flu epidemic in 1916. **49(Vol. 30 No. 3, "New Brighton and the Titanic" pg. 6)**

- **1912** – Pittsburgh & Lake Erie Railroad freight and passenger station in West Aliquippa was built by A. Wishart & Sons. **36(33).**

- **1912** – Potter Township was formed from parts of Raccoon and Moon Townships. **21(141)**

- **1912** – Midland developed telephone service when Crucible Steel began to grow in the area. **5(355)**

- **May 16, 1912** – Thousands of people thronged Beaver Falls to hear famous evangelist Billy Sunday preach the gospel. A tabernacle built to hold 7,500 people was placed at 2nd Avenue and 11th Street and was financed entirely by donations for this event. Area churches generally closed for the occasion. Sunday, a former major league baseball player once spent two seasons with the Pittsburgh Pirates and quit at the height of his career to follow his religion. **45("Billy Sunday's Battle at Beaver to start Tonight," May 16, 1912),**

- **July, 1912** – Steel Workers of German, Irish and English ethnicities began moving into the newly completed Aliquippa Plan 3. **64(23)**

- **July, 1912** – The Keystone Steam Driller Company began producing excavating equipment which they named the "Skimmer." It became the precursor of the backhoe. **93(66)**

- **September 26, 1912** – The Beaver County Fair was re-established at Junction Park. The association working on the fairgrounds to make them the most "up to date in this part of the state, with a race track one-half mile long," was known as the Beaver County Agricultural and Driving Association **5(552), 111("Beaver County to Have County Fair," March 22, 1912)**

Beaver Falls Police Ca. 1912 - BCHRLF Collection

- **October, 1912** – Aliquippa's Plan 9 was finished and was populated by Croatians and Serbians. Plan 10 had no date available but consisted of mill supervisors of mixed ethnicity. **64(23)**

- **December, 1912** – Aliquippa's Plan 4 was finished and was composed of Croatians and Serbians. **64(23)**

- **March 1, 1912** – American Bridge Co. began work on the longest steel arched railroad bridge in the world at that time at Hell Gate, N.Y. for the Pennsylvania

Railroad Company. The bridge was finally completed on September 30, 1916. **(http://structurae.net/structures/hell-gate-bridge)**

- **1913** – Spang-Chalfant opened their new Ambridge plant. In the 1940's Spang-Chalfant was purchased by Armco. Their specialty became welded tubes from coils. **82(231-238)**

- **1913** – New Brighton native Louis B. Hanna was elected the eleventh governor of the state of North Dakota. **(http://history.nd.gov/exhibits/governors/governors11.html)**

- **1913** – The first indoor swimming pool in the county was built inside the Beaver County YMCA in New Brighton. **5(391)**

- **1913** – Dawes Manor opened in New Brighton to care for elderly women until finally closing its doors in 2002. **57(53)**

- **March 10, 1913** – Harriet Tubman, famous for her work as a conductor on the Underground Railroad passed away at her home in Auburn, New York at the age of 92. 129(170)

- **April, 1913** – Plan 5 in Aliquippa became its business district **64(23)**

- **April, 1913** – Plan 6 in Aliquippa was finished and consisted of senior mill managers of mixed ethnicity. **64(23)**

- **July, 1913** – Plan 11 in Aliquippa was finished and consisted of Italians, Polish and African-American mill workers and their families. **64(23)**

- **August, 1913** – Plan 12 in Aliquippa was finished and consisted of Germans, Irish and English mill workers and their families. **64(23)**

- **1914** – Moltrup Steel Corporation, producers of fine quality cold finish steel was founded in Beaver Falls. They also made the currency plate stock for the U.S. Mint as well as crankshafts for WWI airplane engines and automobiles. **1(28), 19(117)**

- **1914** – The Beth Samuel Congregation was chartered in Ambridge and a synagogue was built in 1940. **5(497)**

- **1914** – St. Joseph School opened in West Aliquippa. **5(298)**

- **1914** – The St. Elijah Serbian Orthodox congregation was formed in Aliquippa. **5(495)**

- **1914** – The Beaver Valley Hebrew Religious School was formed. **5(497)**

Strolling Through Time: A Chonology of Beaver County, PA History to 2016

- **August 28, 1914** - Austrian Archduke Francis Ferdinand and his wife, the Duchess of Hohenberg were gunned down by a Bosnian student sparking events that would lead to the outbreak of WWI. **129(183)**

- **November 24, 1914** – Center Township was formed when it was split off from Moon Township. **21(70)**

- **1915** – The Dando Brickyard was built in Industry by George Dando of Beaver, and it had 26 kilns capable of holding 80,000 to 90,000 bricks. In 1978, the plant was shut down due to Pennsylvania pollution standards and moved to Ohio. **49("Beaver County Brickworks," Vol. 35, No. 2, Spring, 2010)**

- **1915** – The Fort McIntosh chapter, Daughters of the American Revolution marked the Legionville site by the erection of a flag pole and flag. **43("D.A.R. to Mark Site," October 24, 1915)**

- **1915** – The Pittsburgh, Harmony, Butler & New Castle Railway (PHB&NC) entered Koppel and Beaver Falls and connected to the Beaver Valley Traction Line. **80(215)**

- **1915** – The Aliquippa-Woodlawn Beth Jacob Congregation was established. **5(497)**

- **July 7, 1915** – New Sheffield Academy in Hopewell closed. **5(279)**

- **1916** – Rochester native and Marine Corps Colonel Joseph Pendleton established Camp Pendleton in southern California. He retired in 1924 as a Major General. **5(232)**

- **1916** – The Holy Trinity Greek Orthodox Congregation was established in Ambridge. **5(495)**

- **1916** – Beaver Falls native Thomas Midgeley created tetraethyl lead or leaded gasoline to reduce engine knock and save gasoline. In 1928, he invented the refrigerant used in air conditioning known as Freon. Midgeley's other accomplishments included creating a process for extracting bromine from seawater, developing both natural and synthetic rubber, as well as acquiring 117 patents. In 1942, he was awarded the Willard Gibbs Medal of the American Chemical Society. (http://invent.org/inductee-detail/?IID=193), **33("Beaver Falls Native Honored," January 19, 1942)**

- **April 27, 1916** – Jan Kurek of Woodlawn invented a shield, in the form of a shirt made of metal rings which covered the chest and abdomen and would protect an infantryman from both rifle and machine gun fire. He presented his idea to the War Department, but it was not adopted. **101(Woodlawn Man is Inventor of "War" Shield," April 27, 1916), 101("Woodlawn Man Invents War Shield," April 27, 1916)**

🐦 **December 4, 1916** – Stanislof Woceshoski of Ambridge became the first county resident to die in the electric chair elsewhere for a murder committed here. **(http://deathpenaltyusa.org/usa1/methods/electrocution_501-750.htm),**

🐦 **April 6, 1917** – The United States Congress voted to enter WWI.

🐦 **April 24, 1917** – The Beaver Valley Traction Company advertised for women to fill the position of trolley car conductor, a position once held only by men. **5(235)**

Trolleys in Beaver Falls – BCHRLF Collection

🐦 **July 2, 1917** – The recruiting station for the Eighteenth Pennsylvania Infantry, N.G.P. set a record in Monaca for short time recruiting. Part of Company "A" of that unit was stationed in Monaca to guard the Pittsburgh & Lake Erie Railroad bridge. **101("N.G.P. Infantry has Record," July 2, 1917)**

🐦 **July 16, 1917** – During WWI, the 5th Engineers became the first troops from the county to arrive in France. **5(234)**

🐦 **March 14, 1918** – Mrs. Jenny DeLucia, the alleged "Blackhand Queen" and one of her confederates were arrested and held for court after being accused of sending threatening blackmail letters to a Woodlawn man. Failing to receive payment, the "Blackhand Queen" had his house blown up with dynamite. DeLucia was convicted and sentenced to one year and six months while her partner was sentenced to five years in a federal penitentiary. **45("Alleged Blackhand Leaders are Held," March 14, 1918), 45("Dynamiter Sentenced," March 27, 1918)**

🐦 **March 8, 1918** – Former President William Howard Taft attended a dinner at Heath Manor, the home of Mr. and Mrs. Fred Beegle in Patterson Township. **127(6)**

🐦 **March 18, 1918** – Daylight Savings Time was enacted into law as a measure to increase productivity, save coal and increase the yields of "victory" gardens during WWI. It was introduced into the United States by part-time Center Township and Sylvan Crest resident Robert Garland. **19(43), 45("Beaver County Distracted by Time Changes," April 29, 1920)** *See entry for August 20, 1919 and 1942*

🐦 **June 23, 1918** – The Pennsylvania State Historical Commission at Harrisburg dedicated a bronze tablet marking the location of General Anthony Wayne's camp at Legionville. **45("Tablet Dedicated to Memory of Wayne at Legionville," June 23, 1918)**

July 1, 1918 – Fulton C. Smith of Ambridge was believed to the first drafted man from Beaver County to die in WWI when he was killed in action in France while serving with an engineering regiment. **33("First Beaver County Soldier Falls in War," July 24, 1918)**

October 1, 1918 – Beaver Falls native Colonel Joseph H. Thompson, wounded three times and gassed by the Germans, earned the Congressional Medal of Honor. The citation wasn't awarded until 1925. **5(230), 44(109)**

October 3, 1918 – The first cases of Spanish Flu were reported in the county. Within two weeks, cases numbered in the thousands and all schools, churches and public places were closed to help stop the spread. The pandemic finally abated by early November, and by November 7th, schools, theaters and churches were reopening. Although no records of deaths from the flu had been kept for Beaver County, it is estimated that hundreds died here. **36(63-68)**

November 11, 1918 – Germany signed an armistice with the allies, effectively ending WWI.

1918 – A part of Ellwood City became a Beaver County community when a strip of North Sewickley Township was annexed from Lawrence County. **21(87)**

1918 – The Central District and Telegraph Printing Company merged with Bell Telephone to provide telephone service throughout Beaver County. **5(356)**

1918 – The Sons of Israel Congregation was chartered in Midland. **5(497)**

1918 – White Mine in Cannelton opened and was the first strip mine in America. **86(110)**

1918 – The Synagogue of the Congregation Tree of Life was established in Rochester. **5(497)**

1918 – The Assumption Greek Orthodox congregation was established in Aliquippa. **5(495)**

1919 – Travers Engineering Company, makers of amusement rides and roller coasters for amusement parks around the country, was founded in Beaver Falls. The company failed in the early years of the Depression and was succeeded by the R.E. Chambers Company. **44(155), 19(135)**

1919 – Patterson Heights Airfield opened. It was the first in the county, and it closed in 1957. **5(81)**

1919 – Tabernacle Baptist Church in Beaver Falls was organized. **5(496)**

- **April 2, 1919** – At midnight, the existing county liquor licenses expired and Judge George A. Baldwin refused to grant any new ones. His action caused Beaver County to become a "dry" county. **115("Judge Ousts Saloons From Beaver County," April 2, 1919)**

- **May 28, 1919** – Seventeen Beaver County men of the 323 Light Field Artillery Regiment who were awarded the Croix De Guerre for bravery were honored at a homecoming in Beaver. **104("17 Beaver County Men With Croix De Guerre Honored at Homecoming," May 29, 1919)**

- **August 9, 1919** – Monaca honored the return of its WWI veterans with a large parade. **55(145)**

- **August 20, 1919** – The Daylight Saving Time law was formally repealed over President Wilson's veto. Some individual communities in Beaver County and throughout the east coast kept it, while others went back to standard time. In the 1920's Midland was the first town in the county to re-adopt Daylight Savings and then repealed it within a day while most others were undecided as to what to do. When the Pittsburgh & Lake Erie Railroad adopted daylight saving time, the county was forced to follow along. **19(43), 45("Beaver County Distracted by Time Changes," April 29, 1920),** *See entries for March 18, 1918 and 1942*

- **December 13, 1919** – The town of Beaver faced a smallpox epidemic and churches and schools were ordered closed. All public gatherings were banned. The disease was believed to have been brought in by a group of young people who attended a dance in New Cumberland, West Virginia. **45("Beaver County Town Under Smallpox Ban," December 13, 1919)**

VIII. The "Roaring Twenties," Depressed Thirties & WWII: 1920 to 1945

During this time, our industries were firmly established and the population was rapidly increasing, making even greater demands on infrastructure. Roads were built as the automobile became more abundant and affordable; electric trolley cars were introduced only to be replaced by buses and cabs; airplane travel became more common; a new dam was built on the Ohio River; and life in general was much better than it had ever been. That is, until the Great Depression hit and plunged many families into poverty. Strikes and labor unrest marked this period as workers fought for better jobs and higher wages, and a Landmark Supreme Court ruling changed the labor landscape. With the start of WWII, county men began serving in large numbers, and county women stepped forward and took their places in such factories as Spang-Chalfant, Curtiss Wright, and American Bridge in order to support the war effort. Once again, business was booming and the populace simply believed that the good times would never end.

- **1920** – The Pittsburgh & Lake Erie Railroad carried approximately 6,780,000 passengers that year, which was the greatest number carried in any year previous. **55(74)**

- **1920's** – Hughes O. McClure of Chippewa operated the first electric car in Beaver Falls. **5(63)**

- **Late 1920's** – Conway Airfield was initially opened and stayed open until the 1960's. **19(121)**

- **1920** – The U.S. Census reported county population at 111,621. **21(47), 33**

- **1920** – The Tabernacle Baptist Church was founded in Beaver Falls. **19(47)**

- **August 26, 1920** – The 19th Amendment to the U.S. Constitution passed giving women the right to vote. **129(269)**

- **June 26, 1921** – Old Economy Village officially opened to the public. At that time it was known as "Old Economy," and it wasn't until the late 1970s that it was known as "Old Economy Village." Old Economy was the first historic site for the Pennsylvania Historical Commission which later became the Pennsylvania Historical and Museum Commission. It was officially deeded to the Commonwealth on February 3, 1916, through an escheat case that lasted 6 years. **(Sarah Buffington Curator OEV)**

🐾 **1921** – Beaver County had just sixteen and three quarters miles of improved roads with plans to pave another fifty two miles with concrete, brick or macadam by year's end. **5(71)**

🐾 **1921** – The first board of Commissioners for Patterson Township was elected. **127(6)**

🐾 **1922** – The first successful production and piercing of seamless stainless steel and pure nickel tubing in America was accomplished at the Beaver Falls Babcock & Wilcox Tube Company plant (Pittsburgh Seamless until 1923). **82(6)**

🐾 **1922** – Mrs. Laura Johnson of Potter Township became the first woman juror in the county. **19(37)**

🐾 **1922** – Miss Melba Stucky of New Brighton became the first female lawyer in Beaver County, and was one of only two women admitted to practice before the state supreme court. Miss Stucky was a graduate of Wellesley College and Pittsburgh Law School. **5(216), 45("Woman Admitted For First Time to Beaver County Bar," October 23, 1922)**

🐾 **1922** – St. John the Baptist Carpatho-Russian Orthodox congregation was formed in Ambridge. **5(495)**

🐾 **1922** – The Beaver Valley School of Nursing was built on Penn Avenue in New Brighton by the Beaver Valley General Hospital. The school was closed in the 1970's, and the building was removed in April of 2010. **57(51)**

🐾 **April 22, 1922** – The Rochester Public Library was formed and leased the downstairs of the American Legion building in 1925. In 1939 the borough purchased the Legion building for a permanent home for the library. **61(44-45),** *See entry for 1922*

🐾 **January 1, 1923** – Pittsburgh Seamless became the Babcock & Wilcox Tube Company in Beaver Falls when the corporate title was changed. **82(5)**

Tuberculosis Sanitorium – BCHRLF Collection

🐾 **February 20, 1923** – Beaver College in Beaver closed after an unsuccessful fundraising campaign. **41, 5(292)**

🐾 **December 7, 1923** – West Mayfield was incorporated as a borough even though the area was settled as early as 1816. It came from a part of White Township, once consisting of scattered farms and homes, and was a station on the Pennsylvania Railroad. **21(158)**

Strolling Through Time: A Chonology of Beaver County, PA History to 2016

- **1923** – Dr. Ruth Wilson became one of the earliest female physicians in the county, who along with her husband, Doctor Fred Wilson, established a tuberculosis sanitarium on the present site of Penn State Beaver. In 1936, she became medical director and served in that position until 1957 when the sanitorium stopped treating tuberculosis patients. Dr. Ruth also appeared in "Who's Who of American Women." **5(309), 34(September 13, 1963, "Four County Women Recognized")**

- **1923** – Aliquippa's Plan 11 Extension was completed and populated by African-Americans, Polish, Ukrainians, Russians and Italians. **64(23)**

- **May 1, 1924** – The Beaver Valley Chamber of Commerce began activities. **39**

- **1924** – Beaver Valley Motor Coach was incorporated and began operations with three routes: Beaver Falls to New Brighton, Rochester to Colona (now a part of Monaca) and Sewickley to Leetsdale, replacing the streetcar route between New Brighton and Beaver Falls. The company ceased operations in 1978. **5(66)**

- **1924** – The Noss Family Horn Band retired from show business after having successfully toured the United States, Canada, Mexico and Europe for many years. **57(60)**

- **1925** – Conway – Freedom Boulevard opened and was described as the "worst stretch of road between New York and Chicago." It was finally resurfaced in 1934. **5(70)**

- **1925** – Fourteen miles of roads were built in Chippewa at a cost of $7,500 per mile. **5(71)**

- **1925** – St. Vladimir Ukrainian Orthodox congregation was formed in Ambridge. **5(495)**

- **1925** – The Christ Temple Church of God in Christ was established by Elder Thomas Griswold in Beaver Falls. **19(47)**

- **1925/1926** – After having closed in 1923, Beaver College merged with the Beechwood School and relocated to Jenkintown a suburb of Philadelphia. In 2001, it was renamed Arcadia University. The Beaver property was sold to the Beaver School District for its high school. **46(90-91), 133(53)**

- **1925** – The first San Rocco Festival was held in what is today Aliquippa. The tradition of the San Rocco Festival was brought to the Aliquippa area by immigrants from Patricia, Italy, where St. Rocco was the patron saint. They settled primarily in the Plan 11 section of Aliquippa. **34("San Rocco Festa Ready to Celebrate in Center", 8/02/2015)**

🍂 **1926** – Woodlawn, already the largest community in Beaver County, annexed New Sheffield from Hopewell Township along with the land in between. *See entry for Woodlawn in 1877.* **21(50)**

🍂 **June 15, 1926** – The Pennsylvania Railroad opened its relocated line through New Brighton over the old Beaver Division Canal bed and a new bridge across the Beaver River was built. In the fall the converted former Fort Wayne Railroad bridge was opened for highway traffic. **4(169), 26**

🍂 **September, 1926** – Saints Cyril and Methodius Church of New Brighton opened a school to serve the Croatian and Slovak Catholic Children of the community. **5(298)**

🍂 **November 19, 1926** – Beaver County banned Sunday football games and threatened to arrest spectators, officials and players. Sunday golf was still permitted. **104("Beaver County Bans Sunday Grid Battles," November 20, 1926)**

🍂 **December 31, 1926** – Jones & Laughlin Steel and the Pittsburgh & Lake Erie Railroad Company spent nearly $500,000 to build a boulevard between South Heights and Woodlawn. The west approach to the new Ohio River bridge connecting Woodlawn and Ambridge linked directly with the boulevard. **101("Corporations Build Ohio River Highway as Real boulevard," December 31, 1926)**

🍂 **Ca. 1927** – Babcock & Wilcox Tube Company successfully pierced stainless steel billet for their famous Croloy tubing, a first for America. **82(7),** *See January 1, 1923*

🍂 **1927** – The Penn Beaver Hotel was built in Rochester for $450,000 by the Beaver Valley Hotel Corporation. Eva Johnston won the contest to name the hotel and her prize was $50. **49("The Last in the Line: The Penn Beaver Hotel," Vol. 24 No. 1, Winter 2006)**

Building Penn Beaver Hotel in Rochester – BCHRLF Collection

1927 – The First Church of Christ was founded in Aliquippa. In 1970, the congregation moved to the new structure and called it the Church in the Round. **19(47)**

1927 – Beaver's Esther Stoll made her professional debut with the German State Opera Company and went on to become a Prima Donna singing Wagnerian Operas. In 1930, she returned to the U.S. and toured the country with the American based Johanna Gadski's Grand German Opera Company. After retiring from the stage, she joined Arthur Godfrey's television show "Talent Scouts" as the Head of Auditions from 1948 to 1958. **(Beaver Area Heritage Museum)**

1927 – St. George's Serbian Orthodox congregation was formed in Midland. **5(95)**

April 21, 1927 – Merle Moltrup, son of the Moltrup Steel Company owner made the first airmail flight between Bettis Field in Pittsburgh and Cleveland. Moltrup was Chief Engineering Test Pilot for Douglas Aircraft and trained pilots during World War II. He became the first manager of the Beaver County Airport from 1953 to 1956. **5(82), 49("Merle Moltrup: Beaver County Aviator," Vol. 36, No.4, Fall, 2011)**

August 15, 1927 – Two men were killed when the private bi-plane that they were flying exploded in mid-air and then dived into the Ohio River near Legionville. George Roth of Monaca was the pilot, and the passenger was Kenneth Hercules of Martin's Ferry, Ohio. The first crash of its kind in Beaver County. **102("2 Men Killed as 'Plane Falls," August 15, 1927), 34("It Happened Here," August 9, 1987)**

December 29, 1927 – The Aliquippa – Ambridge Bridge was dedicated. **5(71)**

1928 – *The News-Tribune* was founded in Beaver Falls and functioned until April 11, 1979 when its last paper was published. **44(83)**

1928 – The Steamboat "Aliquippa" overturned and sank near the Jones & Laughlin plant in Aliquippa while maneuvering to pick up barges. Three persons were drowned. (http://www3.gendisasters.com/pennsylvania/8505/aliquippa-pa-steamer-aliquippa-sinking-aug-1928)

J&L Steamboat Aliquippa - Courtesy of Beaver County Industrial Museum

1928 – Presentation School in Midland was opened under the direction of Father John Breen. **5(298)**

🦫 **January 27, 1928** – A merger of Aliquippa (this section later became known as West Aliquippa), Woodlawn and New Sheffield became the borough of Aliquippa. The new borough kept the name Aliquippa to better identify the name of the steel works. (NOTE: the name "West Aliquippa," like "Aliquippa" came from the Pittsburgh & Lake Erie Railroad as it was west bound on the railroad from Pittsburgh. Hence Aliquippa station and then West Aliquippa station.) *See entries for Aliquippa in 1926 and Woodlawn in 1877.* **21(50), 39**

🦫 **June 26, 1928** – Beaver County Commissioners established the first Milk Control board in the state due to concerns over the amount of bacteria found in the milk of county dairies. **110("Milk Control Board for Beaver County," June 26, 1928)**

🦫 **1929** – American Bridge Company designed and built the first all-welded barge. This construction technique became crucial during WWII when the company began making LST's (Landing Ship Tank) for the war effort. **5(117),** *See entry for 1942*

🦫 **1929** – William Miller became the first African-American mortician in Aliquippa. **19(47)**

🦫 **1929** – A report by the State of Pennsylvania called the Beaver River the worst source of potable water in the entire state with the majority of the pollution entering by way of the Mahoning River from the area of Youngstown, Ohio. **5(572)**

🦫 **1929** – The 1897 Rochester–Monaca suspension bridge was torn down and replaced by a new cantilever truss bridge built by Beaver County. The State Highway Department assumed all future maintenance and construction obligations on June 1, 1930. A third bridge would replace this one in 1986. **68(18)**

🦫 **February 1, 1929** – B.F. Jones Memorial Library opened to the public in Aliquippa. The brass arches over the entrances to the rooms were the work of celebrated artist Oscar Bach. It was listed on the National Register of Historic Places in 1978. **56(121-123)**

🦫 **July 6, 1929** – Laughlin Memorial Library was presented in Ambridge by Mr. And Mrs. Alexander Laughlin, founders of Ambridge's Central Tube Company, as a memorial to their son, Major Alexander Laughlin, Jr. The building cost $300,000. These Laughlins were not related to the Laughlin family of Jones & Laughlin Steel Company. **47(63)**

🦫 **October 1, 1929** – The Commonwealth of Pennsylvania established compulsory motor vehicle inspections. **5(63)**

🦫 **October 29, 1929** – The stock market crashed and the Great Depression began.

- **November 9, 1929** – The crew of a passing Cleveland & Pittsburgh freight train foiled an attempted robbery at the Beaver Station of the C&P. The second break-in within a week. **45("Frustrate Robbers," November 10, 1929)**

- **January 31, 1930** – St. Joseph Lead Co. erected a zinc smelter plant along Route 18 in Potter Township. On Christmas Eve that year, the roaster and acid plants went on stream and were prepared to produce zinc. **5(128)**

- **1930** – Stella Burge Sullivan became the first female pilot licensed in the county. For 16 years, she made stunt flying her career at air circuses and exhibitions throughout the country. **5(82), 19(125)**

Stella Burge Sullivan – BCHRLF Collection

- **May 8, 1930** – Harmony Electric Co. merged with Pennsylvania Power. **5(263)**

- **June 13, 1930** – Freedom Savings & Trust Co. was chartered. **5(102)**

- **1930** – The U.S. Census reported the county population at 146,889, with Aliquippa the largest town at 27,116. **21(47), 33**

- **1930** – Ellwood City native Lewis "Hack" Wilson had a record setting baseball season with the Chicago Cubs when he hit 56 home runs which stood as the National League record for 68 years, and amassed 191 runs batted in, a record that still stands today. He was inducted into the Professional Baseball Hall of Fame in 1979. **(http://baseballhall.org/hof/wilson-hack)**

- **1931** – Moon Township was annexed to the borough of Monaca, constituting the fourth and fifth wards and increasing the town's population by 2,200. **55(60)**

- **1931** – Beaver County's second largest island, Hog Island, was buried by Jones & Laughlin slag operations. **81(290)**

- **1931** – The Pittsburgh, Harmony, Butler & New Castle Railway (PHB&NC Harmony Route) ended service in Western Pennsylvania. **80(224)**

- **September 4, 1931** – The Oriental Theater opened in Rochester and was considered one of the finest "theme" theaters in the country and the most majestic in Beaver County. It was closed on April 23, 1972, and finally demolished in 2001. **5(441), 61(195-196)**

Oliver Shallenberger House Rochester – BCHRLF Collection

🍂 <u>**1932**</u> – A fire destroyed the home of Rochester native Oliver Shallenberger who was credited with the invention of the "Watthour meter" (electric meter). **19(34),** *See entry for 1894*

🍂 <u>**June 1932**</u> – Wilbur N. Phelps of Aliquippa became the first African-American to receive a B.S. degree in printing from Carnegie Tech (now Carnegie Mellon University). Phelps founded and ran the Phelps Printing Company in Aliquippa until his retirement at age 78. He passed away on June 1, 1994. **142("First Degree," July 9, 1932), https://community.aarp.org/t5/AARP-Tribute-To-An-Ancestor/In-Pursuit-of-Excellence/cns-p/1540137**

🍂 <u>**September 3, 1932**</u> – Forty-three cases of typhoid fever were reported in Beaver Falls and New Brighton. A "boil water" advisory was issued. **114("Typhoid fever Hits Beaver County Area," September 3, 1932).**

🍂 <u>**October 20, 1932**</u> – New Brighton was surprised to see a large school of fish in a pool along the banks of the Beaver River, since the river had been free of fish, crabs and mussels for over 50 years due to industrial pollution. By 1974, the Pennsylvania Fish Commission reported that a wide variety of fish were again inhabiting the river. **5(572)**

Fire destroyed the 1876 courthouse – BCHRLF Collection and photo donated by Susan Mitchem

🍂 <u>**1933**</u> – The fourth courthouse was built following an accidental fire caused by a workman's blowtorch on May 26, 1932 that destroyed the original building. Additions were constructed in 1976 and 1993. **5(211-213)**

🍂 <u>**1933**</u> – The Travers Engineering Company was succeeded by the R.E. Chambers Company who continued to make amusement park rides until a devastating fire in 1962. They were noted for making many of the rides for the New York World's Fair 1939 - 1940. **4(155)**

- **January 20, 1933** – The Beaver County "Shanghai" occurred when a police raid was conducted on the Industry home of Virginia Heath, where a party was going on with a group of around 56 people – all African-American. Payoffs were demanded and those refusing were jailed for the night and next morning were taken out of the county by truck in a driving rain and dropped about seven miles south of Waynesburg without proper clothing or transportation and told not to come back. A great outcry occurred across the state. **49("The Beaver County Shanghai," Vol. 30 No. 1, Winter, 2010)**

- **October 5, 1933** – A bystander was shot and killed and a dozen were clubbed and gassed as 200 sheriff's deputies confronted nearly 500 strikers in a riot at the Spang-Chalfant plant in Ambridge. **89("Riots, gun play Feature Steel Iron "Holiday"." October 6, 1933)**

- **1934** – Routes 857 in Ambridge, Route 68, Route 288, Route 51 and portions of Route 19 were blacktopped. **5(71)**

- **1934** – Michael Dioguardi started Rome Monument Works in Rochester to specialize in personalized cemetery memorials and gravestones. As of 2015, the business had grown to fourteen showrooms all located in Western Pennsylvania. **(http://www.romemonuments.com/company_history)**

- **1934** – Route 18 and parts of Routes 51, 68, 351 and 288 were declared state highways. **5(71)**

- **Spring, 1934** – Monaca Public Library was established by the Monaca Junior Women's Club. **55(140)**

- **November 6, 1934** – Although Prohibition had ended with the repeal of the 18th Amendment in 1933, residents of Beaver voted to remain a "dry" town. **34("Waffles InCaffeinated adds beer to menu through deal with Beaver Brewing Company," July 21, 2016.**

- **1935** – The Civilian Conservation Corps built two camps around what is now Raccoon Creek Park and were supervised by the military. The program was to put young men to work during the Depression. Paid $30 per month, the CCC planted over 2 million trees, built roads and trails, and quarried stone for fireplaces and foundations. The CCC disbanded in 1942. **36(117-120),** *See entry for 1945*

- **August 22, 1935** – The first issue of the *Beaver Valley Journal* was published in Aliquippa by John Alexander to "render an accurate and unbiased account of all events affecting colored people locally." **19(47)**

- **1936** – Aliquippa dedicated its United States Post Office. A mural was painted inside by Niles Spencer and showed a mill, billowing smoke, a train and a scenic hillside as the background. The mural now resides in the Smithsonian American Art Museum in Washington, D.C. **56(96)**

- **1936** – Big Knob Grange #2008 was organized. **(http://www.visitbeavercounty.com/outdoor-adventures/fairs)**

1936 Ice jam on the Ohio River - Courtesy of Lillian Stout

- **March 17, 1936** – Ice jammed up the rivers and combined with heavy snowfall, it caused the worst flooding on record on the Ohio and Beaver Rivers. The Ohio crested at 54.5 feet, countless homes were flooded and many bridges were closed. All industrial plants in the county were shut down due to high water or electrical failures. This flood was also known as the "St. Patrick's Day" flood. **5(568), 58(71)**

- **March 20, 1936** – Legendary female aviator, Amelia Earheart visited Geneva College to give a lecture on women's roles in aviation. **44(71)**

- **July 17, 1936** – Beaver County suffered through the worst series of forest fires in its history due to a prolonged drought and hot weather. Five sizeable fires occurred throughout the county resulting in thousands of dollars in damages. **45("Forest Fires Take Big Toll," July 17, 1936)**

- **August 28, 1936** – On the Ohio River, opposite Industry, Montgomery Island Lock and Dam was completed and dedicated, replacing several smaller dams and greatly reducing the threat of recurring flooding in the valley. It was the first non-navigable, high-lift gated structure to be built on the Ohio River. During the dedication, nearly 100,000 people witnessed an 18 mile long parade of river craft and speedboats. **1(75), 27, 45("River Flotilla to Mark Dedication of New Dam," August 8, 1936)**

Montgomery Island Lock & Dam – BCHRLF Collection

- **1937** – By this year, 385 of the county's 902 miles of roads were improved. **5(70)**

- **1937** – Beaver Borough swimming pool was built by the Works Progress Administration in Gypsy Glen Park. **5(391)**

- **March 1, 1937** – The Beaver County Department of Veteran's Affairs was established. **5(246)**

- **1937** – The Darlington Polo Club was formed in Darlington. In 1938 it became the first team in the United States to have a lighted field. **1(15), 64(41)**

- **March 27, 1937** – The Woodlawn Street Railway Company trolley made its last run. It was replaced by the buses of the Woodlawn and Southern Motor Coach Company. **56(93)**

- **April 8, 1937** – Big Beaver Boat Club was chartered. It was located on the east bank of the Beaver River in lower New Brighton. Leroy Kelbaugh was elected as the first Commodore. The club was disbanded in 1942 due to war time restrictions. **5(389), 49(Vol. 22 No 4, Winter, 1997, Pages 1-3)**

- **April 12, 1937** – In the Landmark case, *National Labor Relations Board vs. Jones & Laughlin Steel Corp.*, which originated in Beaver County, the U.S. Supreme Court established the legal basis for collective bargaining between labor unions and employers. For over half a century, this decision also became the regulatory and administrative law that governed labor relations in the United States. It became known as the Wagner Act. **5(219)**

- **April 22, 1937** – The town of Koppel was put up for sale when the Pressed Steel Car Company decided to sell the 560 acres on which the town was built and all of its other property there. The company moved its subsidiary, the Koppel Industrial Car and Equipment Company to McKees Rocks. The company's holdings included the abandoned plant, fifty single houses; fifty double houses; a bank; a hotel and club houses. **115("Beaver County Town on Block," April 22, 1937),** *See entries for 1906 and 1912*

- **May 6, 1937** – After arriving at the Lakehurst Naval Air Station, the German airship Hindenburg caught fire and crashed to the ground killing 33 of its passengers and crew. **127(470)**

- **June 29, 1937** – A picketer was killed during the Moltrup Steel strike in Beaver Falls when a deputy accidently fired a tear gas gun into a crowd of strikers. George Mike was struck in the head and became the 13th death in the seven state steel strike. Ironically, Mike was a WWI veteran who had been wounded twice and gassed by the Germans. **87("When Gas Gun Kills Steel Strike Picket," June 30, 1937), 88("Bystander Injured in Strike Riot at Beaver Falls, Dies." June 29, 1937)**

🍁 **July 18, 1937** – Two Homewood men, Thomas Urista and N. Seaman crash landed their airplane on railroad tracks in front of a speeding Baltimore & Ohio freight train which was barely able to stop a few feet away from the wreckage. Because the accident occurred about three miles north of Beaver Falls in an isolated area, the engineer uncoupled his engine and hurried the injured flyers to that city where they were admitted to Providence Hospital. **123("Close Call!," July 18, 1937)**

🍁 **August 10, 1937** – The last trolley car to operate in the county made its final run to Morado (Beaver Falls) from Junction Park. **10(61), 24, 25, 66(22-23)**

🍁 **1938** – Mildred Custer Baum of Beaver Falls, a former staff soloist for KDKA Broadcasting, was the "Queen of Melody" in a weekly musical show on KDKA Radio, where she sang as part of a quartet until 1941. She studied music at the famous Julliard School of Music as well as the Pittsburgh Conservatory of Music. She was the former President of the Pittsburgh Die & Casting Company and was featured in "Who's Who of American Women." She passed away on February 19, 1987. **34(February 22, 1987, "Mildred C. Baum Obituary"), 34(September 13, 1963, "Four County Women Recognized")**

🍁 **1938** – The Department of Welfare Office was opened in Rochester in the old Majestic Theater building. **61(49-50)**

🍁 **February 7, 1938** – Beaver County banned any bank nights (a free lottery held by movie theaters) and bingo games that were not exclusively held for charity. **113("Beaver County will ban Bank Nights and Bingo Games Beginning Feb. 7," January 21, 1938)**

🍁 **May 18, 1938** – First bag of airmail was flown out of the county from the Conway Airport. **5(82)**

🍁 **November 27, 1938** – The Steubenville, East Liverpool & Beaver Valley Traction's (SEL&BVT) "Yellow Car Line" made its last run from Midland to East Liverpool, Ohio. Prior to October 5, 1935, the SEL&BVT made its last run from Midland to Vanport and back. **78(127, 269)**

Dr. Harrison H. Richardson - Courtesy of Beaver Area Heritage Museum

🍁 **1939** – Harrison H. Richardson of Beaver, then age 19, accompanied Admiral Byrd on his Antarctic expedition and was a member of the 59-man team that stayed on the ice over the winter of 1940-41. He worked as a dog team driver and meteorological observer. Mount Richardson in the Fosdick Mountains in Marie Bird Land, Antarctica was named for him. Dr. Richardson became a radiologist and practiced in Beaver. He passed away on July 17, 1999. **64(81), (New York Times, "Harrison Richardson, 80, Joined Byrd's Expedition to Antarctica",August 1, 1990)**

1939 – The General Anthony Wayne Chapter of the Sons of the American Revolution was founded in Heath Manor in Patterson Township, with Heath Manor's owner, Clifford Beegle as its first president. **49("Mansion to Mystery to Manor", Vol. 34 No. 1, Winter, 2009)**

1939 – Situated on 150 acres of Raccoon Creek State Park, Camp Johnson was established as the first summer camp for African American youth in the Pittsburgh area and one of the first in the country. It was named after James Weldon Johnson, the first director of the National Association for the Advancement of Colored People (NAACP). The camp taught African American history as well as provided outdoor activities and role models for young inner city campers. The camp closed in 1967. **(http://digital.library.pitt.edu/cgi-bin/f/findaid/findaid-idx?c=hswpead;cc=hswpead;rgn=main;view=text;didno=US-QQS-MSS229), http://www.heinzhistorycenter.org/blog/detre-library-archives/camp-james-weldon-johnson)**

1939 – The Great Depression neared its end as America and the world began preparing for war.

May 24, 1939 – Three persons of the Cook family were found shot and hacked to death with an axe in their South Beaver home. Paul Cook, their seventeen year old son was arrested and charged with the murders. **110("Father, Mother and Daughter Are Found Dead," May 24, 1939)**

January 1, 1940 – Beaver Countians who were eligible for Social Security received their first monthly payments under the law passed in 1935. **The Aliquippa Gazette("First Payments Under Insurance Plan to be Made", November 28, 1939), 65.**

February 15, 1940 – Beaver County was hit with a record snowfall of nearly twenty inches in a twenty six hour period, eclipsing the previous record of sixteen inches in 1902. **The Daily Times("County Digs out of Record Snow", 2/15/1940), 65.**

1940 – The current Monaca pump house was built by the Works Progress Administration to resemble a castle. **55(63)**

1940 – The U.S. Census reported the population of the county totaled 156,754; Aliquippa totaled 27,023. **21(47), 33**

- **1940** – Babcox & Wilcox in Beaver Falls acquired the Penn Bridge Company adjacent to their plant and built the "East Work" for the production of Navy boiler tube. **82(8)**

- **1940** – Monaca celebrated its centennial. **55**

- **May 1, 1940** – Michael Baker, Jr. opened his engineering firm in the Penn Beaver Hotel, Rochester. **5(74)**

- **November 5, 1940** – 15 volunteers from Aliquippa filled the first Beaver County draft quota for army service. The very first volunteer was Joseph F. Patuc. **The Aliquippa Gazette("15 Volunteer Here for Army Service", 11/6/1940), 65**

- **1941** – Anthony Wayne Terrace was built in Baden to house workers for the defense industry. **48(123)**

- **Ca. 1941** – The Spang-Chalfant Company in Ambridge began producing shell forgings, bomb casings, and airplane cylinders for the war effort. Nearly 25 million casings were produced. **5(131), 62(circa 32 pages not numbered)**

- **1941** – The United States Army Air Force built a secret aviation gasoline storage facility disguised as a farm in Potter Township on Mowry Road. In 2005, Horsehead Industries which owned the land turned it over to Potter Township. The Army Corps of Engineers then began removing the facility.. **49("Potter Township Tank Farm," Vol. 37 No. 4, Fall, 2012)**

- **March 16, 1941** – A passenger train from Cleveland derailed near Baden into the Ohio River during a snowstorm and was considered to be sabotage. Four people were killed and 113 injured. All spikes from both sides of the track were removed causing the derailment. Although a $5,000 reward was offered, no one was ever arrested. **48(119-120), 60("G-men Probing Baden Train Wreck," 3/17/1945), 65**

- **April 23, 1941** – Curtiss-Wright unveiled plans to erect an airplane propeller plant in Borough Township (now a part of Vanport). Steel for the fabrication of the plant was manufactured at American Bridge Company in Ambridge. Cost of the factory was estimated at $5,221,000. The factory was listed as the #10 target on the Nazi "hit" list because it produced almost 15 percent of all aircraft propellers manufactured in the United States. **5(242), 49("Beaver, Pennsylvania: Nazi Target"), 60("County to Welcome Curtiss-Wright," 4/23/1941), 65**

- **September 11, 1941** – The Federal Works Agency chose a site in Monaca's Fourth Ward (Monaca Heights) for a 100 unit defense housing project. A special meeting of council was called to consider the proposal. **60("Monaca Site is Chosen for Unit of Defense Homes," September 11, 1941)**

🌿 **December 7, 1941** – Louis Moslener, Jr. of Monaca was the first Beaver Countian and possibly the first American serviceman killed in WWII when his B24A bomber was destroyed on the ground during the Pearl Harbor attack. **34("First Area Serviceman Killed in WWII....", 7/15/2013), 60("Armed Guards on Duty at County Highway Bridges, 12/09/1941), 65 (http://www.pearlharborattacked.com/cgi-bin/IKONBOARDNEW312a/ikonboard.cgi?act=Print;f=14;t=39)**

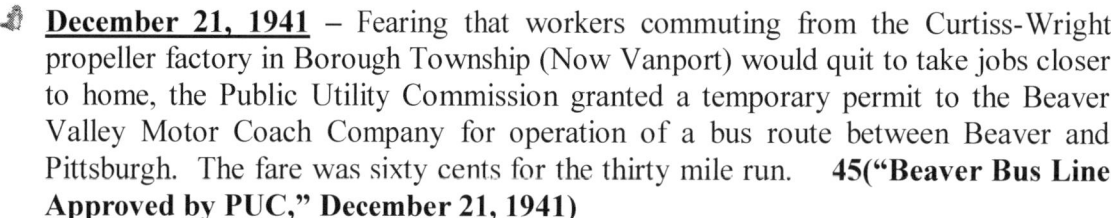

🌿 **December 21, 1941** – Fearing that workers commuting from the Curtiss-Wright propeller factory in Borough Township (Now Vanport) would quit to take jobs closer to home, the Public Utility Commission granted a temporary permit to the Beaver Valley Motor Coach Company for operation of a bus route between Beaver and Pittsburgh. The fare was sixty cents for the thirty mile run. **45("Beaver Bus Line Approved by PUC," December 21, 1941)**

American Bridge LST launch – BCHRLF Collection

🌿 **1942** – American Bridge Company in Ambridge began producing LST's (Landing Ship Tanks) for the navy using a welding versus a rivet technique. In July, 1945, American Bridge delivered the final LST to the Navy. Approximately 125 LST's were produced throughout this period at the Ambridge plant and launched into the Ohio River. Many of these Landing Ship Tanks were used in successful amphibious operations in both the Atlantic and Pacific theaters and were very helpful in winning the war. **5(242), 62(pages not numbered)**

🌿 **March 8, 1942** – The War Production Board passed order L-85 which restricted the public use of certain fabrics and materials deemed essential to the war effort. As a result, L-85 prompted a change in the ladies ready-to-wear industry that we still see today with shorter and tighter fitting clothing and two piece bathing suits, The manufacture of nylon stockings stopped altogether in order to make parachutes, airplane tires, netting and tents for the troops. To work around the stocking shortage, some women actually coated their legs with pancake makeup or gravy browning and painted a dark seam line on the backs of their legs with an eyebrow pencil to mimic stockings. Some shoe and cosmetic stores offered leg painting and even used a "stocking bar" that enabled women to paint a straight line down the back of her legs. **(WPB L-85, NARA), (http://www.oldmagazinearticles.com/WW2_fashion_and_WW2-fabric_rationing_of_World_War_Two#.WRmw22yGN9C)**

🌿 **June, 1942** – Babcock & Wilcox (B&W) built the Wallace Run Steel Mill that eventually grew to 4 electric furnaces, two of which specialized in stainless steel.

Between 1947 & 1950, B&W operated the world's first continuous caster at this location. **82(9)**

🍂 **August, 1942** – President Franklin Roosevelt signed a new Daylight Savings Time law, once again making it the standard for the entire country. **19(43-44)**, *See entries for August 20, 1919 and March 18, 1918.*

🍂 **August 26, 1942** – The first county air raid test was conducted. **40**

🍂 **December 22, 1942** – A landslide on Constitution Boulevard in Aliquippa sent tons of rock and earth falling 100 feet onto a bus loaded with 25 war workers from the Jones & Laughlin Steel Company Plant. The bus was crushed under the weight killing 22 people and injuring three others. (Note that earlier sources claim 21 killed and 2 to 4 injured, but later sources put the number at 22 killed and 3 injured). **84("Avalanche Buries Pennsylvania Bus," December 23, 1942).**

🍂 **December 30, 1942** – Another flood hit the county causing widespread devastation when the Ohio River crested at 39 feet. **58(71)**

🍂 **January 6, 1943** – Jones & Laughlin's Aliquippa Works was awarded the "Army and Navy Award for Excellence in Production" by Lieutenant Colonel John Swauger, executive officer of the Pittsburgh Ordinance District. **85("3000 Witness Army-Navy "E" Award", January 7, 1943), 65**

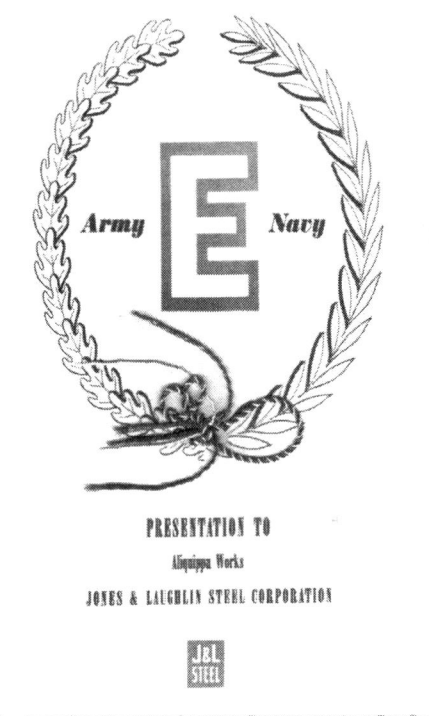

Army-Navy "E" Award – Courtesy of the Beaver County Industrial Museum

🍂 **February 19, 1943** – The *Aliquippa News Gazette* ceased publication on this day due to a lack of funds. **43("Aliquippa Paper Quits," February 24, 1943)**

🍂 **1943** – The Kobuta plant was established in Potter Township for the manufacture of butadiene and styrene. The name is a combination of "Koppers" and butadiene. Known today as Nova Chemical. **5(121)**

🍂 **March 3, 1943** – Geneva College played host to approximately 300 Army Air Cadets known as the 36th Detachment for training and classes. They were housed in Alumni and North Halls. **44(112)**

- **March 16, 1943** – Ingram–Richardson Manufacturing Company was awarded the "Army and Navy Award for Excellence in Production" by Lieutenant Colonel Harold Garvis of the Pittsburgh Ordinance District for their outstanding contribution to the war effort. **25("Ing-Rich to get Army and Navy "E" Award Tomorrow", March 15, 1943), 65**

- **August 2, 1944** – A small seaplane flown by John E. Kennedy of Beaver, hit some power lines in Potter Township and crashed into the Ohio River killing both Kennedy and his passenger. Kennedy was well known throughout the valley as a musician and orchestra leader. **103("Two Men Drown as Plane Crashes," August 2, 1944)**

- **August 9, 1944** – Aliquippa native and OSS operative, George Vujnovich put into operation his successful plan to rescue nearly 500 downed airmen hiding in Yugoslavia from the Germans. **42**

- **December 6, 1944** – Due to a shortage of factory and defense workers in the county industries, the War Manpower Commission sent special recruiting crews throughout the county to urge men and women to take jobs in the essential war material producing plants. **60("War Workers Being Recruited on Street", 12/6/1944), 65**

- **1944** – The Jewish Congregation Beth El of Beaver Valley was formed. **5(497)**

- **March 8, 1945** – A Beaver and Ohio River flood caused damage estimated at $450,000. **40**

- **March 12, 1945** – Fourteen year old diarist Anne Frank passed away in the German death camp at Bergen-Belsen. Starving and unconscious from fever, she fell off her bunk and rolled lifeless to the floor. **129(586)**

- **May 7, 1945** – Germany officially surrendered ending the war in Europe.

- **August 14, 1945** – WWII ended with the Japanese surrender. Beaver County suffered 479 casualties with 296 of them killed in action. **53(Tabulation by county)**

- **1945** – War bond rallies were held at American Bridge.

- **1945** – Raccoon Creek State Park was created. During the 1930's it was the Raccoon Creek National Recreation Demonstration Area. Men from

American Bridge War Bond Rally 1945 – BCHRLF Collection

the Civilian Conservation Corps and Works Progress Administration built the recreation facilities. In 1945, the land was transferred by the Federal Government to Pennsylvania to create Raccoon Creek State Park. **5(398),** *See entry for 1935*

1945 – The Beaver Falls Historical Commission was formed to organize the celebration of the town's Diamond Jubilee. When the task was finished, the group was reconstituted as a historical society under the same name. In 1953, the Commission was incorporated as the Beaver Falls Historical Society and Museum. **(Beaver Falls Historical Society and Museum)**

1945 – Former Priesthood student, Robert Marjanovich returned to his home in Aliquippa after six years, having been stranded in Yugoslavia when the Germans invaded. Marjanovich joined the ranks of General Darha Mihailovich's Chetniks as a fighter and helped to rescue downed American airmen. **33("Saving Stranded U.S. Fliers Thrills Aliquippa Man Serving Chetniks," September 24, 1945)**

IX. The Post War Years: 1946 to 1980

As life attempted to return to normal following the end of WWII, the county was once again in an economic boom, and the emphasis turned to recreation. This period saw the establishment of our county parks, a new county airport in Chippewa, and many of our local libraries. The Beaver County River Regatta was born as well as the Maple Syrup Festival, the ice arena, the Beaver County Sports Hall of Fame and Brodhead Cultural Center to cater to a renewed interest in our local culture and as a way to spend increased leisure time.

This era also saw Beaver County connected to the Pennsylvania Turnpike, the opening of the new Beaver Valley Expressway, the first shopping center established, the building of the modern Beaver Medical Center and county residents ushered into the atomic age with the dedication of the world's first nuclear power plant in Shippingport.

With the unrest surrounding the Vietnam War, civil rights for not only African-Americans but women as well came to the forefront and those struggles for equality added a diverse texture to the fabric of our society.

- **1947** – George Charles Izenour born on July 24, 1912, in New Brighton, developed an electronic dimming system for stage lighting, the first of its kind. The invention, which came to be known as the Izenour system, was used in television and theaters throughout the country. **(New York Times, "George Izenhour, 94, Designer of Technologies for Theaters, Dies," March 30, 2007)**

- **February 5, 1947** – A United States Navy fighter jet having instrument problems crashed in Harmony Township while en-route from St. Louis to the naval air station at Patuxent River, Maryland. Crash investigators determined that the plane had run out of fuel. The pilot, Lieutenant Commander William Kelly, a native of New Castle, Pa., was able to bail out safely. **34("Jet Slammed into Ground," 9/7/2003)**

- **May 5, 1947** – Attorney Harry L. Garrett became the first African-American member of the Beaver County Bar Association. **5(216)**

- **1947** – Aliquippa works of Jones & Laughlin became the world's fastest rolling mill for tin plate. **84(281)**

- **1947** – Located in Independence Township, the last covered bridge in Beaver County collapsed. The bridge was the oldest covered

Independence Covered Bridge – BCHRLF Collection

bridge in the state as well and was believed to be 130 years old.   **1(82), 110("Old Covered Bridge Drops into Creek in Beaver County," September 4, 1947)**

- **September 29, 1947** – Jerry Reed opened the iconic Jerry's Curb Service restaurant in Bridgewater. **(http://www.jerryscurbservice.com/history.html)**

- **1948** – WBVP became the first radio station in Beaver County. The original studio and offices were located on the third floor above the Rio Grille on 7th Avenue in Beaver Falls. In 2000, the station was purchased by Iorio Communications and merged with WMBA. Both stations were sold to Sound Ideas Media owned by Mark and Cynthia Peterson in 2014.   **5(358), 34("Riding the airwaves: Beaver County's radio history," February 16, 2016), (Mark Peterson, WMBA/WBVP)**

- **1948** – Gertrude Trobe became the first female radio personality in the county when she joined WBVP with her weekly show "You and Your Home."   **19(38), 45("Gertrude Trobe Even Finds Time to Cook," May 5, 1954)**

- **1948** – Edith B. Goosby of Beaver Falls became the first black notary in Beaver County. She served until 1982. **34(2/28/1999, "Miss Edith was a Mother to Everyone")**

- **1948** – Ben Mauro moved Taylorcraft, an airplane manufacturing firm, to Conway from Alliance, Ohio, and developed the first fiberglass composite airplane. **5(83)**

- **1949** – WRYO radio in Rochester Township was on the air until 1950, and had studios in Ambridge and Aliquippa. **5(358)**

- **1949** – Bell Telephone began the installation of a transcontinental microwave radio relay system that consisted of relay towers located approximately every 25 miles between New York to San Francisco. Using high frequency microwaves, the system could carry telephone, television and radio communications. One tower stands in Ohioville and was named the "Fairview" tower. **(http://long-lines.net/places-routes/1st_transcon_mw/LL0949/02.html)**

- **March 3, 1949** – A Capital Airlines DC-3 en-route from Chicago to New York was having engine and landing gear problems and was forced to make an emergency landing in a cow pasture in Beaver County. None of the 12 passengers or crew was injured. **110("Emergency Landing Made by Plane in Beaver County," March 3, 1949)**

- **November 18, 1949** – Beaver Area Memorial Library opened. **5(527)**

- **1950** – Brady's Run Park opened to the public. **5(395)**

- **1950's** – Service Creek Reservoir was created by the Ambridge Water Authority. **21(144)**

Willowbrook Lake Fishing Derby – BCHRLF Collection

- **1950** – Willowbrook Lake Resort was opened in Ohioville by Charles Luzell. The resort featured fishing derbies and dog/raccoon races across the lake. **49("Willow Brook Lake Resort," Vol. 33 No. 3, Summer, 2008)**

- **1950** – The U. S. Census reported county population at 175,192. **21(47), 33**

- **June 10, 1950** – Ellwood City council opened the Veteran's Memorial swimming pool, dedicated to WWII veterans at a cost of $95,980. **63(126)**

- **June 25, 1950** – The Korean War began as North Korean troops invaded South Korea.

- **September 24, 1950** – A strange yellowish haze settled over the county that Sunday morning, eventually turning to a dark black sky as if it were night. By 5:00 the sky started to lighten and returned to normal again. A lot of fear and panic ensued. **44(136-137)**

- **November 23, 1950** – Beginning on Thanksgiving Day and continuing for nearly 36 hours, a massive snowstorm blanketed our region. The storm dropped a record of over 27 inches of snow on the ground with high winds creating 8 to 10 foot drifts that paralyzed the county. The record still stands today. **34("Blizzard of 1950 buried Beaver County region," January 26, 2016), 44(139)**

- **1951** – St. Theresa School was opened in Koppel and closed in 1966. **5(299)**

- **November 26, 1951** – Beaver Valley Interchange of the Pennsylvania Turnpike opened to traffic at Route 18 near Koppel. **5(71)**

- **January 1, 1952** – Babcock &Wilcox East Works developed the first extrusion process in America to press short stainless billets into tubes and shapes. **82(9-10)**

- **February 28, 1952** – The Federal Rent-Control Office declared that a critical housing situation existed in Beaver County communities north and east of the Ohio River due to the tremendous industrial expansion, and imposed ceilings on rents for all hotels and rental units built within the past five years. **45("Government Slaps Tight Rent Lid on Beaver Towns," February 28, 1952)**

- <u>September, 1952</u> – St. John the Baptist School in Monaca opened. **5(299)**

- <u>September, 1952</u> – Ten year old Betty Bennett of Beaver County became the youngest person ever to fly solo when she eclipsed her brother Al Jr.'s record by one year. She did so in Cuba because the minimum solo flying age in the United States was 16. LIFE Magazine photographed the ten minute flight. Her record stood until 1982 when her nephew Ken flew at the age of nine. **33("Pittsburgh Soaring Club finds thrill in challenge of," August 21, 2011), 45("10-Year-Old District Girl Youngest to Fly," January 15, 1952), 130("Life's Camera Solos with a Ten-Year-Old," January 28, 1952)**

- <u>1952/1953</u> – The Beaver Borough School District merged with Borough (Vanport), Bridgewater and Brighton Township to form the present Beaver Area School District. **46(113)**

- <u>1953</u> – The last class was taught at the Mercer School house in Greene Township. The school originally opened around 1874. In 1995, the Mercer School was moved to the Hookstown Fair Grounds. **19(191)**

- <u>May 2, 1953</u> – Beaver County Airport in Chippewa was dedicated. It was built on 210 acres and cost $267,238. **5(81)**

- <u>July 27, 1953</u> – The Korean War ended when all parties agreed to an armistice.

- <u>September 23, 1953</u> – Cora Blackledge, who was a county juvenile probation officer for nearly 30 years prior to her retirement in 1940 passed away. **34("Cora Blackledge Dies in Hospital," September 24, 1953)**

- <u>1954</u> – Our Lady of Fatima Shrine was dedicated in Ambridge outside of the former St. Stanislaus Roman Catholic Church. It was dedicated to Ambridge war veterans and is unique because it included more than 220 pieces of rock, coral and seashells embedded below each bronze plate bearing a soldier's name. The rocks were sent back by soldiers and were taken from places in which they had served. **36(93)**

- <u>March 13, 1954</u> – An Air Force T-33 jet trainer crashed on a farm near Hookstown when it ran out of fuel. The pilot was killed, but a second airman was able to parachute to safety. **110("Pilot is Killed in Plane Crash in Beaver County," March 13, 1954)**

- <u>1955</u> – WRYO Radio went off the air. **(Mark Peterson, WBVP/WMBA)**

- <u>June 26, 1955</u> – Ambridge celebrated its Golden Jubilee (50 years). **59(93)**

🔹 **May 22, 1955** – Ground was broken for the Aliquippa Hospital. The hospital was dedicated on May 5, 1957. **56(107-108)**

🔹 **September, 1955** – A 100 foot long state highway bridge over a stream in Fombell collapsed into the stream below. A crane hauled the bridge from the creek and placed it on the stream bank. From that time on, despite conflicting claims, the bridge vanished and no one knows what really happened to it. **110("Beaver County Puzzled, Who Stole the Bridge?," October 9, 1958)**

🔹 **August 1956** – Our Lady of Fatima School opened in Chippewa. **5(299)**

🔹 **1956** – Old Economy Park opened to the public. It was our second county park. **5(396)**

🔹 **1956** – The Northern Lights Shopping Center opened as the area's first major shopping mall. **5(166-167)**

Shippingport Nuclear Power Plant – BCHRLF Collection

🔹 **December 2, 1957** – The world's first commercial electric plant powered by atomic energy went on line in Shippingport. **1(89)**

May 12, 1957 – The first patients were admitted to the newly built Aliquippa Hospital. **5(317)**

🔹 **July 5, 1957** – The first greater Ambridge Soap Box Derby was held. **62(pages not numbered)**

🔹 **1957** – Joe Letteri, Oscar winning visual effects wizard, was born in Aliquippa. He won Oscars for his work on *The Lord of the Rings: The Return of the King* (2003), *Avatar* (2009), *The Lord of the Rings: The Two Towers* (2002) and *King Kong*. He was the 1975 Valedictorian of his graduating class at Center High School which after the merger with Monaca is now Central Valley.
(http://www.imdb.com/name/nm0504784/)

🔹 **1957** – Allencrest Juvenile Detention Center opened in Brighton Township to house juvenile offenders being held for trial. The facility closed in 2009 due to rising costs and lack of state reimbursement. **34("Beaver Detention Center to Close," April 4, 2009)**

- **1957** – WMBA, originally a class "D," daytime only A.M radio station was founded by Miners Broadcasting Service, Inc. from Pottsville, Pennsylvania. **(Mark Peterson, WBVP/WMBA)**

- **January 1, 1958** – Economy Borough received borough status. It was formerly a township created from New Sewickley Township in 1827. **21(85)**

- **1958** – Saint Philomena School was built in Beaver Falls. **5(299)**

- **1958** – Aliquippa celebrated its Golden Jubilee (50 years). **56(109)**

- **1958** – Big Beaver changed its status from a township to a borough. **21(64)**

- **1958** – Jones & Laughlin Aliquippa Works operated America's first experimental Basic Oxygen Furnace, and in 1968, operated the first BOF to melt and process scrap into steel. **81(251)**

- **1958** – The highway bridge built between Beaver and Rochester as a bypass to connect to Route 65 was completed. It was designed by Michael Baker, Jr. to bypass downtown Rochester. **5(77)**

- **1958** – The weldings and fittings operation for Babcock & Wilcox was moved from Milwaukee, Wisconsin, to a new plant located in Koppel. **82(10-11)**

- **December 28, 1958** – An explosion and fire erupted at the Valvoline Oil Company in Freedom, resulting in an estimated $100,000 in damages. **33("Explosion, Fire Rip Refinery," December 29, 1958)**

- **1959** – The East Rochester – Monaca Bridge was built over the Ohio River. It was a toll bridge until 1973. **31(22)**

- **1959** – Beaver County Home and Hospital was built in Brighton Township (built on the former Haffey farm) and eventually become known as the Beaver Valley Geriatric Center and in 1993, Friendship Ridge. It was sold to a private company in 2013. **21(68), 5(324)**

- **July, 1959** – The Keystone Steam Driller Company, then known as the Stardrill Keystone Company, which had earlier been purchased by the Koehring Company of Milwaukee closed the Beaver Falls plant, moving operations to Buffalo, New York. **93(91)**

- **October 24, 1959** – Joseph Tonti of Midland, once called the "World's Strongest Upside Down Man," passed away at a Midland football game. He was nationally known and celebrated for his strongman performances and was once featured in "Ripley's Believe it or Not." **36(113-116)**

November 29, 1959 – The original Brighton Hot Dog Shoppe was opened in New Brighton by Victor and Francis Trevelline. As of 2015, the company operated nine company owned locations and also three licensed locations.
(http://www.brightonhotdogshoppes.com/aboutus.html)

1960 – The 1785 Pennsylvania – Virginia boundary stone was stolen from its location west of Georgetown. It was recovered and returned to its original location by Jack Lanam of the East Liverpool Ohio Historical Society in 1976. **109("How History was Stolen", Saturday December 5, 1987)**

1960 – Industry Borough was incorporated and changed from a township to a borough. It included the neighboring villages of Ohioview, Merrill and Industry. **21(114)**

1960 – To foreshadow the demise of American Steel, Armco shuttered its Butt Weld process of tube making because of foreign competition. It was the first mill to do so locally. Between 1961 and 1972, Armco built the most highly automated pipe making operation in the United States. By 1972, the automated plant was lost to foreign competition and the building sold to Babcock & Wilcox for their Ambridge Works. **82(231-238)**

1960 – Ohioville Borough was incorporated from Ohio Township. **21(136)**

August 18, 1960 – Ray W. Snyder Elementary School, Western Beaver, was dedicated. Due to low enrollment, the school closed in 2010. **5(287), Western Beaver School District**

July 24, 1960 – Beaver County Council of Girl Scouts purchased Camp Fombelina in Fombell. **41**

November 23, 1960 – Dr. Charles R. Cephas of New Brighton, one of the earliest black physicians to receive hospital privileges in the county, passed away. Dr. Cephas was a member of the staffs of the New Brighton, Providence and Beaver Valley General Hospitals as well as a progressive and constructive force in the medical profession. **141(92-93)**

1960/1970's – Native American site 36BV9 was excavated on Midland-Beaver Road. Artifacts covering a span of 8,000 to 9,000 years were found there by members of the Amockwi Chapter 17 Society for Pennsylvania Archaeology in the 1960s and 1970s. This stratified site was located on a flood plain with periodic floods sealing habitats 8 to 9 feet deep. **(BCHRLF historical marker)**

April 12, 1961 – The Soviet Union sent Major Uri Gagarin into orbit making him the first man in space. **129(864)**

- **April 15, 1961** – Ground was broken for Western Beaver Junior-Senior High School. **5(287). 41**

- **May 15, 1961** – Beaver County Commissioner J. Gordon Camp was killed while piloting his Cessna 172 when it crashed near Harrisburg. A passenger, John Licker, Jr. was also killed. **110("Hunt Mountains for Lost Plane," May 15, 1961)**

- **1961** – Evelyn Faye Javens became the first female mayor of Beaver Falls and the first female mayor of a town in Pennsylvania. **34("Four County Women Recognized," 9/13/1963), 45(11/11/1961)**

- **1961** – Aliquippa – Hopewell airport closed. **19(121)**

- **1962** – John P. O'Leary and Thomas Woolaway founded Tuscarora Plastics on Fifth Avenue in New Brighton. It became the nation's largest producer of expandable polystyrene foam packaging with over 30 manufacturing plants. Tuscarora was purchased by the Swedish firm SCA in 2001 and eventually relocated from New Brighton in 2009. **57(18), (David O'Leary, formerly Tuscarora Plastics)**

- **September, 1962** – Saint John the Baptist School opened in Baden. It closed after the 1971-1972 school year. **5(300)**

- **October 12, 1962** – President John F. Kennedy visited Aliquippa and gave a speech on a platform in the parking lot of the municipal building just four days before the Cuban Missile Crisis began. **33("When the Commander-in-Chief Comes Calling," November 3, 1996)**

- **September 18, 1962** – The Little Beaver Historical Society was incorporated. **Little Beaver Historical Society**

- **1963** – McGuire Memorial Home was founded and run by the Felician Sisters of North America and the Diocese of Pittsburgh for individuals who were severely physically and developmentally challenged. **(http://www.mcguirememorial.org/aboutus.html)**

- **June, 1963** – Captain Howard Eakin, Jr. became the first Beaver County casualty in what was the very early stages of America's entry into the Vietnam War. He was a member of the Army's 96th Advisory Team and was buried in Arlington National Cemetery. **(VVA Post 862), (http://www.vvmf.org/Wall-of-Faces/14467/HOWARD-M-EAKIN-JR)**

- **August 9, 1963** – Ellwood City officially annexed 76 acres in Beaver County when it voted to add an old brickyard located on the southern edge of the borough. **110("Ellwood Adds 76 Acres in Beaver County," August 9, 1963)**

Shippingport Ferry – BCHRLF Collection

October 1, 1963 – The Shippingport Ferry boat collided with a tow boat towing eleven empty barges during a heavy fog, resulting in two deaths. **34(5/19/2004)**

November 22, 1963 – President John F. Kennedy was assassinated in Dallas, Texas.

Ca. 1964 – Beaver County's Donnie Ierace, under the stage name of "Donnie Iris" helped to form the group "Jaggerz" which went on to create the 1970's hit song "The Rapper." Iris would have a long career in music. **(http://www.donnieiris.com/donnie/)**

1964-1968 – Crow Island, once Beaver County's largest, was buried beneath slag for the new Jones & Laughlin Basic Oxygen Furnace operation. **81(290)**

1964 – Shippingport Bridge was constructed over the Ohio River to connect with Midland. Designed by Michael Baker, Jr., the bridge put the Shippingport Ferry out of business. **5(78),** *See April, 1964*

1964 – Beaver County Restauranteur Lou Pappan opened his first Pappan's Family Restaurant in the College Hill section of Beaver Falls, eventually growing to 20 restaurants. In 1971, he acquired the Roy Roger's franchise and operated 19 of those. His interests turned to real estate with properties in Beaver and Allegheny Counties as well as Phoenix, Arizona. Mr. Pappan retired in 1997, and the Pappan's Family Restaurant Corporation declared bankruptcy in 2007. **34("Local Restaurant Owner to Retire," 5/21/1997),** *See entry for May, 2007*

1964 – Joines Radio Communications became the only radio communications carrier headquartered in Beaver County. The first beepers and mobile phones were introduced by the local firm in 1967. The company was started by Gladys Joines in her home in New Brighton for taking messages for other businesses. **5(357-358)**

Franciscan Manor – Courtesy Angela Modany

1964 – Steel for the Verrazano Narrows Bridge, one of the longest suspension bridges in the world connecting Staten Island and Brooklyn, New York, was fabricated at American Bridge Co. They also fabricated the steel for the New Orleans Superdome in 1974 and the steel for the New River Gorge Bridge in West Virginia in 1975. **5(118)**

- **1964** – The Fetterman Bridge that once connected Beaver Falls and Eastvale was demolished and the new Eastvale Bridge was built to replace it. The initial cost of the old bridge was $47,500 as compared to $2,239,418 for the new bridge. **25("Fetterman Bridge Comes Down," April 25, 1964)**

- **January 19, 1964** – The First Annual World Championship Snow Shovel Riding Contest was scheduled in Economy Park. **5(400)**

- **March 24, 1964** – Groundbreaking ceremonies were held in Bridgewater for Union Building & Loan. **5(163)**

- **April, 1964** – The Shippingport Ferry, the last ferry in Beaver County, made its final trip. **(BCHRLF historical marker),** *See 1964 Shippingport Bridge*

- **September 9, 1964** – Driver Improvement School for traffic offenders was begun. **5(65)**

- **February, 1965** - The Beaver Valley General Hospital in New Brighton and Providence Hospital merged to become the Beaver Valley Providence General Hospital. **5(319),** *See entries for 1980 and December, 1971*

- **1965** – The first American combat troops entered South Vietnam.

- **1965** – Heath Manor, owned by the Beegle family in Patterson Township, was sold to the Croatian Franciscan Brothers for $100,000 to be used as a monastery. The monastery was sold in 1996 to Scott Gordon, who renovated the old mansion-turned-monastery into Franciscan Manor, the assisted living home that it is today. **49("Mansion to Mystery to Manor", Vol. 34 No. 1, Winter, 2009)**

- **1965** – Penn State Beaver campus opened. **5(296)**

- **1965** – Ambridge held its first Nationality Days Festival. **33("Ambridge Marks 50th Year for Nationality Days Festival", 5/08/2015)**

- **April 17, 1966** – Police officers from Atwater, Ohio, chased a UFO nearly 80 miles through Ohio and into Pennsylvania where their speeds at times exceeded 100 miles per hour. The chase finally ended up in Harmony Township, PA, where they and a Conway police officer watched the UFO hover for a time and finally fly away at high speed. **34("Spooky History of Beaver County," 10/27/2015)**

- **October 11, 1965** – New Brighton Public Library opened. **39**

- **1966** – Construction was begun on Route 60, the Beaver Valley Expressway (current I 376), and it was finally completed to New Castle on November 20, 1992. **5(72)**

- **October 15, 1966** – The "Point of Beginning" was listed on the National Register of Historic Places. **(National Register of Historic Places)**

- **October 15, 1966** – Old Economy Village in Ambridge was listed on the National Register of Historic Places. **(National Register of Historic Places)**

- **1967** – Beaver Area Heritage Foundation was established. The museum opened in 1998, the log house was established in 2002 and the train station was renovated and opened in 2015. **(http://www.beaverheritage.org/)**

- **1967** – Community College of Beaver County began classes in the Freedom Bank Building. The present campus in Center Township was dedicated June 6, 1971. **5(294)**

- **1967** – The Roman Catholic Diocese of Pittsburgh opened Quigley Catholic High School in Economy Borough. **5(300)**

- **1967** – New Brighton Historical Society was founded in 1967 by Dr. A. E. Chadwick, and the meetings were originally held in the Merrick Art Gallery. **(New Brighton Historical Society)**, *See entry in 1974*

- **1968** – Jones & Laughlin's open hearth furnaces at their Aliquippa Works ceased operation. **81(132, 305)**

- **1968** – Midland's Crucible Steel Works was purchased by Colt Industries. **(https://www.crucible.com/history.aspx?c=21)**

- **1968** – Vanport Bridge for The Beaver Valley Expressway (now I 376) was built at a cost of $10.4 million, making it the second most expensive bridge built in state history. It was the first bridge to use curved steel girders. **5(78), See entries for 1966 & 1975**

- **1968** – Babcock & Wilcox constructed a special metals expansion in Koppel. In conjunction with B&W East Works, tubing was made and finished for nuclear steam generators in nuclear power plants for U.S. Navy submarines and aircraft carriers. **82(12)**

- **April 5, 1968** – Dr. Martin Luther King was assassinated on a hotel room balcony in Memphis, Tennessee. **129(981)**

- **January 12, 1969** – Joe Namath of Beaver Falls quarterbacked the New York Jets to a 16 – 7 win over the Baltimore Colts in Super Bowl III. Namath was inducted into the Pro Football Hall of Fame in 1985. Also on that championship team was Rochester's Babe Parilli who served as Namath's backup quarterback.

(http://www.bcshof.org/halloffamers/namath1982.htm), 5(375)

- **July 20, 1969** – Apollo 11 became the first successful lunar landing mission when Neil Armstrong became the first man to walk on the moon.

- **1969** – Rochester's Charles Asche, known throughout the valley as "Charlie the Radio Man," passed away. He was a self-educated pioneer in the early days of both radio and television, as well as the owner of Asche Radio & Television Service. **(Email remembrance 7/4/2017 from Elizabeth Asche Douglas)**

- **1969** – Ambridge Area Catholic School was created by a merger of St. Stanislaus School, St. Veronica's and Divine Redeemer. **5(300)**

- **1969** – Beaver County Christian School opened in Beaver Falls. **5(301)**

- **1969** – Dr. Jesse Steinfeld of West Aliquippa served as Surgeon General of the United States until 1973. **56(56)**

- **1970** – The name Vanport Township was officially recognized even though its unofficial history dated back to 1804 and took its name from former President Martin Van Buren. Originally known as Borough Township, it was created in 1804 to be identical in boundaries with the Borough of Beaver, hence, "Borough Township." (Beaver Borough, incorporated in 1802, was not completely independent of its parent, South Beaver Township, until Borough Township was formed.) Beaver's boundaries were reduced in 1804 leaving Borough Township as a separate entity. **21(156)**

- **1970** – The eight remaining Isaly's stores in the county were closed. **54(94-97)**

- **April, 1970** – An explosion rocked the Apollo 13 spacecraft crippling it on its trip to the moon. Aliquippa graduate Ralph Salaya who was on the design team for the command module assisted in creating the strategy that returned the spacecraft and its astronauts safely to earth. **34("Aliquippa Grad Helped Bring Apollo 13 Astronauts home," August 5, 2013)**

- **July 1, 1970** – The Blackhawk School District began operations. The new district was created from two earlier school districts: Highland Suburban School District and the Northwestern Beaver County School District. **5(274)**

- **1970** – Former New Brighton high school athlete, Ray Tannehill returned to the area to anchor Pittsburgh's WIIC television evening newscast. Tannehill had a long career as a newscaster and television correspondent. **5(358)**

- **September, 1970** – The Beaver Valley Mall opened in Center Township on the site of the former Pettibon Raccoon Golf Course. The course was opened on July 3, 1937 and closed in 1965 when it was sold to a developer. **5(167), 34("Now the Mall**

Once a Golf Course," by Mike Bires June 19, 2007), 60("Official Opening of Raccoon Creek Golf Course on July 3," June 16,1937)

- **September 4, 1970** – A tornado ripped through the Center Township and Monaca area causing an estimated $500,000 in damages. **34("Tornado Expert Reports Threat Exists in Area," April 12, 1974)**

- **September 10, 1970** – The restored Little Red School House on Dutch Ridge Road was dedicated. Originally known as Richmond School, this one room school was built in 1844 and closed its doors in 1954. **41, 19(176)**

- **November 16, 1970** – Ground-breaking ceremonies were held in Center Township for the Gateway Rehabilitation Center, a 135 bed 28 day facility for treating patients suffering from drug and alcohol addiction. **5(325)**

- **1970** – County population was 208,418.

- **1971** – Baden and Ambridge Area School Districts merged. **48(118)**

- **1971** – The Research Center for Beaver County was founded, and the Beaver County Genealogical Society was founded in 1974. In 2008 the Research Center for Beaver County and the Beaver County Genealogical Society merged to form the Beaver County Genealogy and History Center. It is presently located in the new Beaver Station Cultural & Event Center. **(http://beavercountyhistory.org/)**

- **1971** – The Beaver County Historical Research & Landmarks Foundation was incorporated. **(BCHRLF)**

- **July, 1971** – Through a mandate from the Department of Education, the Ambridge Area School District came into existence. The new district consisted of Ambridge, Baden, Economy, Harmony Township and South Heights. **62(pages not numbered)**

- **July 1, 1971** – Beaver Valley Intermediate Unit began its work as a regional service agency serving the school districts in Beaver County. **5(289)**

- **July 2, 1971** – Beaver Valley Expressway (now I-376) was completed to Vanport. **5(72)**

- **August 30, 1971** – Baden Memorial Library opened to the public. **48(128)**

- **December, 1971** - The Beaver Valley Providence General Hospital and Rochester Hospital agreed to a merger with the end result to be one large hospital built either in Brighton Twp. or in Rochester. Aliquippa Hospital refused to participate. Many years of law suits etc. followed until building began on the new Medical Center of Beaver County around 1977. **5(319),** *See entries for 1980 and February, 1965*

- **December, 1971** – Ambridge adopted an ordinance to create a historic district to preserve the Old Economy Village area. **47(169)**

- **1972** – The Beaver County Community College "Golden Dome" was built. **5(295)**

- **1972** – The Youngstown and Southern Railroad stopped using the former Greersburg Academy as a freight station, and the building was turned over to the Little Beaver Historical Society. **86(250)**

- **April 1, 1972** – Ambridge native General George Axtell was promoted by President Nixon to three star general. Axtell, a World War II ace and Navy Cross recipient, was the youngest commanding officer of a Marine Fighter Squadron. He also served in the Korean and Vietnam Wars. Axtell who passed away in 2011 was buried in Arlington National Cemetery. **(https://en.wikipedia.org/wiki/George_C._Axtell), (http://www.findagrave.com/cgi-bin/fg.cgi?page=gr&GRid=75239849)**

- **June 24, 1972** – A flood hit the county due to the remnants of Hurricane Agnes. **58(71)**

- **September 11, 1972** – A massive explosion ripped through the county courthouse causing nearly $700,000 in damage. A bomb was planted by five West Virginia men who wanted to destroy their criminal records, but their plan failed. **5(213)**

- **1973** – A cease fire was agreed upon which effectively ended the United States involvement in Vietnam. South Vietnam would fall in 1975. Beaver County lost 73 of her sons in that war. **(http://www.vva862.org/memoriam)**

- **1973** – Babcock & Wilcox rebuilt the former Armco buildings in Ambridge with a modern piercer and two lines of steel making for mechanical and oil well tubing that was completely computerized. Completed in 1976, this plant was considered the most modern computerized tube plant in the world. **82(14, 260)**

- **1973** – Verna Dorsey became the county's first African-American policewoman to join the Pennsylvania State Police. **19(47)**

- **1973** – The first steel swimming pool in Beaver County was built in Rochester in the area of lower Case Street with steel produced by the American Bridge Company. It closed in 1978. **5(391)**

- **1973** – The Anthony Wayne Historical Society was formed to save the 1792 Legion Ville training camp of General Anthony Wayne and his legions in present day

Harmony Township. In 1996 it was renamed the Legion Ville Historical Society. **(Legion Ville Historical Society)**

- **October 15, 1973** – The Gee Bee store opened in the Center Township Plaza and closed in 1989. It is the site of present-day Wal-Mart Plaza. **34("Gee Bee Store Opens Monday", October 12, 1973)**

- **December, 1973** – Patterson Township formed its first full time police force with David Hayes as chief. **127(10)**

- **1974** – Local archaeologists, with assistance from the University of Pittsburgh and the Carnegie Museum, began excavations to locate the remains of Fort McIntosh. They found stone footers marking walls and fireplaces. The dig continued for four years, turning up more than 80,000 identifiable artifacts and fragments of archaeological significance.
Digging was completed in 1978.
(http://www.beaverheritage.org/ftmcintosh.htm), 21(59), 46(30)

- **1974** – Jones & Laughlin Steel became a wholly owned subsidiary of the LTV Steel Corporation. In 1984 the J&L name was no longer used with the merger of LTV Corporation and Republic Steel, becoming LTV Steel. **83(284)**

- **November 1, 1974** – Ellwood City's National Tube Company owned by United States Steel closed. The seamless tube plant had been in operation since 1896. It would be the first of many steel mills to collapse in the county. **82(22)**

- **November 8, 1974** – The Captain William Vicary Mansion in Freedom was listed on the National Register of Historic Places. **(National Register of Historic Places)**

- **1975** – Beaver Valley Expressway (I-376, formerly Route 60) was opened between Vanport and Chippewa. **5(72)**

- **February 24, 1975** – Greersburg Academy in Darlington was listed on the National Register of Historic Places. **(National Register of Historic Places)**

- **March 27, 1975** – Legion Ville near Ambridge was listed on the National Register of Historic Places. **(National Register of Historic Places)**

- **April 24, 1975** – Fort McIntosh in Beaver was listed on the National Register of Historic Places. **(National Register of Historic Places)**

- **May 15, 1975** – The Matthew Stanley Quay house in Beaver was listed on the National Register of Historic Places. **(National Register of Historic Places)**

🪶 **August, 1975** – The Beaver County River Regatta was born as a rehearsal for the 1976 National Bicentennial Celebration. Both years were so successful it became an annual event. In 1993 due to a lack of funds, the Regatta left Bridgewater for Rochester. The Regatta was dissolved in 1994 and returned to Bridgewater in 2006. **34(8/10/1980), 58(46)**

🪶 **August 1, 1975** – Beaver County began a three day celebration to mark its 175 year anniversary. The festivities were marked by parades and a special visit from the President's Honor Guard who performed a flag raising ceremony at the courthouse. **108("Beaver County Set to Mark 175 Years," July 31, 1975)**

🪶 **September 30, 1975** – The Beaver County Sports Hall of Fame was organized by Alex Scassa, Sr. **5(369)**

🪶 **October, 1975** – Brush Creek Park was officially opened to the public. **5(397)**

🪶 **1976** – Beaver Valley Christian Academy was founded by Pastor Henry Howells in Bridgewater. **5(301)**

🪶 **1976** – Brodhead Cultural Center was opened at Penn State Beaver to celebrate the country's bicentennial. **5(447)**

🪶 **October 26, 1976** – President Gerald Ford visited the Aliquippa Jones & Laughlin Steel Plant and spoke with the workers there before heading off to a campaign appearance in Chicago. **33("When the Commander-in-chief Comes Calling," November 3, 1996)**

🪶 **February 22, 1977** – Michael Baker, Jr., founder of Michael Baker Jr. Incorporated, died. **5(74)**

1978 Phoenix Glass Fire – Courtesy of David Kramer

🪶 **February 24, 1977** – Pennsylvania Transportation Secretary William Sherlock, a Beaver native, was killed when his state leased plane crashed into a suburban house while taking off from the Harrisburg airport. Seven others died in the crash. He was interred in the Beaver Mausoleum. **33("Plane Crash Kills Sherlock, Frame," February 25, 1977)**

🪶 **September, 1977** – Beaver County Ice Arena opened in Brady's Run Park. **5(395)**

🪶 **September, 1977** – Beaver County

Community College celebrated its tenth anniversary with a special dedication ceremony. **111("Area News-Beaver County," September 22, 1977)**

- **1977** – Lapic Winery was founded in New Brighton. **64(84)**

- **1977** – Henry Mancini performed before a packed house at the CCBC Golden Dome. **19(197)**

- **1978** – A 44 seat passenger plane crash landed in the Ohio River near Shippingport. The three crewmembers were rescued by a tugboat and the plane was removed by the Coast Guard. **33("Plane Crashes in Ohio River," May 13, 1978)**

- **1978** – The first pancake dinner was held at the Maple Syrup Festival. **5(400)**

- **1978** – First organized and sponsored by the Crucible Steel Corporation, the town of Midland held its initial Fourth of July Parade and Celebration. **(http://www.midland4th.com/about/)**

- **1978** – The West Mayfield Christian School and the Pleasant Hills Wesleyan Methodist School opened. **5(301)**

- **July 15, 1978** – The Phoenix Glass plant in Monaca sustained heavy fire damage to its finishing, decorating, carton and warehousing facilities. The plant was acquired in 1970 by Anchor Hocking. **33("Phoenix Glass rises again", 9/5/1980)**

- **August 11, 1978** – Amber Brkich Mariano was born in Beaver. She appeared on reality television shows such as: *Survivor* (2000), *The Amazing Race* (2001) and *Rob and Amber Against the Odds* (2007). She married fellow *Survivor* contestant Rob Mariano on April 16, 2005. **(http://www.imdb.com/name/nm0110317/)**

- **September, 1978** – Beaver County Vocational Technical School opened its doors to students. **5(270)**

- **November 2, 1978** – President Jimmy Carter vetoed a bill that would have turned the Legion Ville site in Harmony Township into a national park. The President felt that Legion Ville was not of sufficient national significance. **33("Legionville Park Historical Status Vetoed by Carter," November 3, 1978)**

- **November 3, 1978** – President Jimmy Carter made a campaign stop at Aliquippa High School to attend a town meeting for several local candidates. **33("When the Commander-in-Chief Comes Calling," November 3, 1996)**

- **December 15, 1978** – B.F. Jones Memorial Library in Aliquippa was listed on the National Register of Historic Places. **(National Register of Historic Places)**

1979 – Kim Clements joined the County Detective Bureau, becoming the first female detective in county history. She would retire as a Detective Lieutenant in 2013 after an accomplished career. **34("County's First Female Detective Retires," 10/21/2013)**

1979 – Candy Young set the world record in the 55-yard hurdles and established the American Junior record for the 100 meter hurdles. In 1980, she became a member of the U.S. Olympic team but never competed due to an Olympic boycott that year. **19(47)**

1979 – The Sylvanian Hills Christian School opened in Rochester. **5(301)**

1979 – The 5,000th barge built at U.S. Steel's American Bridge Division plant in Ambridge was launched. The first vessel was launched at the Ambridge plant in 1903. **62(pages not numbered)**

1980 – County population was 204,441.

1980 – The Medical Center of Beaver County was dedicated in Brighton Township and cost $54 million. No local or federal taxes were used as it was financed entirely by bonds. It was built on the former Cook-Anderson farm and was the merger of the Rochester Hospital and United Hospital (former Beaver Valley Providence General Hospital). **5(322),** *See entries for February, 1965 and December, 1971*

1980 – Beaver Valley Transit Authority was formed. In 1991 they introduced the Demand and Response Transit (DART). **5(70), 61(33)**

1980 – Bell of Pennsylvania opened its first PhoneCenter Store in the county on Route 51 in Monaca. **5(357)**

1980 – Beaver native Ed Schaughenecy retired from a distinguished broadcasting career with KDKA radio that spanned nearly 48 years. He was known to the radio world as "Uncle Ed." **5(358)**

August 29, 1980 – The William B. Dunlap Mansion in Bridgewater was placed on the National Register of Historic Places. The mansion was torn down due to its neglected and dilapidated condition in 2016. **58(35)**

September 14, 1980 – Merrill Lock Number 6 was listed on the National Register of Historic Places. **(National Register of Historic Places)**

October 20, 1980 – President Jimmy Carter visited Beaver Falls and made a speech from the steps of the Carnegie Library. **33("When the Commander-in-chief Comes Calling," November 3, 1996)**

X. Death of big steel: 1981 to 1989

All good things come to an end, and so it was with the decline of the steel industry and the closing of our large steel plants along with many of the dependent industries which, in turn, idled thousands of workers. Within a short number of years, almost our entire industrial production capacity had nearly disappeared and all hope of recovery stood expectantly beside the grave of big steel. With the loss of jobs came the loss of population as many younger workers left the county in search of their next job while a lot of their elders simply retired to an uncertain future. Hard times had come to Beaver County.

- **1981** – This was a very significant year in Beaver County Steel. This year saw the beginning of the end of the American steel economy in Beaver County and Western Pennsylvania. Extensive layoffs began this year, and within a dozen years, Babcock & Wilcox, Crucible Steel, what was left of Armco, Wykoff, Moltrup, Pittsburgh Bridge and Iron, Superior Cold Draw Steel were gone. **82(78)**

J&L Steel Aliquippa - BCHRLF Collection

- **1981** – Aliquippa's Dr. James Frank became the first African American president of the National Collegiate Athletic Association (NCAA) until 1983. He was also president of Lincoln University in Missouri at the time. **5(380)**

- **1981** – Famous composer Henry Mancini returned to Beaver County and conducted the Aliquippa High School band. **19(197)**

- **1981** – Metropolitan Brick Company in Cannelton closed. The buildings were demolished in 2015-2016. It originally opened in 1927 as Alliance Brick Company, and it was the next to last brick plant to close in the county. Beaver County once had over 50 clay and brick plants. **86(114)**

- **September, 1981** – Rhema Christian School was established in Hopewell Township. **5(302)**

- **October 15, 1982** – Crucible Steel Company closed its Midland plant. **Gettysburg Times("Crucible Steel Closes Midland Plant," August 18, 1982)**

- **1983** – Beaver County Model Railroad Club (now the Beaver County Model Railroad & Historical Society) opened in the Century National Bank Building in Freedom. Circa 1994, the club moved into the former Pittsburgh and Lake Erie Railroad station in Monaca. **(http://bcmrr.railfan.net/overview.html)**

1983 – Air Heritage of Western Pennsylvania was established. In 1990 it became Air Heritage, Inc. and opened its 14,400 square foot hangar at the Beaver County Airport that August. **(http://airheritage.org/about/history/)**

1983 – The American Bridge Division, Wychoff Steel and Armco Steel Company plants in Ambridge ceased operations. **59(121), 62(pages not numbered)**

July 21, 1983 – A large explosion ripped apart the sewage disposal plant (which belonged to Chippewa but was actually located in Patterson Township) along Route 51 killing two employees and injuring thirteen firemen. **127(57)**

June 24, 1983 – Sally Ride became the first American woman in space. Ride was a member of the shuttle Challenger crew. **129(1220)**

August 5, 1983 – The Merrick Art Gallery in New Brighton was listed on the National Register of Historic Places. **(National Register of Historic Places)**

1984 – Several Beaver County towns became part of one of the longest Olympic Torch Runs ever. Local runners carried the torch through Ambridge, Baden, Freedom, Rochester, Beaver Falls and finally to Ellwood City where the torch exited the county toward New Castle. **5(382), 34("Olympic Torch Passing Through County," February 26, 1984)**

August 21, 1984 – An explosion and fire killed three workers at the Ashland Oil Company Valvoline plant in Freedom. A second fire occurred just four months later in December with no fatalities or injuries. **19(221), 34("Fire strikes Freedom refinery twice in four months," 12/21/1984)**

1985 – The Holy Trinity Roman Catholic Church in Beaver Falls celebrated its 75th Diamond Jubilee. The church was established primarily for parishioners of Polish descent. **72(2)**

1985 – Following years of cleanup efforts, the Ohio River was finally judged to be suitable for use as a water supply, for recreation use and safe for aquatic life throughout nearly ninety percent of its length. **5(573)**

January 25, 1985 – Keystone Bakery in Bridgewater closed its doors for good. It had been in business since its beginnings in Beaver in 1864. **58(42)**

January 26, 1985 – Mike Ditka formerly of Aliquippa, coached the Chicago Bears to a 46-10 victory over New England Patriots in Super Bowl XX. Also on that championship team was Conway's Jim Covert who went on to All Pro honors. **33("Mike Ditka Huddles with the Quips of his Alma Mater," 8/16/2011)**

May 17, 1985 – LTV Steel Corporation announced the closure of most of its facilities including the Aliquippa Works (leaving only the tin mill running), laying off about 8,000 workers. **5(157), 83(201)**

May 21, 1985 – The Economy Historic District was listed on the National Register of Historic Places. **(National Register of Historic Places)**

May 31, 1985 – A tornado ripped through 13 miles of Beaver County resulting in nearly $10 million in damages. Three people were killed and 107 injured. The Big Beaver Shopping Plaza, along with nearly 200 homes, was destroyed. The county was declared a disaster area by the federal government. **5(331), 34("Three Killed by Twister; Shopping Center Leveled," June 2, 1985)**

June 11, 1985 – Ray Robinson, the real person behind the legend of "Charlie No Face" passed away at the Beaver County Geriatric Center and was buried in Grandview Cemetery. **36(102)**

College Hill Station – BCHRLF Collection

July 12, 1985 – This was the last run of Pittsburgh & Lake Erie passenger railroad service in the county. Its last stop was at the College Hill station. **36(36)**

September 5, 1985 – Carnegie Free Library in Beaver Falls was listed on the National Register of Historic Places. **(National Register of Historic Places)**

November 1, 1985 – Armco Steel Corporation closed its Ambridge Works, permanently laying off 1,200 workers. **82(231-238)**

1985 – Demand and Response Transit (DART) merged with Phone-a-ride. **5(70)**

1985 – The second Rochester-Monaca bridge was torn down and replaced by the present continuous steel truss bridge which was completed in 1986 using the same piers. Between 1987 and 2009, the bridge

1930 Rochester-Monaca bridge being torn down in 1985 – BCHRLF Collection

took its name from the winner of the Rochester Versus Monaca football game each year. **68(18)**

🌿 **October 31, 1986** – The David Littell House in Hanover Township was listed on the National Register of Historic Places. **(National Register of Historic Places)**

🌿 **1986** – LTV sold the Midland Specialty Steel Plant to a group which included former Jones & Laughlin executives and became known as J&L Specialty Steel, Inc. A few years prior, in 1983, J&L had purchased this same Specialty Steel Plant from Colt Industries, and in 1990, 54% of its share was sold to a French company named Usinor. **83(203)**

🌿 **1986** – Beaver County bought the Beaver Train Station and expanded it to 8,500 square feet to create the county's first 911 Center. **(Beaver Area Historical Foundation)**

🌿 **1987** – Aliquippa native "Pistol" Pete Maravich was inducted into the Pro Basketball Hall of Fame following a stellar career in which he won an NBA scoring title and participated in five NBA all star games. He passed away of a massive heart attack while playing a half- court basketball game at a California church on January 5, 1988. **(Beaver County Sports Hall of Fame)**

🌿 **1987** – Logstown Associates Historical Society was formed. The first American Indian Gathering was held that year. In 1991, the American Indian Gathering moved to the CCBC Golden Dome. **(Logstown Associates)**

🌿 **May 18, 1987** – The Raccoon Creek Recreational Demonstration Area in Hanover Township was listed on the National Register of Historic Places. **(National Register of Historic Places)**

🌿 **August, 1987** – McDermott International Corporation announced the pending closing of its Babcock & Wilcox plants in Beaver Falls, Koppel and Ambridge, idling more than 1,500 workers by January 31, 1988. **44(156)**

🌿 **September 23, 1987** – Babcock & Wilcox had shut down most of its operation. However, Special Metals in Koppel was not affected and would continue another ten years under McDermott International. Special Metals is still in production as of 2015 as Penn State Special Metal. **82(20)**

🌿 **December 1, 1987** – Babcock & Wilcox Koppel Steel poured its last cast. Between 1985 and the summer of 1987, East Works, Beaver Falls, Wallace Run Steel mill, most of Koppel and B&W Ambridge were "mothballed." Most of the B&W Beaver Falls plants were eventually demolished. **82(20)**

🌿 **1987-1988** – Archaeological excavations were done at the Standard Slag Company in Georgetown that uncovered three sites spanning the Early Archaic through the Early

Woodlands periods which covered the time between 6300 B.C to 1600 A.D. with more than 14,000 artifacts recovered. In addition, Standard Slag discovered Mammoth or Mastodon tusks thought to be 26,000 years old buried in the slag during normal operations in 1989. **34("Mammoth Discovery made in Georgetown Excavation," March 18, 1990)**

- **January 4, 1988** – Theresa Ferris-Dukovich became the first female District Attorney for Beaver County, and the first in the state. **5(217)**

- **1988** – William Alston became the first African American police chief of Aliquippa. **34("Aliquippa Lauds Outgoing Police Chief," April 9, 2001)**

- **June 22, 1988** – Watts Mill Road Bridge over little Beaver Creek was listed on the National Register of Historic Places. **(National Register of Historic Places)**

- **March, 1989** – A miracle was reported at the Holy Trinity Roman Catholic Church in Ambridge. A witness claimed that the eyes of Jesus were miraculously closed when they had been open before. Large numbers of believers crowded the church. A panel from the Catholic Diocese of Pittsburgh disputed the "miracle." **62(pages not numbered), 33("'Miracle in Ambridge' church pastor resigns," August 14, 1989)**

- **May 17, 1989** – The James Beach Clow House in North Sewickley Township was listed on the National Register of Historic Places. **(National Register of Historic Places)**

XI. A New Era Begins: 1990 to 2016

The outlook to this point was bleak indeed, but typical of the hardy breed of Beaver Countians, recovery began, although sometimes painfully and slowly. Local industry was forced to re-invent itself from the ashes of a manufacturing economy to a more service oriented one. With the invention of fracking, oil and gas have once again become an important part of our economy.

This period has so far seen major steps forward for women as they moved into county leadership roles as: District Attorney, Constable, Commissioner, Treasurer, Recorder of Deeds, Coroner and Common Pleas Court Judge. African-Americans have also seen progress with the first black judge, and several mayors of major Beaver County towns, with more work to be done.

Transition to the digital age has seen the establishment of innovative cyber and charter schools, as well as faster and more secure communications helped along by the extensive use of the internet streamed to us through cable and telephone modernization. The county and the world have become smaller places.

- **1990** – County population was 186,093.

- **1990** – Former Emmy Award winning actress and star of the "Brady Bunch," Ann B. Davis moved to Ambridge along with her friend, former Episcopal Bishop William Frey and others, where Frey served as the dean and president of Trinity Episcopal School for Ministry. While living in Ambridge, Davis was active in the local community, volunteering at Trinity and even narrating Ambridge High School's "T'was the Night Before Christmas" play in 1992. In 1996, she and her group moved to San Antonio, Texas, where she passed away on June 1, 2014. (http://www.ambridgeconnection.com/local-news/brady-bunch-actress-ann-davis-former-ambridge-resident-dies), **33(Obituary: Ann B. Davis / She was beloved TV housekeeper, June 2, 2014)**

- **1990** – Dr. Corrado Baglio and Mark Ondrusek opened the Beaver Super in downtown Beaver. The market was still in business as of 2016. **34("Celebrating Independency: Owner's Work ethic, loyal staff make Beaver market super," July 6, 2016)**

- **April 26, 1990** – The Pittsburgh and Lake Erie Passenger Station in Aliquippa was listed on the National Register of Historic Places. **(National Register of Historic Places)**

- **October 5, 1990** – The former Babcock & Wilcox Koppel and Ambridge plants were purchased from McDermott International and Koppel Steel was formed. The UHP furnace, continuous caster and ladle refiner from the 1984 modernization helped to save steel in Beaver County. The Koppel plant would specialize in oil well tubing. **82(21-22)**

🌿 **January 16, 1991** - The United States and our allies launched Operation Desert Storm with a series of devastating air attacks to force Iraq out of Kuwait. The ground war began on January 24th and lasted 100 hours until President Bush declared a cease-fire following the liberation of Kuwait on February 27, 1991.

🌿 **1991** – Ownership of both Georgetown and Phillis Islands in the Ohio River was transferred to the National Park Service to become part of the Ohio River Islands National Wildlife Refuge in order to protect their natural habitats. **(http://www.water.ohiorivertrail.org/index.php/en/2012-12-26-22-31-55)**

🌿 **April 1, 1992** – Construction was underway at the former Center Township Plaza on the first county Wal-Mart store. Tentative opening date was set at August 1st. **(Allegheny Times article April 1, 1992)**

🌿 **1992** – Connie Tuccinard Javens became the first female treasurer in county history. **(http://www.beavercountypa.gov/treasurer/connie-tuccinard-javens-treasurer)**

🌿 **1992** – The Monaca Community Hall of Fame opened. **(http://www.monacapa.net/index.asp?Type=B_BASIC&SEC=%7B7F796FA5-F8DF-4E09-BD53-4186D6227E53%7D)**

🌿 **October 3, 1993** – President Bill Clinton and First Lady Hillary Clinton visited Ambridge High School to introduce their national health care plan. **33("When the Commander-in-chief Comes Calling," November 3, 1996)**

🌿 **1993/1994** – The East Liverpool (Ohio) City School District - located only two miles from the Midland Borough line signed an agreement in the 1993-94 academic year to accept Midland's students in its high school. Midland became the only district in Pennsylvania whose students attended school in another state. **33("Ohio Teaches Pennsylvania a Lesson", June 13, 1997)**

🌿 **1994** – Ellwood City Historical Society was formed and moved to their current location in 1997. **(Ellwood City Historical Society)**

🌿 **January 29, 1994** – Rochester native and Hopewell High star Tony Dorsett was inducted into the Professional Football Hall of Fame following a record setting twelve year career. Dorsett was the only player in the history of football to have played on a collegiate national championship team, won the Heisman Trophy, been inducted into the College Football Hall of Fame, played on a team that won the Super Bowl, and been inducted into the Pro Football Hall of Fame. He has

also been well known locally for his charitable work and fundraising efforts for McGuire Homes. **(http://www.profootballhof.com/players/tony-dorsett/highlights/), (http://www.imdb.com/name/nm0234132/bio)**

- **February, 1994** – Papa John Creach, born in Beaver Falls in 1917, passed away from pneumonia. Creach was one of the best known 20th century blues violinists who toured with Jefferson Airplane, Hot Tuna, Jefferson Starship and who also made many solo recordings. He was skilled equally in pop, rock, jazz, and blues. **(https://sites.google.com/site/pittsburghmusichistory/pittsburgh-music-story/blues/papa-john-creach)**

- **June 14, 1994** – Former Aliquippa native and world famous composer Henry Mancini passed away at his home in Los Angeles, California. On April 30, 1995, the Henry Mancini Bridge in West Aliquippa was named after him. **(http://www.miami.edu/frost/index.php/henry_mancini_institute/about_us/henry_mancini_biography/), 19(197)**

- **September 8, 1994** – USAirways flight 427 mysteriously crashed into a wooded area of Hopewell Township killing all 132 persons on board due to a rudder problem. The subsequent four and a half year crash investigation became the longest in the history of the National Transportation Safety Board up to that time. **33("Lessons from Flight 427," September 7, 2014), 84("Crash of Flight 427: The Crash Site," September 10, 1994)**

- **1995** – Southside Historical Village was setup at the Hookstown Fairgrounds. **(https://sshva.wordpress.com/)**

- **May, 1995** – The four local branches of the NAACP merged to form the Beaver County branch. **19(47)**

- **September 1, 1995** – Judy Moore, Beaver County's first female constable passed away. She served as constable in New Brighton's first ward. (**NOTE: RIVERS OF DESTINY ON PAGE 37 CLAIMS THIS HONOR FOR GERTRUDE TINSMAN OF BEAVER FALLS 1940-1944). 34("Beaver County's First Female Constable Dies," 9/6/1995)**

- **November, 1995** – Bea Schulte and Nancy Loxley were elected as the first female commissioners in county history. **34("Stunning Local Election Heads Top Stories of '95", 12/29/1995)**

- **March 31, 1996** – With the closure of Babcock & Wilcox in 1988, McDermott kept one part of the Koppel plant (Special Metals) open to make nuclear tubing for South Korea. On this date, it was sold first to Teledyne, and in 1998 to a Management Buy-out group. **82(23),** *See entry for August 21, 2006*

- **June 24, 1996** – Harold Trobe, the son of a rabbi born in Beaver Falls, passed away at his home in Gainesville, Florida. Trobe spent most of his adult life working for the American Jewish Joint Distribution Committee and the Hebrew Immigration Aid Society, helping to resettle, feed and train Jewish refugees from war torn Europe. Following WWII, he served at different times as the Director General of the Hebrew Immigration Aid Society for Europe, all of Latin America and finally Israel. **84("Harold Trobe is Dead at 82; Helped Resettle War Refugees," June 26, 1996)**

- **June 28, 1996** – Bridgewater Historic District was placed on the National Register of Historic Places. **(National Register of Historic Places)**

- **August 1, 1996** – Former U.S. Representative Joe Kolter, who had represented Beaver County, was sentenced to six months in prison and fined $20,000 for defrauding tax payers in the House Post Office scandal by converting stamps and stamp vouchers into cash. **84("Ex-Congressman Gets 6 Months in Prison," August 1, 1996),**

- **October 24, 1996** – The Beaver Historic District was listed on the National Register of Historic Places. **(National Register of Historic Places)**

- **January, 1996** – Another flood hits the county. **58(71)**

- **January, 1996** – Janice Jeschke Beall became the first female Recorder of Deeds in Beaver County history. **(Janice Jeschke Beall)**

- **April 12, 1997** – Aliquippa firefighters burned the St. Nicholas Russian Orthodox Church and parish house in a controlled blaze as practice for putting out fires. The church had opened on December 19, 1921 and closed in 1991 due to low attendance and lack of funds. **34("It's Really Heartbreaking," April 11, 1997)**

- **1998** – Beaver County had 6,384 registered boaters enjoying the county waterways. **64(102)**

- **1998** – Beaver Area Heritage Foundation (BAHF) completely renovated the adjacent 1910 freight house converting it to the Beaver Area Heritage Museum. **(BAHF)**

- **January 20, 1998** – The Beaver County Industrial Museum was founded at Geneva College in Beaver Falls and eventually moved to historic Darlington in 2010. **(Beaver County Industrial Museum)**

- **October 31, 1998** – French steel giant Usinor purchased the remaining 46% of the Jones & Laughlin Specialty Steel Plant in Midland. **84("Company News; USINOR BID FOR J & L SPECIALTY STEEL IS ACCEPTED," October 31, 1998)**

- **November, 1998** – George "Tookie" James became the county's first African American judge. **38**

- **December 31, 1998** – All 155 Hills Department Stores, including both sites in the county, were acquired and converted into Ames Department Stores. Ames went out of business in 2002 partly due to the debt absorbed when acquiring Hills. **Bloomberg Business("Hills Stores Company," 10/1/2015), 33("Bankrupt Ames Hanging it Up," 8/15/2002)**

- **September, 1999** – The Brighton Township Historical Society was formed. **(http://brightontwp.org/historical-society/)**

- **2000** – LTV Corp. sold the tin mill, the only remaining section of the plant that still operated, to U. S. Steel Corp. That Pittsburgh-based steel maker announced it would close the tin mill, resulting in the layoff of 400 steel workers.
(http://www.aliquippapa.gov/aliquippa_history.php)

- **2000** – Beaver County celebrated its bicentennial. **33("Beaver County Celebrates 200 Years," June 16, 2000)**

- **2000** – The Census put county population at 181,416.

- **2000** – The Pennsylvania Cyber Charter School (PA Cyber) was founded in Midland. It was the first online school in Beaver County and became the first in Pennsylvania to accept students from throughout the state in grades K through 12. **(http://www.paschoolchoice.org/school-choice/cyber-charter-schools/)**

- **2000** – The new 174,000 square foot Beaver County Jail was dedicated in Hopewell Township. To save taxpayer money, it relied on geothermal energy for heating and cooling. **33(7/13/2000)**

- **February, 2001** – President Bush visited Control Concepts in Vanport to talk about his plan for dealing with the inheritance tax and its effect on small businesses. **33("Beaver County firm excited about its 15 minutes of fame," February 28, 2001)**

- **September 11, 2001** – A series of coordinated attacks by the Islamic terror group Al Queda used four airliners; two to crash into the World Trade Center in New York; one into the Pentagon; and a fourth which crashed into a field in Pennsylvania killing thousands of Americans.

- **May 24, 2002** – The 1859 Beaver County Jail was demolished in Beaver. The jail closed officially in November of 2000. **34("Photo of the Day- Old Jail Demolished," 5/27/2002), 49(Vol. 26 No. 3 page 1)**

Lewis & Clark Keelboat visits Rochester 2003 - Applegate Collection

🦫 **January 17, 2003** – The fifth county courthouse was dedicated. **33("Beaver County Dedicates Courthouse," January 18, 2003)**

🦫 **March 19, 2003** – The United States and our allies invaded Iraq following an ultimatum for Iraqi leader Saddam Hussein to leave Iraq.

🦫 **2003** – A re-enactment of the Lewis and Clark Expedition stopped at Rochester and Georgetown on their way across the United States to commemorate the 1803 journey of the Corps of Discovery to explore the Louisiana Purchase. **(Author present)**

Logstown native re-enactors 2003 – Applegate Collection

🦫 **2003** – A re-enactment of Logstown was held in Economy Park in order to help celebrate the young Major George Washington's 1753 visit. The event was sponsored by the Beaver County Historical Research & Landmarks Foundation as well as the Commissioners of Beaver County. **(Author present)**

🦫 **August, 2003** – The new $4.1 million visitors Center for Old Economy Village opened. **62(pages not numbered)**

🦫 **August 12, 2003** – Pfc. Timothy R. Brown of Conway became the first Beaver County soldier killed in Operation Enduring Freedom when his vehicle struck a land mine in Afghanistan. He was interred at Arlington National Cemetery. **34("Pfc. Tim R. Brown, Jr. Honored," 8/30/2003)**

🦫 **December 12, 2003** – St. Veronica's High School (Ambridge) alumnus David Zubik was named Bishop of the Diocese of Green Bay. **62(pages not numbered)**

🦫 **2004** – New Brighton native Terry Francona managed the Boston Red Sox to their first World Series title since 1918 and ended the "curse of the Bambino." He would go on to win a second World Series title with Boston during the 2007 season.

(http://www.baseball-reference.com/bullpen/Terry_Francona)

🔹 **2004** – The remnants of Hurricane Ivan caused the Ohio River to flood. Damage was not nearly as bad as from some previous floods and was confined mostly to boats and docks. **58(71)**

🔹 **2004** – USAirways abandoned its hub at Pittsburgh International Airport and moved operations to Charlotte, North Carolina, affecting many Beaver County jobs. **34("Promises Made and Broken," October 11, 2015)**

🔹 **2004** – Rochester native Lauryn Williams won a silver medal at the summer Olympic Games in Athens in the 100 meter dash. In 2012, she won an Olympic Gold Medal while setting a world record with the 4 x 100 relay team. During the 2014 Winter Olympics, she won a silver medal in the bobsled competition, and became the first American woman to win medals in both the summer and winter Olympic Games, as well as only the fourth person ever to accomplish this feat.
(http://www.usatf.org/athletes/bios/Williams_Lauryn.asp&http://articles.sun-sentinel.com/2014-02-19/sports/sfl-williams-silver-medal-bobsled-20140219_1_sochi-games-jamie-greubel-heather-moyse)

🔹 **June 1, 2004** – Allegheny Ludlum purchased the Jones & Laughlin Specialty Steel plant in Midland from Usinor for $67.2 million. **90("Allegheny Technologies paid $67M to buy J&L," June 15, 2004)**

🔹 **August 22, 2004** – Beaver Mayor Robert Linn passed away. In 1995, he was recognized by the "Guinness Book of World Records" as the nation's longest serving mayor. **34("New Mayor for Beaver", 10/08/2004), (http://www.beaverheritage.org/2005-exhibit-mayor-linn-nations-longest-serving-mayor.htm)**

🔹 **January 9, 2005** – Due to recent heavy rains, the tugboat *Elizabeth M* sank after being swept over a spillway of the Montgomery Island Lock and Dam in Industry while pushing six barges. Three crewmembers were killed and three others were rescued. **33("3 dead, 1 missing as towboat goes over dam, sinks in Ohio River," January 10, 2005)**

🔹 **January 20, 2005** – George Walker was appointed the mayor of Rochester following the resignation of Mayor Matthew Cuccinelli, making him the first black mayor of Rochester and first African-American mayor in Beaver County history. **34("Rochester Appoints Beaver County's First Black Mayor," 1/20/2005)**

🔹 **March 1, 2005** – Emil Alam, known as the "Dean of Beaver County Amateur Archaeologists," and recipient of the James L. Swauger Award from the Carnegie Museum of National History for his writings and contributions to the field, passed away. **34("Alam, Emil A. obituary, March 3, 2005)**

- **November, 2005** – Deborah Kunselman was elected the first female Common Pleas Court Judge for District 36.
  (http://www.beavercountypa.gov/courts/courts-common-pleas/courts-common-pleas-judge-deborah-kunselman)

- **December 1, 2005** – Aliquippa native and former American case officer and Afghan Task Force Chief for the Central Intelligence Agency, Gust Avrakotos, passed away. Avrakotos was best known for his role in leading Operation Cyclone, the largest covert operation in the CIA's history which armed the Afghan Mujadeen to help drive out the Soviets. This operation was dramatized in the movie "Charlie Wilson's War." **(Washington Post, "CIA Agent Gust L. Avrakotos Dies at Age 67," 12/25/2005)**

- **April 6, 2006** – Darlington Brick Company, a subsidiary of General Shale announced that it was permanently closing its operations and moving to Tennessee. It was the last brick and clay plant in Beaver County. **34("Darlington Brick Co. announces its closing," April 6, 2006)**

- **August 21, 2006** – The Koppel Special Metals plant was bought by a group of former employees and was named Penn State Special Metals. That plant was still in operation as of 2016. **82(23)**, *See entry for March 31, 1996*

- **October 20, 2006** – A Norfolk Southern Railway train en-route from Chicago pulling 83 cars of ethanol derailed in New Brighton due to a defective rail near Third Avenue and Fifth Street. Ethanol was released into the Beaver River and surrounding area. A large fire resulted and more than 500 people and businesses were evacuated.
  33("Tanker Cars burn in New Brighton; 500 residents evacuated," Oct. 21, 2006), (http://www.ntsb.gov/investigations/AccidentReports/Pages/RAR0802.aspx)

- **May, 2007** – Pappan's Family Restaurants filed for Chapter 11 bankruptcy. **37 ("Beaver County's Pappan's files Chapter 11," May 30, 2007),** *See entry in 1964*

- **2007** – Wild Waterways Conservancy bought the 100 acre Rock Point property near Ellwood City from the Nastas family, renamed it the Rock Point Nature Area and opened it to the public. **36(18)**

- **2007** – Huntington Bank of Columbus, Ohio, merged with Sky Bank to become the 24th largest domestically controlled bank in the country. **(http://huntington-ir.com/ne/news/hban122006.pdf)**

- **2008** – Teri Tatalovich-Rossi became the first female coroner of Beaver County. **(http://www.bsddigital.com/bc-gov/coroner/teri-tatalovich-rossi-coroner)**

- **2008** – Geneva College's Mike "Doc" Emrick received the Foster Hewitt Award from the Hockey Hall of Fame for his outstanding contributions to hockey broadcasting. **(Beaver County Sports Hall of Fame)**

- **2008** – Koppel Steel in Ambridge and the Koppel Works become Russian owned when purchased by a firm named TMK IPSCO. **82(23)**

- **May 31, 2008** – McCarl Industrial Museum opened in Darlington. **49("Little Beaver Historical Society Celebrates 50th," Vol. 37 No. 3, Summer, 2012)**

- **August 29, 2008** – Democratic presidential candidate Barack Obama and running mate Joe Biden toured the Pennsylvania Biodiesel plant in Monaca. **34("Obama, Biden visit Beaver County biodiesel plant," August 29, 2008)**

- **December 16, 2008** – Ground was broken in Ambridge for the new Beaver County 911 building located on the former H. H. Robertson Steel Decking Company property. **(http://www.beavercounty911.com/News/News.html)**

- **July 1, 2009** – Center and Monaca school districts officially and voluntarily merged to become Central Valley. It was the first merger of Pennsylvania school districts in nearly 20 years. **33("Central Valley Celebrates Merger," 7/9/2009)**

- **November 6, 2009** – Route 60 was officially re-designated as Interstate 376. The process was started locally circa 2001. **43**

- **2010** – County population dropped to 170,539. **(http://www.census.gov/)**

- **2010** – Beaver County moved the 911 Center from Beaver Station to its new site in Ambridge. **(Beaver Area Historical Foundation)**

- **March 23, 2010** – Mike Veon, former state representative from the 14th Congressional District, was convicted by a Dauphin County jury of 14 counts related to using taxpayer-paid bonuses to reward state workers for campaign efforts and illegal campaign fund-raising among other charges. Veon previously had been instrumental in the formation of Beaver Initiative for Growth, also better known locally by its initials as BIG for which he received an additional one to four year sentence in 2012. **33("Veon could face up to 73 years in prison," March 24, 2010),** *See entry for June 19, 2015*

- **May 24, 2010** – Swimmer Mimi Hughes, a teacher from Tennessee and U.S. Army Veteran, began her epic swim of the length of the Ohio River from the Mon Wharf in Pittsburgh through Beaver County and on to the Mississippi River in order to highlight women's causes. Hughes left the river for the night at Baden Beach. She successfully completed her journey at Cairo, Illinois, on July 19, 2010. Hughes had previously completed swims such as the Tennessee, Danube, Drava and Mura Rivers

as well as a trip across the Bering Strait. **(http://blog.al.com/breaking/2010/07/mimi_hughes_completes_ohio_riv.html), 124("Woman sets out to swim length of the Ohio River," May 24, 2010)**

December 24, 2010 – John Warhola of Freedom passed away from pneumonia at Allegheny General Hospital at age 85. Warhola was the older brother of famed artist Andy Warhol. Following his brother Andy's death in 1987, Mr. Warhola was one of three board members who oversaw the Andy Warhol Foundation. He became a key player in setting up the museum that bears the artist's name, as well as another Andy Warhol museum in the family's ancestral home in Medzilaborce, Slovakia. **33("Obituary: John Warhola / Brother who was told, 'Your role is to take care of Andy,'" 12/25/2010)**

February 11, 2011 – Noted local historian Denver Walton passed away. Walton was the author of numerous books and publications on local history as well as having served many years as President of the Beaver County Historical Research & Landmarks Foundation. **49("Denver Walton: Beaver County Historian," Vol. 36, No. 1, Winter, 2011)**

May 11, 2011 – Armstrong World Industries (formerly Armstrong Industries) closed in Beaver Falls. The plant was opened in 1902 in Beaver Falls to produce clay bounded cork products. **49(6-7)**

September, 2011 – Center Township resident Eileen Battisti lost her $280,000 home to a sheriff's sale over $6.30 owed for interest on her school tax bill. In 2015 Commonwealth court overturned the sale and allowed Mrs. Battisti to keep her home. **34("Beaver County woman has lost her home – again – because she owed $6.30," April 28, 2014), 37("Beaver County widow won't lose home over $6.30 late fee," 7/29/2015)**

December 12, 2011 – Geneva's Mike "Doc" Emrick was the first member of the media inducted into the U.S. Hockey Hall of Fame. He was awarded the Vin Scully Lifetime Achievement Award for his distinguished broadcasting career in 2015. **134("Emrick to receive Lifetime Achievement Award," June, 19, 2015)**

January 3, 2012 – Dwan Walker took office as the first African-American mayor of Aliquippa. **(http://www.aliquippapa.gov/aliq_city_dwan_walker.php)**

March, 2012 – Shell Chemical Company announced that it was considering a site in Beaver County for its ethane cracker plant. Shortly afterward, they were given a 25-year tax break worth about $66 million a year starting in 2017, or $1.7 billion over the life of the tax break. **34("Shell Confirms It Will Build Cracker Plant in Potter Township," June 7, 2016)**

May 16, 2012 – After nearly 42 years, Specialist Four Leslie Sabo, Jr. of Ellwood City was posthumously awarded the Medal of Honor for bravery in action during the Vietnam War. 33("**Vietnam War hero may finally get his due: Soldier who died to save his comrades recommended for Medal of Honor,**" **May 9, 2010**).

- **June 26, 2012** – Demolition began on the Kenwood School in New Brighton which had been built in 1855. 34("**Kenwood School Building Demolition,**" **June 27, 2012**)

- **July 6, 2012** – President Barack Obama made a surprise visit to Kretchmar's Bakery in Beaver. 33("**Obama Visits Beaver,**" **July 6, 2012**)

- **January 22, 2013** – During the early morning hours, the cooling towers from the Beaver Valley Nuclear Power Plant in Shippingport produced a narrow band of snow that traveled east from the stacks across the greater Pittsburgh area. The snow band was about 2 miles wide and extended east about 30 miles over southeast Beaver County and northern Allegheny County. Residents reported an accumulation of over an inch of fluffy snow. **(http://www.newsnet5.com/weather/weather-news/beaver-valley-nuclear-power-plant-produces-band-of-snow)**

- **2013** – The old Babcock & Wilcox East Works was demolished and, as of 2015, the grounds were an open field. **82(24)**

- **May 16, 2013** – Beaver County Commissioners announced the sale of Friendship Ridge (formerly the Beaver County Geriatric Center) to Comprehensive Healthcare Management Services LLC of New Jersey for $37.5 million. 37("**Beaver Nursing Home Sale Finalized,**" **3/26/2014**)

- **November 22, 2013** – Former Bridgewater Councilman Gregory Scott Hopkins was convicted of third degree murder in the September 1, 1979, strangulation death of Catherine Janet Walsh. The 34 year-old case was revived due to DNA evidence that was not available at the time. 33("**Verdict ends 34 year old odyssey for Victim's Brother,**" **11/22, 2013**)

- **May 21, 2014** – Beaver County began issuing marriage licenses to same sex couples. 34("**Beaver County Now Issuing Marriage Licenses to Same Sex Couples,**" **5/22/2014**)

- **May 21, 2014** – The first legally sanctioned same sex marriage was performed in Beaver County. 35("**Beaver County Legally Marries its First Same Sex Couple,**" **5/21/2014**)

- **May 21, 2014** – Wal-Mart opened its third county location in Economy Borough behind the Northern Lights Shopping Center. 34("**Economy Walmart Opens in May 21,**" **May 14, 2014**)

May 26, 2014 – Veteran's Memorial Bridge was built across the Beaver River connecting Bridgewater with Rochester Township. It was the first bridge built in the county in many years. Also, the Veteran's Memorial, located on the Bridgewater side was dedicated on this date. **(author was in attendance), 37("Bands to key Beaver County bridge opening," May 21, 2014)**

Veteran's Memorial Bridge under Construction – BCHRLF Collection

July 11, 2014 – Beaver County Sheriff George David was acquitted of charges that he threatened a reporter and intimidated a deputy sheriff. In May of 2015, David lost the Democratic primary race, ending his tenure as sheriff.
34("David Says it's Over.....," May 19, 2015), (http://triblive.com/news/adminpage/6427374-74/david-vranesevich-county#axzz3pJKuxMSP)

August, 2014 – The Ambridge Family Theater closed its doors as the last independent theater in the county. **(WPXI. Com, "Last Independent Movie Theater in Beaver County Closing," Friday, August 15, 2014)**

August 1, 2014 – Following fifteen years in the NFL, Aliquippa's Ty Law was inducted into the New England Patriot's Hall of Fame following a stellar career in which he helped to win three Super Bowls and was a five time Pro Bowl selection and one time Pro Bowl MVP.
(http://archive.patriots.com/team/index.cfm?ac=playerbio&bio=270), (http://www.patriots.com/news/2014/05/20/fans-vote-ty-law-2014-patriots-hall-fame-inductee)

December 7, 2014 – Kmart in Rochester closed, idling 78 workers. **34("Loss of Kmart Leaves Big Hole in Rochester Business District," October 3, 2014)**

December 12, 2014 – A disembodied woman's head was found in a wooded area along Mason Road in Economy Borough. The head had been previously embalmed and someone had taken out her eyes and substituted red rubber balls. On December 12, 2015, the still unidentified remains were buried in Beaver Cemetery. **34("Who Was She?," December 6, 2015), 34("'Jane Doe,' whose remains were found last year in Economy, buried in Beaver," December 13, 2015)**

- **February, 2015** – East Liverpool (Ohio) City School District terminated its contract to educate Midland students. **34("In surprise move, East Liverpool voids contract with the Midland School District," 2/26/2015)**

- **February 10, 2015** – WesBanco consummated a merger with ESB Financial Corporation and ESB Bank, Ellwood City, PA. **(http://www.wesbanco.com/AboutUs/History.aspx)**

- **March 4, 2015** – Officials announced that the Fallston Bridge would be permanently closed to both pedestrians and vehicles. **34(3/4/2015)**

- **April 23, 2015** – Beaver County's Donnie Iris (Donnie Ierace) was inducted into the Pittsburgh Rock 'n Roll Legends Hall of Fame. **33("Pittsburgh Rock 'N Legends Awards to induct Donnie Iris, Lou Christie and Porky Chedwick," March 19, 2015)**

- **April 30 - May 3, 2015** – A memorial and wreath laying ceremony was held at the Sewickley Cemetery's Tuskegee Airmen Memorial of Western Pennsylvania to honor Beaver County's five Tuskegee participants in WWII. Air Heritage hosted a P-51 Mustang of the CAF Redtail Squadron and accompanying exhibit honoring the Tuskegee Airmen program through the weekend. The weekend was sponsored by the Beaver County Historical Research & Landmarks Foundation and the Tuskegee Airmen Memorial of the Western Pennsylvania Region, Inc. **(Author was present)**

- **June 23, 2015** – Former Representative Mike Veon was released from prison for good behavior after having served five years for his convictions in the "Bonusgate" and Beaver Initiative for Growth scandals. He will remain on parole for nine years. **37("Veon comes out of jail swinging, vows to be Pa.'s 'Comeback Kid'," June 19, 2015),** *See entry for March 23, 2010*

- **June, 2015** – Shell Chemical Company purchased the former Horsehead Corporation site in Potter Township for $13.5 million. Horsehead began the demolition of its buildings and the remediation of the site thanks to Shell paying more than $80 million for the work. **34("Shell Confirms It Will Build Cracker Plant in Potter Township," June 7, 2016)**

- **July 31, 2015** – Rochester Heritage Society opened their Vintage Room Museum in the Rochester Municipal Building. **34("Rochester's History Showcased in New Museum," 7/28/2015)**

- **August 21, 2015** – A series of arsons broke out in Beaver Falls targeting abandoned buildings. By September 28th thirteen separate fires had been investigated, and a suspect was taken into custody. **34("Three more fires plague Beaver Falls," September 29, 2015)**

- **September 9, 2015** – Developer Chuck Betters purchased eight acres of the Bridgewater Crossing land for $1 million from the Beaver County Corporation for Economic Development, with plans to build three apartment buildings along with a commercial development nearby. The remaining four acres were being used for roads and a park. **34("Bridgewater Crossing sold to developer Betters; residential and commercial development planned," 9/09/2015)**

- **September 12, 2015** – Former Hopewell High School soccer player April Goss became only the second female in NCAA history to score points in a Division 1 football game. Goss kicked an extra point for her Kent State team in a game against Delaware State. **73("Inside the game: How April Goss came to kick for Kent State", 9/18/2015)**

- **September 25, 2015** – Midland School District and Beaver Area School District announced the signing of a 20 year tuition agreement that was effective earlier on July 1, 2015. **34("Midland-Beaver Area school districts sign 20-year tuition agreement," September 25, 2015).**

- **October 3, 2015** – The bones of several bodies from the 1800's that were found during the remediation of the old Horsehead Corporation site in Potter Township were prepared for reburial in Beaver Cemetery. The remains were determined to be of early resident Adam Stone and his family. **34("Stone Bones burial set for Beaver," 9/29/2015)**

- **October 21, 2015** – The Kane Road Drive-In in Hopewell Township was demolished to make room for a new apartment complex. The Drive-In which was owned by the Gray family had operated since 1954 and was officially closed in 2013. **34("Memories go up in Dust....", October 2, 2015), 49(Lights Going Out at Kane Drive In," Vol. 37 No. 3 Summer, 2012 pg. 5)**

- **October 23, 2015** – AES Corp. announced that it was closing its coal fired power plant in Potter Township. The company could not find a buyer for the electricity that it produced. By a prior agreement, the plant reverted to Nova Chemical which planned to begin demolition in early 2016. **34("Burned Out," October 23-24, 2015), 34("Coal plant will be reduced to soot," 11/19/2015)**

- **November 5, 2015** – For the first time since 1955, two Beaver County Republican commissioner candidates (Sandie Egley and Dan Camp) were elected and will constitute the majority on the Board of Commissioners. **34("Republican revolution comes at no surprise to Beaver County's GOP leadership," November 5, 2015)**

- **November 12, 2015** – Beaver County Commissioners purchased existing park and riverfront land at the confluence of the Beaver and Ohio Rivers next to the proposed Bridgewater Crossing Development from the Beaver County Corporation for Economic Development. **34("Beaver County takes over control of riverfront park," 11/13/2015)**

Newly remodeled Beaver Station Cultural & Events Center – Courtesy of Beaver Area Heritage Foundation

🦫 **November 17, 2015** – The Beaver Area Heritage Foundation held its first public membership meeting in the newly renovated train station which has become the Beaver Station Cultural & Event Center. **(Author was present)**

🦫 **December 2, 2015** – The towns of Aliquippa and Patricia, Italy approved proclamations to become sister cities. Many of the early Italian immigrants to Aliquippa came from the Patricia area. **34("Aliquippa and Patricia, Italy further ties," 12/02/2015)**

🦫 **December 10, 2015** – Allegheny Technologies Incorporated idled its Midland plant. Unable to reach an agreement since August, ATI locked out its 220 employees at this location. **(http://triblive.com/news/adminpage/9607897-74/ati-company-plants)**

🦫 **December 31, 2015** – The Youngstown and Eastern Railroad through Darlington is currently America's oldest operating short line. It began operations in 1883. **86(267)**

🦫 **June 7, 2016** – Shell Chemical Company officially announced that they will be building their ethane cracker plant at the old Horsehead site in Potter Township with plant construction to begin within 18 months. **34("Shell Confirms It Will Build Cracker Plant in Potter Township," June 7, 2016)**

🦫 **December 6, 2016** - Elizabeth Asche Douglas of Rochester Township, a noted local artist whose paintings and sculptures have been exhibited throughout the world, received the Lifetime Service Award for her contributions to the county as an artist, educator, musician, advocate and community leader. This was only one of many other awards that she has received throughout her lifetime. **19(49), Rochester Chamber of Commerce Awards 2016.**

APPENDIX A – Evolution of the Boroughs and Townships of Beaver County

(Diagrams courtesy of the 1976 Beaver County Centennial Atlas)

East Side Communities

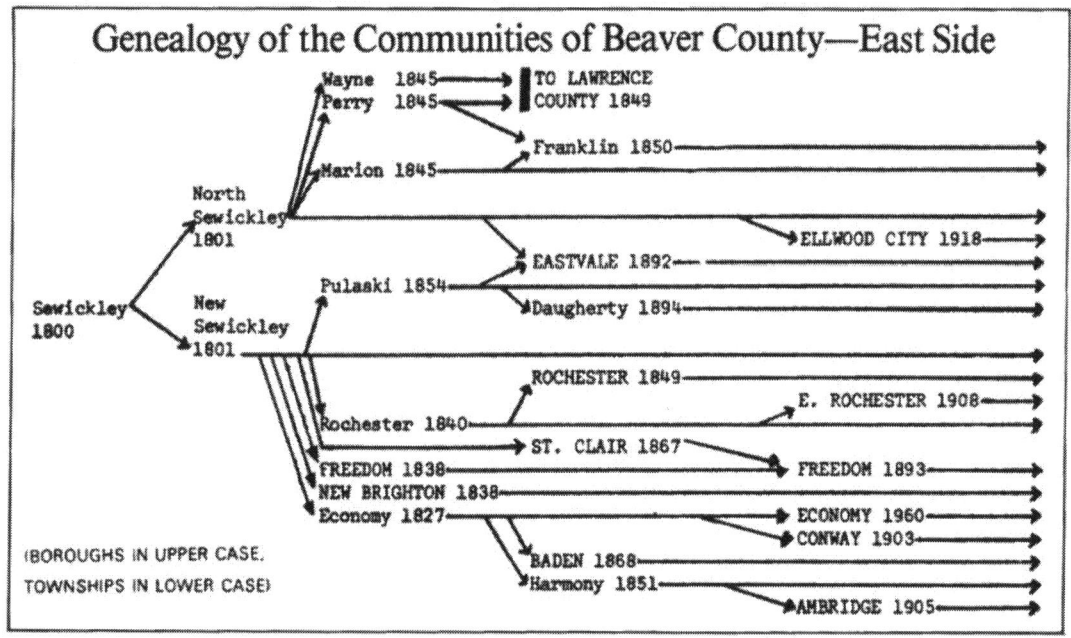

North Side Communities

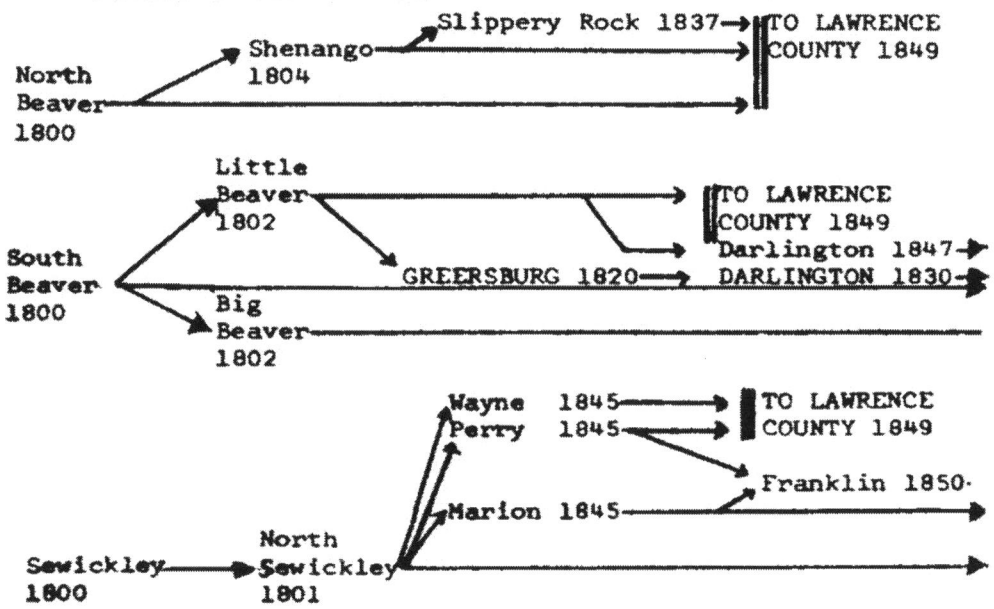

Appendix A – Continued

West Side Communities

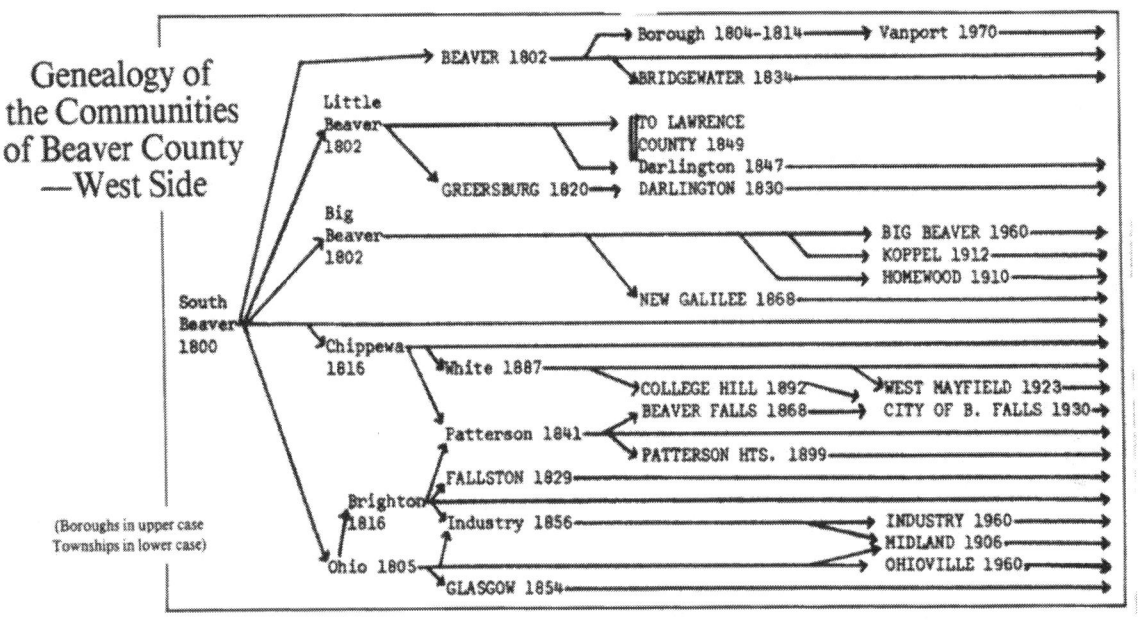

South Side Communities

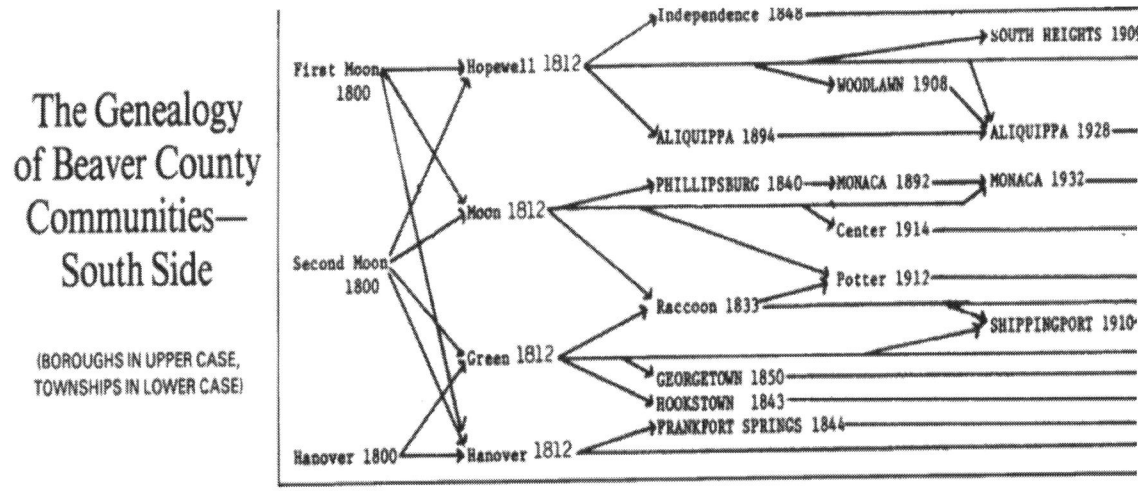

APPENDIX B – Evolution of Beaver County
(Diagrams courtesy of the 1976 Beaver County Centennial Atlas)

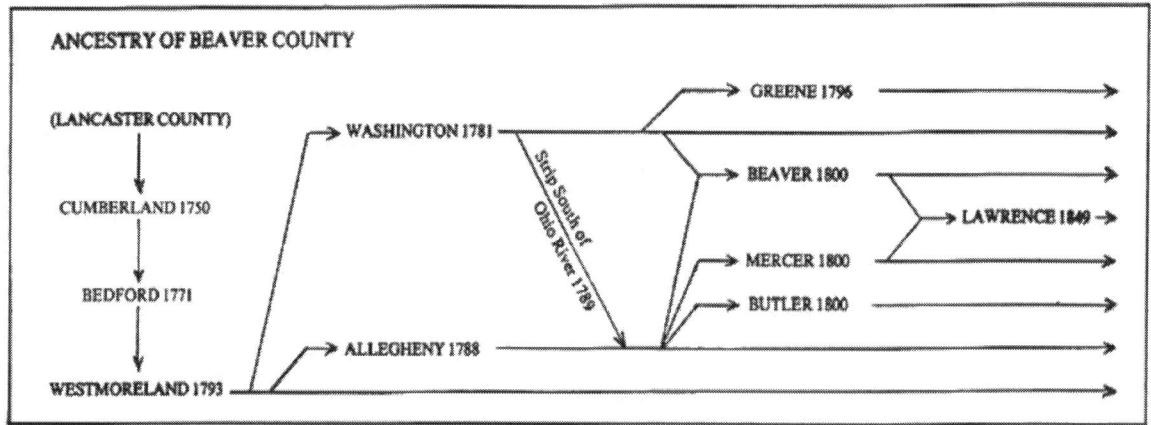

APPENDIX C – National Register of Historic Places Listings in Beaver County

1. **1966** – "Point of Beginning" in Ohioville on the PA/Ohio line.
2. **1966** – Old Economy Village in Ambridge.
3. **1974** – The Captain William Vicary Mansion in Freedom.
4. **1975** – Greersburg Academy in Darlington.
5. **1975** – Legion Ville near Ambridge.
6. **1975** – Fort McIntosh in Beaver.
7. **1975** – The Senator Matthew Stanley Quay House in Beaver.
8. **1978** – The B.F. Jones Memorial Library in Aliquippa.
9. **1980** – The former William B. Dunlap Mansion in Bridgewater.
10. **1980** – Merrill Lock Number 6 in Industry.
11. **1983** – The Merrick Art Gallery in New Brighton.
12. **1985** – The Economy Historic District in Ambridge.
13. **1985** – Carnegie Free Library in Beaver Falls.
14. **1986** – The David Littell House in Hanover Township.
15. **1987** – The Raccoon Creek Recreational Demonstration Area in Hanover Township.
16. **1988** – Watts Mill Road Bridge over little Beaver Creek.
17. **1989** – The James Beach Clow House in North Sewickley Township.
18. **1990** – The Pittsburgh and Lake Erie Passenger Station in Aliquippa.
19. **1996** – Bridgewater Historic District.
20. **1996** – The Beaver Historic District.

Source: National Register of Historic Places

APPENDIX D – State Historical Markers in Beaver County

1. **Beaver County** – Located: County Courthouse, at park on 3rd St., Beaver. Erected 1982.

2. **Fort McIntosh** – Located: 3rd St. at Insurance St., Beaver. Erected 1946.

3. **General Anthony Wayne's Camp** – Located: Duss Ave. at Anthony Wayne Drive. Erected 1918.

4. **Harmony Society Cemetery** – Located: Church St. center of cemetery, Ambridge. Erected 1963.

5. **Harmony Society Church** – Located: Church St. near Creese St., Ambridge. Erected 1967.

6. **Ingram-Richardson Mfg.** – Located: 24th St. Ext. and 31st St. Ext., Beaver Falls. Erected 2001.

7. **King Beaver's Town** – Located: 3rd St. at Wilson Ave., Beaver. Erected 1946.

8. **Legionville** – Located: Duss Ave. at Anthony Wayne Drive, Ambridge. Erected 1946.

9. **Logstown** – Located: Duss Ave. (old PA 65) at Anthony Wayne Drive North of Ambridge.

10. **Logstown Plaque** – (Plaque missing), Ambridge. Erected 1918.

11. **Matthew S. Quay** – Located: 3rd St. at Insurance St., Beaver. Erected 1947.

12. **NLRB Vs. J&L Steel** – Located: Franklin Ave. & Route 51, Aliquippa. Erected 2000.

13. **Old Economy** – PA Route 65 across from site, Ambridge. Erected Ca. 1948.

14. **Old Economy Memorial** – Located: 13th & Church Sts., Ambridge. Erected 1947.

15. **Pennsylvania** – (Missing) Located: U.S. 30 .State Line. Erected 1949.

16. **Pennsylvania** – (Missing) Located: Pa 51 at State Line. Erected 1949.

17. **White Cottage** – Located: 1221 3rd Ave., New Brighton. Erected 1969.

Sources: A Guide to State Historical Markers of Pennsylvania, by George R. Beyer, Commonwealth of Pennsylvania: 2000. Pages 43-46 & (http://www.phmc.state.pa.us/apps/historical-markers.html#.VvxkYGz2Z9A)

APPENDIX E – Beaver County Historical Markers

No.	Marker	Location
1.	Mill Creek Presbyterian Church	Greene Twp.
2.	Nelson Bauer House	Greene Twp.
3.	Greersburg Academy #1	Darlington
4.	Merrick Art Gallery	New Brighton
5.	Thiel College Site	Monaca
6.	Logstown	Harmony Twp.
7.	Tuscarawas Trail	Brighton Twp.
8.	Legion Ville (Anthony Wayne's Camp)	Harmony Twp.
9.	Fort McIntosh	Beaver
10.	Brodhead Road	Center Twp.
11.	Geneva College	Beaver Falls
12.	Rev. Bausman's Home	Rochester
13.	Beaver Division Canal	New Brighton
14.	Bassenheim Furnace	Franklin Twp.
15.	Methodist Church	Greene Twp.
16.	First Colonial Residents	Aliquippa
17.	Frankfort Springs	Hanover Twp.
18.	Vicary Mansion	Freedom
19.	St. Matthews Church	Economy
20.	St. Luke Episcopal Church	Georgetown
21.	Mt. Pleasant Church (1st site)	Big Beaver
22.	Little Red Schoolhouse	Brighton Twp.
23.	Matthew Stanley Quay House	Beaver
24.	Site of first Catholic Mass	Harmony Twp.
25.	Providence Baptist Church	North Sewickley
26.	McMinn Mill	Darlington
27.	Trinity Evangelical Church	Freedom
28.	St. Peter's Lutheran Church	New Sewickley
29.	Free Presbyterian Church	Darlington
30.	Buttonwood (Arthur B. Bradford home)	Darlington Twp.
31.	St. Peter's Evangelical Lutheran Church	Monaca
32.	Carnegie Free Library	Beaver Falls
33.	Darlington Borough	Darlington
34.	Mt. Pleasant Presbyterian Church	Darlington Twp.
35.	Sprott's Delight (Wallace home)	Darlington
36.	Levi Dungan Home Site	Hanover Twp.

APPENDIX E – Beaver County Historical Markers - Continued

No.	Marker	Location
37.	First Building in Ambridge	Ambridge
38.	Oakland United Presbyterian Church	New Sewickley
39.	Oak Grove United Presbyterian Church	New Sewickley
40.	Elder's Woolen Mill	Darlington Twp.
41.	Cannelton Settlement	Darlington Twp.
42.	Wallace City	Economy
43.	Merrick House	New Brighton
44.	Mt. Carmel Presbyterian Church	Aliquippa
45.	Aaron Burr boats built	Bridgewater
46.	Sandy & Beaver Canal	Glasgow
47.	Point of Beginning	Ohioville
48.	New Philadelphia Society	Monaca
49.	Greersburg Academy #2	Darlington
50.	Cook's Ferry	Industry
51.	Benvenue Manor	Marion Twp.
52.	Fry Glass	Rochester Twp.
53.	Beaver County Fairgrounds	Beaver
54.	Seceder Church & Cemetery	South Beaver
55.	Major General Joseph Pendleton	Rochester
56.	George Foulks House	Darlington Twp.
57.	Patterson Heights Incline	Beaver Falls
58.	American Bridge	Ambridge
59.	Foulks, Martin, Watt's Mill 1798-1863	South Beaver
60.	Always a River	Rochester
61.	New Salem Presbyterian Church	Ohioville
62.	White's Mill	Hanover Twp.
63.	James Beach Clow House	North Sewickley
64.	Union Drawn Steel	Beaver Falls
65.	Water Cure/Soldier's Orphan Home	Monaca
66.	Stephen Stone House	North Sewickley
67.	Pa Canal Beaver Division #2	New Brighton
68.	Homewood Junction	Homewood
69.	Mill Creek	Greene Twp.
70.	PA/WVA Boundary	Georgetown
71.	Smith's Ferry (town)	Ohioville
72.	Chippewa United Methodist Church	Chippewa Twp.

APPENDIX E – Beaver County Historical Markers - Continued

No.	Marker	Location
73.	Swearingen Cemetery	Hanover Twp.
74.	Jones & Laughlin Steel Co.	Aliquippa
75.	36 BV-9 Indian Site	Industry
76.	Loganstown	Rochester
77.	Littell House	Hanover Twp.
78.	Henry Mancini – boyhood home	Aliquippa
79.	Rochester Masonic Temple	Rochester
80.	Second Baptist Church	Beaver Falls
81.	Baker Cemetery	Center Twp.
82.	Freedom Boat Yards	Freedom
83.	McKinley School	Chippewa Twp.
84.	Fombell House	Franklin Twp.
85.	Townsend Company	Fallston
86.	Caughey Mill	South Beaver
87.	Christ Episcopal Church	New Brighton
88.	Robert Townsend House	New Brighton
89.	Ohio U.P. Church	Hopewell Twp.
90.	St. John's AME Church	Bridgewater
91.	Junction Park	Rochester Twp.
92.	Daugherty Cemetery	Daugherty Twp.
93.	Michael Camp House	Rochester Twp.
94.	Second Baptist Church	Rochester
95.	Georgetown Marker/Lewis & Clark	Georgetown
96.	Midland Schools	Midland
97.	White Cemetery	Darlington Twp.
98.	Conway Yards	Conway
99.	Grove Cemetery	Daugherty Twp.
100.	Tried Stone Baptist Church	Aliquippa
101.	Wayman Chapel AME	New Brighton
102.	Hill Cemetery	Pending
103.	Passavant Memorial Homes	Pending
104.	McGuire Chapel Cemetery	Pending
105.	Providence Hospital	Pending
106.	Baker Baldwin Cemetery	Pending

Source: Beaver County Historical Research & Landmarks Foundation

APPENDIX F – Original Depreciation Lands Owners

There is a fascinating story to be told about who some of the first landowners in Beaver County were that purchased lots in the area known as the Depreciation Lands which lay along the north side of the Ohio River. When viewing copies of the original patent maps for that area, the names listed there read as a virtual "Who's Who" of the rich and famous from the Revolutionary War Era.

The concept of Depreciation Lands ownership has been one of the most misunderstood settlement issues in Beaver County and remains so to this day. Many people are of the mistaken belief that the Depreciation Lands were given away by the government as payment to soldiers who had served in the Revolutionary War. The simple truth is that this land was actually sold to raise money in order to redeem the Depreciation Certificates (think IOU's) issued to anyone who received payment in the nearly worthless Continental Money, so this land was never given away. All confusion aside, for various reasons, the vast majority of Depreciation Lands were purchased by wealthy and/or notable eastern speculators as an investment, and a very few others who actually lived here.

Listed below, in no particular order, are just a few of the fascinating people who once owned Beaver County Depreciation Land.

A Few of the Original Depreciation Land Owners

Timothy Matlock: Matlock served as the assistant to Charles Thomson who was the Secretary of the Continental Congress. When the final version of the Declaration of Independence was agreed upon, it was Matlock who was directed to personally copy the final draft for publication. It is his handwriting that is immortalized on that famous document today.

George Meade: Meade was the Grandfather of Union General George Gordon Meade who was the commander of the Army of the Potomac during the American Civil War. Grandfather George came from Barbados, became one of the most successful Philadelphia merchants, and contributed heavily to the revolutionary cause. He invested a great deal in western lands, but his business failed during the panic of 1796 and he died bankrupt.

Henry Knox: Knox was the General of Artillery for the Continental Army during the Revolution. Knox was a member of the court martial board for British officer and spy Major John Andre who was found guilty and hung. In 1783 he commanded the army during its demobilization and became the Secretary of War under President Washington in March, 1785. He organized an expedition led by Anthony Wayne that resulted in the 1794 Battle of Fallen Timbers. Retiring to Maine, Knox built a large landed estate, and invested in large tracts of land in the western areas. He died in 1806 as a result of swallowing a chicken bone that stuck in his throat and became infected. Fort Knox, Kentucky, is named in his honor.

Edmund Randolph: During the Revolution, he served as an aide-de-camp to General Washington. In 1779, he became a delegate to the Continental Congress from Virginia. In

1786 he became Governor of Virginia and later worked to help draft the Constitution. Randolph served as Attorney General and later Secretary of State under President Washington. Following his retirement from politics in 1795, he resumed his law practice and served as head counsel for Vice President Aaron Burr's defense during the latter's trial for treason in 1807. *Refer to 1805-1806 in the timeline*.

Benjamin Chew: Chew served as attorney for the William Penn Family in America. Benjamin Chew refused to take the Oath of Allegiance to the Revolutionary cause and was imprisoned near Winchester, Virginia, along with other notable Philadelphia citizens until the British left Philadelphia in 1778. His country home "Clivedon" became the focal point of the battle of Germantown.

Andrew Swearingen: He was the sheriff of Washington County in 1793 and was appointed by the Governor of Pennsylvania as a commissioner to sell the town lots of the City of Beaver. During the Revolutionary War Swearingen served as a Washington County, Pennsylvania, militia colonel and fought numerous engagements along the western frontier. These included the siege of Fort Henry and the ill-fated Crawford expedition against the Ohio Indians. Swearingen served at both Fort McIntosh and Fort Laurens.

James Moore: Born in Massachusetts in 1747, Moore enlisted in the Continental Artillery in 1775 and served in several New York companies as a private, working his way up to lieutenant. In 1785, Lt. Moore came up the eastern side of the Beaver River looking for a place to make a home on land for which he had been granted a warrant. Danger from the Indians still had to be considered, so he built his cabin about opposite the mouth of Brady's Run and near enough to flee to the (now New Brighton) Block House if danger threatened. When the Indian wars had ended and the settlers began to arrive, he opened a ferry across the Beaver River which became known as Moore's ferry.

John McKee: John McKee was born in Ireland in 1746 and left there to settle in Philadelphia about 1755. At some point prior to 1769 the family relocated to the site of present day McKeesport on the confluence of the Youghiogheny and Monongahela Rivers. As a young man, he became one of the largest landholders in Allegheny County. His purchases and claims were in Beaver County, Allegheny County, Pittsburgh, Beaver and other towns in this area. In fact, he was one of the earliest settlers to improve his land in Fallston, Beaver County, which he later sold to David Townsend in 1799.

John McKee was nearly ruined when he agreed to use his land as surety for his brother-in-law, Judge John Redick. Redick's business venture was to supply General Anthony Wayne's army in 1793. In any event, Redick failed to live up to his obligations to supply the army and McKee was forced to assume liabilities amounting to thousands of dollars. As a result, much of his property was seized by United States Marshals and put up for sale. In order to reclaim his losses, McKee partitioned off his remaining land at the mouth of the Youghiogheny River and laid it into plots to form a town known as McKeesport.

Michael Hillegas: Hillegas was the first Treasurer of the United States from 1775 to 1789, and he was charged with preserving all documents related to the Revolutionary War including the Declaration of Independence, Articles of Confederation, etc. Thanks to him, these precious documents still survive today.

Sam Ewing: He was a Philadelphia publisher. As a young man, Ewing fell madly in love with a Jewish girl named Rebecca Gratz, but because of her faith, she refused to marry him. Rebecca herself never married and devoted her life to charitable causes. Ewing eventually entered a loveless and unhappy marriage with a Presbyterian girl and died several years later. To the shock of his widow and those gathered at the funeral, Rebecca suddenly appeared dressed all in white with her face covered by a veil. She walked quietly to the casket and placed a small portrait of herself along with three white roses over his heart leaving as swiftly as she had appeared. Some believe her to be the model of the character "Rebecca," heroine of Sir Walter Scott's famous novel *Ivanhoe*.

Jonathan Grant: Grant was a Revolutionary War veteran. He left Beaver County in 1809 and became the first settler in Holmes County, Ohio. During his time on the frontier, Grant became known as a great hunter and skilled woodsman who also happened to speak several Indian languages. He is buried beside his son, Parkinson, in McCulloch Cemetery in Holmes County.

Joseph Nourse: He was elected Registrar of the Treasury in 1781, and as Registrar, Nourse had to personally sign each piece of Continental Currency to ensure its authenticity. His Washington, D.C. home, the Dumbarton House, is a house museum open to visitors today.

Dr. John Redman: He was one of the first physicians at the Pennsylvania Hospital and first President of the Philadelphia College of Physicians. Redman was considered one of the most eminent physicians of his time. Interestingly enough, Dr. Redman believed that swallowing your own saliva was harmful to your health, and he always kept a chew of tobacco in his mouth to avoid doing so.

William Foulkes (Also spelled Fulks): Reported to be one of the first permanent settlers north of the Ohio River in 1792. He settled in Ohio Township between Salem Meeting House and the Little Beaver Creek. The Pennsylvania Population Company won a lawsuit against him in Federal Court in Philadelphia, and the court, finding for the company, ordered Foulkes removed from the land on which he had lived for seventeen years and had made many improvements. In 1808 when the United States Marshal and his posse came to remove Foulkes, they were fired upon and one man was killed. It is believed that the shot was intended for the man riding beside the U.S. Marshal who happened to be the agent of the Pennsylvania Population Company. In the first murder trial in the history of Beaver County, Nathanial Eakin was found "not guilty" by a jury. ***Refer to November 5, 1807.***

George McElheny: In 1782 he was an Indian scout who settled in Independence Township south of the Ohio River. He bought 400 acres in Ohio Township. He was originally from Lancaster and married a woman named Martha Stringer without the permission of her parents. The newlyweds fled to his western property to escape their wrath.

John Nixon: He is best known to history as the first person to publicly read the Declaration of Independence on the steps of the Pennsylvania State House on July 8, 1776.

John Phillips: He settled in Philadelphia after selling a cargo of slaves in the West Indies, and with the profits, started a successful rope making business. During the British occupation of Philadelphia, British General Howe chose to stay in Phillips' large luxurious home even though Phillips was an ardent patriot. Phillips continued to own slaves and eventually emancipated them during the early national period. He died by falling down the grand staircase in his home while drunk.

William Rawle: Rawle was a noted attorney and a delegate to the Pennsylvania Constitutional Assembly in 1789. He became the first United States Attorney for the District of Pennsylvania and was instrumental in helping to suppress the "Whiskey Rebellion" and prosecute its leaders. Now known as Rawle & Henderson, his law firm, founded in 1783, is the oldest continuous law office still operating in the United States.

James Reynolds: He was a former Commissary officer in the American Revolution. In 1791, Reynolds began blackmailing then Treasury Secretary, Alexander Hamilton, a married man, for having an affair with Reynold's wife, Maria. Hamilton paid him over $1,000 in blackmail, and the affair only came to light when a group of congressmen believed that Hamilton had given treasury money to Reynolds to speculate with – which he had not. Reynolds' blackmail plans were finally undone when he was caught up in a different scandal involving unpaid wages to Revolutionary War veterans.

Isaac Melchior (sometimes called Melcher): During a 1776 meeting of the Continental Congress, Isaac Melchior stood in front of the assemblage and proceeded to "damn" both the Continental Congress and its President, John Hancock for only offering him a Captain's commission when he believed that he deserved a higher rank. Later called back before Congress to answer for his conduct, Melchior apologized but claimed not to remember having behaved as charged. After purchasing several Depreciation lots in what is now Harmony Township, Melchior laid out the plan for a town called "Montmorin" in 1787 on the site of former Logstown. The proposed town was named after French Minister of Foreign Affairs, Count Montmorin, who as a child was a playmate of the King of France. Due to economic issues, the town was never built and the land was eventually sold to the Harmony Society in 1824 which built its own town on the site.

Clement Biddle: Before the Revolutionary War, Biddle worked in his father's shipping and import business. In 1775, Biddle helped raise a company of Philadelphia volunteers called the "Quaker Blues," and was later commissioned a colonel as Deputy Quartermaster-General for the Pennsylvania and New York militia. Biddle was a close friend of President Washington and handled his business affairs in Philadelphia.

Thomas Shields: He was a gold and silversmith in Philadelphia and was the father of David Shields who settled in Sewickley and was a friend of Captain Vicary. Shields owned over 40,000 acres in Northumberland County and established the town of Damascus. Some of his silver work can be seen today in the Metropolitan Museum of Art.

John Dunlap: Dunlap became an officer in the First Troop Philadelphia City Cavalry which acted as a bodyguard to General Washington at the battles of Trenton and Princeton. In 1782, he contributed nearly $20,000 of his own money to help supply the Continental Army with clothing and food. He was a printer who printed the first 200 copies of the Declaration of Independence which are known today as the "Dunlap Broadsides." Dunlap was also a speculator in western lands and died a drunkard in Philadelphia.

Elias Boudinot: Son of a prosperous silversmith, he was a neighbor of Benjamin Franklin in Philadelphia. General Washington asked Boudinot to serve as Commissary General of Prisoners, in which he was responsible for the well-being of both British captives and those American prisoners in British captivity. He spent over $30,000 of his own money for his charges. In 1778 he was elected as a delegate to the Continental Congress from New Jersey and in 1781 became its President. He was a signer of the preliminary peace treaty with Great Britain in 1783.

Mark Wilcox: His father established the first paper mill in Pennsylvania in 1723. Mark became an associate judge in Chester (now Delaware County) and continued his father's paper making business. He created the first bank note paper in America. In 1781 Wilcox was commissioned to create the paper to be used for continental money through the Bank of America as well as the bank note paper for the bank of the United States, the Bank of Pennsylvania and other banks throughout the United States. Taken by the British from his home on the day after the battle of Brandywine, Wilcox was being held approximately three miles away. That night, Wilcox became cold and asked the British sergeant holding him to go to his neighbor's home and ask for a blanket. The kind sergeant did so, and when he returned, he told Wilcox that the neighbor was no friend of his. The sergeant related that "he must be a great scoundrel; for he has given me a catalogue of your political sins." Fortunately, for Wilcox, the sergeant did not repeat the stories to higher authority or Wilcox could have been hung for treason.

Thomas McKean: McKean was a signer of the Declaration of Independence. He was appointed Chief Justice of Pennsylvania, an office that he held for nearly twenty years. McKean was elected President of Congress in 1781, and Governor of Pennsylvania on the Federalist ticket in 1799. He died on June 24, 1817, at the age of 83. His daughter, Sally married the Marquis De Casa Yrujo, Spanish Minister Plenipotentiary, and he was also a land partner with Captain William Vicary.

Sally McKean (Sarah Maria-Theresa Marchioness De Casa Yrujo): Although Sally's name does not appear as an original land owner, she did inherit a number of lots after her father Thomas McKean died. Captain William Vicary served as the attorney and land agent for some property near Sewickley owned by Sarah Maria-Theresa Marchioness De Casa Yrujo, the daughter of his old land partner, Governor Thomas McKean. Sarah McKean had married the Marquis De Casa Yrujo, Spanish Minister Plenipotentiary and Envoy Extraordinary to the United States. De Casa Yrujo and his wife were frequent visitors to Presidents Thomas Jefferson and James Madison, and Sarah was also a close friend of First Lady Dolley Madison. Later, the Marquis became minister at Rio de Janeiro, and, afterward, at Paris. Sally would never again live in America, and died in Madrid in 1841. Their son Carlos Martínez de Yrujo y McKean became Prime Minister of Spain briefly in 1847.

Richard Somers: U. S. Navy Master Commandant Richard Somers was killed sailing a fireship into the harbor at Tripoli in an effort to destroy part of the pirate fleet during the war with the Barbary pirates in September, 1804. His second in command was Acting Lieutenant Henry Wadsworth, uncle of famous poet Henry Wadsworth Longfellow. Something went wrong as the fireship ignited and exploded prematurely killing all on board, but causing no damage at all to any of the pirate fleet, the harbor or Tripoli. The charred and blackened remains of the crew washed ashore and were buried in the Old Protestant Cemetery in Tripoli, Libya. In 2011, the House passed a resolution to return the remains of Somers and his twelve man crew to the United States, but action is still pending due to the unrest in that country. In recognition of his bravery and that of his twelve comrades, the United States Navy placed a monument in their honor at Annapolis, known as the Tripoli monument, making it the oldest monument commemorating combat in the United States. In addition, since 1812, six different naval vessels have carried his name.

Daniel Leet: Surveyor of District #2 of the Depreciation Lands. He was appointed quartermaster of the 12th Virginia Regiment on January 1, 1777, and later was commissioned brigade-major. He served at the battle of Trenton and later spent the winter of 1777-78 at Valley Forge. Leet served under General McIntosh at Fort Laurens, and in 1782 was a brigade-major during General Crawford's massacre where he commanded the right wing of Crawford's force. In 1785, Leet surveyed a large section of Depreciation Lands in Beaver County, and in 1792, he laid out the town of Beaver.

John Nicholson: Nicholson was Comptroller General of Pennsylvania between 1782 and 1794 and was instrumental in solving the state's debt problem following the Revolutionary War. In 1787 he was made Escheator General, to liquidate the estates of those accused of treason. He then became the partner of Robert Morris in land speculation and promoted the development of Washington, D.C. Along with James Greenleaf and Robert Morris, he created the North American Land Company, which claimed to own six million acres of land in Pennsylvania, Virginia, North Carolina , South Carolina, Georgia, and Kentucky. During the winter of 1799, Nicholson was imprisoned for debt, and he died in prison on December 5, 1800 leaving his family approximately four million dollars in debt.

For those brave souls who would like a much more in depth study of the very complex subject of Depreciation and Donation Lands, I would recommend the following books:

Daniel Agnew's *A History of The Region of Pennsylvania North of The Ohio and West of The Allegheny River, of The Indian Purchases, And of The Running of The Southern, Northern, and Western Boundaries.*

Donna Bingham Munger's . *Pennsylvania Land Records: A History and Guide for Research.*
Reprinted from: Milestones Volume 40 Number 2, Spring, 2015

Key to Sources

1. **A Guide to Historic Landmarks in Beaver County, PA**, Townsend, Bauder & Walton. BCHR&LF, 2002.

2. **History of Beaver County, Pennsylvania, Vol. I & II**, Bausman. The Knickerbocker Press, New York, 1904.

3. **Beaver County Centennial Directory**, Wyand & Read, 1876.

4. **History of New Brighton, 1838-1938**, The Historical Committee of the New Brighton Centennial, New Brighton, PA, 1938.

5. **The Twentieth Century History of Beaver County, Pennsylvania, 1908-1988**, C.W. Beck, Ed. Walsworth Publishing, Inc. 1989.

6. **Historic Western Pennsylvania**, Mulkearn and Pugh, University of Pittsburgh Press, 1954.

7. **Beaver Falls Area Centennial Booklet, 1868-1968**, Beaver County Historical Research Library, Beaver.

8. **The Planting of Civilization in Western Pennsylvania**, Buck and Buck. University of Pittsburgh Press, 1939. Page references from second paperback printing, 1979.

9. **History of Beaver County, Pennsylvania**. A. Warner & Co., Publishers, 1888.

10. **Beaver Falls - Images of America**, Britten and Beaver Falls Historical Society, Arcadia Press, 2000.

11. **Spies, Scoundrels and Rogues of the Ohio Frontier**, Gary S. Williams. Buckeye Book Press, 2005.

12. **Measuring America**, Andre Linklater, Walker Publishing Co., New York, NY, 2002.

13. **History of Monaca, 1840-1940**, The Historical Committee of the Centennial, publishers.

14. *The Beaver Falls News Tribune*, 25 Aug. 1934.

15. **Caldwell's Illustrated Atlas of Beaver County, Pennsylvania**, 1876, J.A. Caldwell, Gondil, OH, 1876. Reprinted 1972 by Pennsylvania Record Press with supplemental section. (Page references are from the supplement)

16. **The Indian Wars of Pennsylvania**, C. Hale Sipe, Wennawoods Publishing, Lewisburg, PA, 1999, Reprint.

17. **Bayonets in the Wilderness, Anthony Wayne's Legion in the Old Northwest**, Alan D. Gaff, University of Oklahoma Press, Norman, OK, 2004

18. **The Journals of Lewis and Clark, Meriwether Lewis & William Clark,** Anthony Brandt, Ed. National Geographic Society, 2002.

19. **Rivers of Destiny**, Denver Walton, Eugenia Walton, Bob Bauder & Charles Townsend, Beaver County Historical Research & Landmarks Foundation, 1999.

20. *Beaver Argus*, 30 July1851, Reprinted in *The Beaver Countian*, Vol. 11 No. 111 (1991) by the Resource and Research Center for Beaver County & Local History, Inc., Beaver.

21. **Beaver County Bicentennial Atlas**, D. Walton, Ed., Beaver County Bicentennial Committee, 1976.

22. **The Pittsburgh & Lake Erie Railroad**, Harold H. McLean, Golden West Books, 1980.

23. **Pennsylvania Historical and Museum Inventory of Historic Places**, 19 December 1979, Compiled from the records of the U.S. Army Corps of Engineers, Pittsburgh.

24. *Beaver County Argus*, 14 Aug. 1837.

25. *The News-Tribune*, Beaver Falls.

26. **Pennsylvania Railroad Day**, Program Booklet. New Brighton Borough Council, Businessmen's Association, et al.

27. *"Water over the Dam"*, Robert A. Smith, Winter 1986 quarterly newsletter of the Beaver Area Heritage Association.

28. **St. Peter's Evangelical Lutheran Church**, Paul Miller Ruff, Monograph, Jan. 2000. From the German Church Records of Western Pennsylvania.

29. **Encyclopedia of American History**, Richard B. Morris, Harper Brothers, 1953.

30. *Milestones*, "The Journal of Beaver County History," Published quarterly by the Beaver County Historical Research & Landmarks Foundation Vol., 23, No. 1.

31. **I Remember Monaca**, Booklet, The Historical Committee of the Centennial, 1940.

32. **Souvenir booklet, Formal Opening of the Rochester-Monaca Bridge.**

33. *Pittsburgh Post-Gazette,* Pittsburgh, Pennsylvania.

34. *Beaver County Times,* Beaver, Pennsylvania.

35. *The Beaver Countian,* www.beavercountian.com.

36. **Looking Back Moments in Beaver County History**, Bob Bauder and presented by the Beaver County Times, Published by PEN Publishing, MO, 2009.

37. *Pittsburgh Tribune Review Article.*

38. "James appointed First Black Beaver County Judge", N. Treshea, *New Pittsburgh Courier,* November 28, 1998.

39. *Beaver County's Main Streets 1993 Historical Calendar,* published by the Beaver County Historical Research & Landmarks Foundation.

40. *1971 – 1991 Historical Calendar,* published by the .Beaver County Historical Research & Landmarks Foundation.

41. *1995 Historical Calendar,* published by the Beaver County Historical Research & Landmarks Foundation.

42. **The Forgotten 500** by Gregory A. Freeman, New American Library, 2007.

43. Schmitz, Jon (November 6, 2009). "Highway now I-376 from Monroeville to Mercer". *Pittsburgh Post-Gazette.*

44. **Beaver Falls: Gem of Beaver County**, Kenneth Britten, Arcadia Publishing, 2002.

45. *Pittsburgh Press,* Pittsburgh, Pennsylvania.

46. **Beaver Town 2002: A Place in History-Then...and Now**, Beaver Area Heritage Foundation, 2002.

47. **Old Economy – Ambridge Sesqui-Centennial Historical Booklet**, Ed. Reverend Norman C. Young, May, 1974.

48. **Baden Pennsylvania Hundred Seventy Five Year Anniversity 1838-2013,** This is a compilation of stories and information from various eras of Baden history.

49. *Milestones,* "The Journal of Beaver County History," Published quarterly by the Beaver County Historical Research & Landmarks Foundation.

50. **The History of Frankfort Springs & Hanover Township**, by Betty Brodmerkel and Charles Townsend, January, 2008.

51. *"The Pennsylvania Population Company"*, by R. Nelson Hale, Pennsylvania History Vol. 16 No. 2, April, 1949.

52. **One Hundred Fiftieth Anniversary, April 11, 1998 Rochester Lodge No. 229**. Robert Batto, Published by Lodge No. 229.

53. **WWII Honor List of Dead and Missing – State of Pennsylvania**. Compiled by the War Department, Adjutant General's Office, June, 1946.

54. **Klondikes, Chipped Ham & Skyscraper Cones The Story of Islay's**, by Brian Butko, Stackpole Books, 2001.

55. **History of Monaca 1840-1940,** The Historical Committee of the Monaca Centennial, 1940.

56. **Aliquippa**, by Cindy and Ed Murphy, Arcadia Publishing, 2013.

57. **New Brighton**, by Karen Helbling, Arcadia Publishing, 2013.

58. **Bridgewater: A Narrative History of a Pennsylvania River Town**. By Valentine J. Brkich, Bridge Street Books, 2009.

59. **Ambridge**, By Larry R. Slater, Arcadia Publishing, 2008.

60. *The Beaver Valley Times/The Daily Times.*

61. **A History of Rochester In Words and Pictures 1849 – 1999**. Ed. Robert Batto, no publication information.

62. **Ambridge Centennial 1905** – 2005, By the Ambridge Centennial Committee 2005.

63. **Ellwood City: Postcard History Series**, by Everett E. Bleakney Jr., Arcadia Publishing 2011.

64. **Celebrate the Valley: Life in Beaver and Western Allegheny Counties**, Ed. Alan Buncher, Marsha Keefer and Tom Bickert, Published by the *Beaver County Times*, 1998.

65. **50th Anniversary of WWII: As Recorded in the Newspapers that Became the Beaver County Times**, Assembled By the *Beaver County Times*, Published by Historical Briefs, Inc. 1992.

66. **Beaver County Trolleys**, by Benson W. Rohrbeck, published by Ben Rohrbeck Traction Publications: West Chester, PA, 1985.

67. **Rudyard Kipling: A Life** by Harry Ricketts, Carroll & Graf Publishers: New York, 1999.

68. **Monaca** by Carol Dietrich Ripper, Arcadia Publishing:Charleston, 2015.

69. **The Frederick Douglass Papers: 1842-1852 Vol. 1.** By Frederick Douglass and Edited by John R. Mckivingan, Yale University Press 2009.

70. **The Harmony Society at Economy, Penn'a: Founded by George Rapp, A.D. 1805,** by Aaron Williams D.D., Pittsburgh: W.S. Haven, 1866.

71. "*100th Anniversary First United Methodist Church Beaver Falls, Pennsylvania 1868 – 1968*" Booklet published by the church.

72. "*Holy Trinity R.C. Church 75th Diamond Jubilee 1910 – 1985*" Booklet published by the church.

73. *USA Today Newspapers,* Fairfax County, Virginia.

74. **Neither Bullets nor Ballots: Women Abolitionists and the Civil War.** By Wendy Hamand Venet, University of Virginia Press Charlottesville, 1991.

75. **The American Woman's Rights Movement: A Chronology of Events and Opportunities from 1600 to 2008**, by Paula D. Buchanan, Branden Books, Boston 2009.

76. **The Survey, Vol. XXXIII, October, 1914 – March, 1915.** New York Survey Associates, Inc.

77. **The Greersburg Academy and The Station House**, by Wayne A. Cole, Colebooks, 2003.

78. **Ghost Rails III Electrics**, By Wayne A. Cole, Colebooks, 2007.

79. **Ghost Rails IV Industrial Shortlines**, By Wayne A. Cole, Colebooks, 2008.

80. **Ghost Rails VI Harmony Route**, By Wayne A. Cole, Colebooks, 2009.

81. **Ghost Rails X Iron Phantoms**, By Wayne A. Cole, Colebooks, 2013.

82. **Ghost Rails XII Seamless, *The B&W History***, By Wayne A. Cole, Colebooks, 2015.

83. **Portraits in Steel; An Illustrated History of Jones & Laughlin Steel Corporation**, by David H. Wollman and Donald R. Inman, Kent State University Press 1999.

84. *New York Times,* New York City, New York.

85. *The Aliquippa News Gazette,* Aliquippa, Pennsylvania.

86. **Rails of Dreams**, by Wayne A. Cole Colebooks, 2002.

87. *The Evening Times,* Sayre, Pennsylvania.

88. *The Kane Republican,* Kane, Pennsylvania.

89. *The Tyrone Daily Herald,* Tyrone, Pennsylvania.

90. *Pittsburgh Business Times,* Pittsburgh, Pennsylvania.

91. **The History of United Methodism in Western Pennsylvania**, by Wallace Guy Smeltzer, Ed. The Parthenon Press/Nashville, Tennessee, 1975.

92. **Thirty Years of Labor 1859-1889**, by Terence Vincent Powderly, Excelsior Publishing House: Columbus, Ohio, 1889.

93. **Where Earth Dissolves Like Snow: The Keystone Driller Story**. By Wayne A. Cole, Colebooks.

94. **Historical Events of South Side Beaver County and Homecoming Week Celebration**, Compiled by Robert M. Bryan, Hookstown, PA, August 18th to 23rd, 1924.

95. **Boundaries of the United States and Several States, Geological Survey Bulletin 1212**, By Franklin Van Zandt, United States Government Printing Office: Washington, 1966.

96. **A Guide to State Historical Markers of Pennsylvania,** by George R. Beyer, Commonwealth of Pennsylvania: 2000.

97. **George Washington in the Ohio Valley,** by Hugh Cleland, University of Pittsburgh Press, Pittsburgh:1955.

98. **Encyclopedia of Pennsylvania Biography: Illustrated, Volume 1**, by John R. Jordan, New York:Lewis Historical Publishing Company, 1914.

99. *The Gazette Times,* Pittsburgh, Pennsylvania.

100. **A Traveler's Guide to Historic Western Pennsylvania**, by Lois Mulkearn and Edwin V. Pugh, University of Pittsburgh Press, 1953.

101. *The Daily City News*, New Castle, Pennsylvania.

102. *The Morning Herald*, Uniontown, Pennsylvania.

103. *Harrisburg Telegraph*, Harrisburg, Pennsylvania.

104. *Pittsburgh Daily Post*, Pittsburgh, Pennsylvania.

105. *Pittsburgh Dispatch*, Pittsburgh, Pennsylvania.

106. *The Kane Leader*, Kane, Pennsylvania.

107. *The Valley Tribune*, Beaver Falls, Pennsylvania.

108. *The Evening Review*, East Liverpool, Ohio.

109. *The Saturday Review*, East Liverpool, Ohio.

110. *New Castle News*, New Castle, Pennsylvania.

111. *New Castle Herald*, New Castle, Pennsylvania.

112. *The Times*, Philadelphia, Pennsylvania.

113. *The News-Herald*, Franklin, Pennsylvania.

114. *The Record-Argus*, Greenville, Pennsylvania.

115. *Wilkes-Barre Evening News*, Wilkes Barre, Pennsylvania.

116. *The Indiana Gazette*, Indiana, Pennsylvania.

117. *The Pittsburgh Daily Commercial*, Pittsburgh, Pennsylvania.

118. *Lebanon County Weekly Republican*, Lebanon, Pennsylvania.

119. *The Lewisburg Chronicle*, Lewisburg, Pennsylvania.

120. *The Adams Centennial*, Gettysburg, Pennsylvania.

121. *The Pittsburgh Gazette*, Pittsburgh, Pennsylvania.

122. **History of the Great Trail From the Forks of the Ohio – to the Tuscarawas Valley**, by Gary Winterburn, Osprey Publishing, London, England, 1993.

123. *The Cincinnati Enquirer*, Cincinnati, Ohio.

124. *The Ellwood City Ledger*, Ellwood City, Pennsylvania.

125. **Indians in Pennsylvania**, by Paul A.W. Wallace, 2nd Edition Revised by William A. Hunter, Pennsylvania Historic and Museum Commission, Harrisburg, 2005.

126. *The Independent Gazeteer*, Philadelphia, Pennsylvania

127. **Patterson Township 175th Anniversary 1841-2016**, By Donald R. Inman, Published 2016.

128. *The Pittsburgh Weekly Gazette*, Pittsburgh, Pennsylvania.

129. **Chronicle of the 20th Century**, Edited by Clifton Daniel, Mount Kisco, NY: Chronicle Publications, Inc. 1987.

130. *LIFE Magazine.*

131. **The First American Women Architects**, by Sarah Allaback, University of Illinois Press: Urbana 2008.

132. *Public Debt News*, Spring, 1973, Published by the Department of the Treasury.

133. **A 150-Year History of Beaver College and Arcadia University**, Ed. by Samuel M. Cameron, Mark P. Curchak, & Michael L. Berger, Glenside, Pa:Arcadia University, 2003.

134. *The Times Herald, Port Huron*, Michigan.

135. **Great Surveys of the American West**, by Richard A. Bartlett, University of Oklahoma Press:Norman, 1962.

136. **Powell of the Colorado**, by William Culip Darrah, Princeton University Press:New Jersey, 1951.

137. **The Olden Time** Volume I, by Neville Craig, Wennawoods publishing: Lewisburg, 2002. Reprint of original 1846.

138. **The French Invasion of Western Pennsylvania**, by Donald H. Kent, Pennsylvania Historical Museum Commission:Harrisburg, 1981.

139. **Historic Logstown the Story of an Indian Village**, By A. R. Temple, unpublished manuscript, BCHRLF archives.

140. **William Trent and the West**, by Sewell Elias Slick, originally published in 1947, Reprinted 2001 by Wennawoods Publishing, Lewisburg, PA.

141. *Journal of the National Medical Association*, January, 1961, Vol 53(1).

142. *The Pittsburgh Courier*, Pittsburgh, Pennsylvania.

Index

1

100th Regiment Pennsylvania Volunteer Infantry, **46**
101st Regiment Pennsylvania Volunteer Infantry, **47**
10th Pennsylvania Reserves, **46**
10th Regiment Pennsylvania National Guard, **73**
134th Pennsylvania regiment, **47**
134th Regiment Pennsylvania Volunteer Infantry, **47**
139th Regiment Pennsylvania Volunteer Infantry, **47**
140th Pennsylvania Voluntary Infantry, **48**
15th Amendment: Celebraion, **53**
162nd Regiment, 17th Cavalry, **47**
1785 Pennsylvania – Virginia boundary stone, **61**, **118**
19th Amendment, **94**

3

323 Light Field Artillery: Croix De Guerre, **93**
38th regiment, 9th Regiment Reserve Pennsylvania Volunteer Infantry, **46**

7

76th Regiment Pennsylvania Volunteer Infantry, **46**
77th Regiment of Pennsylvania Volunteer Infantry, **48**
78th Regiment Pennsylvania Volunteer Infantry, **49**

A

A.F. Smith & Co.: New Brighton, **36**
A.M.E. Church: Bridgewater, **36**
A.S. & R.W. Hall Carriage Works, **56**
Aaron Burr: Boats, **21**
Abolitionists: Abby Kelly and Stephen Symond Foster; Married in New Brighton, **36**; Anna Dickinson, **42**; Bradford, Arthur Bullus, **36**; Chippewa First Abolition Society, **34**; Douglass, Frederick, **37**; Garrison, William Lloyd, **37**
Acme Oil Company: Industry Twp., **59**
Act passed by the state for common schools, **31**
Adams, Captain Samuel: Exlporer, **55**
Adams, Dr. Samuel: Builds first Eastvale Dam, **20**; First physician in county, **19**
Adena: Culture in County, **2**
AES Corp., **148**
Agnew, Daniel, **76**; State Supreme Court Justice, **55**
Agudath Achim: First synagogue, **78**
Air Heritage of Western Pennsylvania, **131**
Alam, Emil, **141**
Alexander, John: Beaver Valley Journal, **102**
Algeo & Sons Coffin Works: Relocates to Beaver Falls, **58**
Aliquippa, **80**, **96**, **123**, **130**; Celebrates Golden Jubilee, **117**; Hospital, **116**; Hospital, **116**; Park Built by P&LE, **60**; Park Dance Hall, **83**; Plan 1, **84**; Plan 10, **88**; Plan 11, **89**, **96**; Plan 12, **89**; Plan 2, **86**; Plan 3, **88**; Plan 4, **88**; Plan 5, **89**; Plan 6, **89**; Plan 7, **87**; Plan 8, **84**; Plan 9, **88**; public school system, **84**; Steamboat sinks, **98**; telephone service, **78**
Aliquippa – Hopewell airport: Closed, **119**
Aliquippa P&LE station: National Register of Historic Places, **86**
Allegheny County, **14**
Allegheny Ludlum: Buys J&L Specialty, **141**
Allencrest Juvenile Detention Center, **116**
Allison, James: First District Attorney, **21**
Alllison, John: Representative & Register, **52**
Alston, William, **134**
Ambridge, **81**, **131**, **140**; Area School District, **124**; Baden School Merger, **124**; Catholic School, **123**; Celebrates Golden Jubilee, **115**; Family Theater, **146**; First Nationality Days, **121**; Incorporated, **80**; Soap Box Derby, **116**; telephone service, **80**
American Axe & Tool Company, **53**
American Bridge Company, **76**, **77**, **80**, **88**, **107**, **120**; First all welded barge, **99**; LST, **108**
American Bridge Division, **129**, **131**
American Grate & Fender Company, **63**
American Indian Gathering, **133**
Ames Tool & Shovel Company, **52**
Amockwi Chapter 17 Society for Pennsylvania Archaeology, **118**
Anderson and Cook Construction, **86**
Anderson, Dr. John, **17**
Anderson, William: Shot by Indians on Raccoon Creek, **11**
Anderton Brewing Company, **52**
Anderton, James, **52**
Andre, Major John: Sentenced to death, **15**
Andriessen, Hugo, **53**
Anthony Wayne Historical Society: Becomes Legion Ville, **125**
Anthony Wayne Terrace: Baden, **107**
Anti-masonic movement: meeting, **27**
Arcadia University: former Beaver College, **96**
Armco: Buys Spang-Chalfant, **89**; closes Ambridge plant, **131**; Closes Ambridge Works, **132**; Closes Butt Weld process, **118**
Armstrong World Industries, **76**, **144**
Asche, Charles: Asche Radio & Television Service, **123**
Ashe, Thomas, **21**
Ashland Oil Company: 1984 fires, **131**
Assumption Greek Orthodox: Aliquippa, **92**
ATI: Idled Midland plant, **149**
Atlantic Tube Company, **73**
Automobile Act, **81**
Avrakotos, Gust, **142**
Axtell, General George, **125**

B

B&W, **79**, **97**, **118**, **122**, **125**, **133**, **135**; Acquires Penn Bridge Company, **107**; East Works demolished, **145**; First etrusion process, **114**; First nickel tubing, **95**; Formerly Pittsburgh Seamless, **95**; Moves welding fittings, **117**
B&W:, **108**
B.F. Jones Library: National Register of Historic Places, **99**
B.F. Jones Memorial Library, **99**, **128**
B.O. Fair: Earliest garage and auto dealer, **81**
Baden, **33**, **40**; Incorporated, **52**; Memorial Library, **124**
Baglio, Dr. Corrado: Beaver Super, **135**
Baker Brothers: Flour mill, **52**
Baker Forge Company, **71**
Baker, George: Captured by Indians, **10**; Early settler, **10**
Baker, Michael Jr.: Died, **127**
Baltimore & Ohio: Engineer rescues downed pilots, **105**
Bank of Beaver, **24**, **64**; First chartered bank in county, **42**
Baptist Church: Beaver Falls, **61**
Barth, Harold: Studied Smtih's Ferry Petroglyphs, **83**
Basse, Baron Detmar: Bassenheim Furnace, **24**
Battisti, Eileen, **144**
Battle of Fallen Timbers, **16**, **17**
Baum, Mildred Custer: KDKA personality, **105**
Bausman, Dr. Joseph, **79**
Beall, Janice Jeschke: First recorder, **138**
Bean, John: One of the earliest teachers, **17**
Beaver, **16**, **131**; Borough School District merger, **115**; Borough swimming pool, **104**; Cemetery, **24**, **50**, **62**, **78**; First cemetery, **14**; First county court held, **21**; Freight station, **86**; Historic District National Register of Historic Places, **138**, **153**; Incorporated, **20**; Move Railroad Station, **86**; Naming squares, **78**; Presbyterian Church of, **24**; public school system, **34**; Reserved Tract First sale of lots, **16**; School District formed, **31**; School District Tuition agreement, **148**; Smallpox epidemic, **93**; Votes to remain "dry", **102**
Beaver Academy, **35**; Teacher's Association; First, **35**
Beaver Area Heritage Foundation, **122**, **149**; Renovates freight house, **138**; Train Station, **149**
Beaver Area Memorial Library, **113**
Beaver Argus, **56**
Beaver Clay Manufacturing Works, **77**
Beaver College, **67**, **95**; Relocated to Philadelphia, **96**
Beaver College and Musical Institution, **41**
Beaver County, **11**, **16**, **77**, **79**, **112**, **113**, **120**, **146**, **148**; "Shanghai", **102**; 175th anniversary, **127**; 2nd courthouse, **22**; 3rd courthouse, **57**; 4th courthouse, **101**; 5th courthouse, **140**; 911, **143**; 911 established, **133**; 911 moves to Ambridge, **143**; Airport, **115**, **131**; Airport, **98**; Bans Bingo, **105**; Bans Sunday football, **97**; Becomes "dry", **93**; Celebrates Bicentennial, **139**; Centennial Celebration, **74**, **75**; Colonization Society, **33**; Community College, **122**, **125**, **128**; Courthouse bombing, **125**; Department of Veteran's Affairs, 104; Fair, 88; First murder trial, **22**; Forest fires, **103**; Formed, 19; General Hospital, **73**; Geriatric Center, **132**, **145**; Home and Hospital Brighton Twp., **117**; Home for Indigent Residents, **82**; Ice Arena, **127**; Jail, **43**, 139; Milk Control Board, **99**; Temperance Society, **30**; WWII casualties, 110
Beaver County Agricultural Society, **40**
Beaver County Christian School: Beaver Falls, **123**
Beaver County Genealogy and History Center, **124**
Beaver County Historical Research & Landmarks Foundation, **124**
Beaver County Industrial Museum: Darlington, **138**
Beaver County Institute, **32**
Beaver County Jail, 139
Beaver County Model Railroad Club, **130**
Beaver County River Regatta, **127**
Beaver County Sports Hall of Fame, **127**
Beaver County Times, **40**, **56**
Beaver County Vocational Technical School, **128**
Beaver CountyRegistered boaters, 138
Beaver Division Canal, **32**, **35**, **39**, **97**; Closes, **53**; opened to New Castle, **31**
Beaver Drugstore & Natural History Museum: Hugo Andriessen, **53**
Beaver Fair, **40**
Beaver Falls, **22**, **44**, **51**, **52**, **53**, **86**, **113**; Arsons, **147**; County's first telephone exchange, **73**; Earliest track meet, **77**; First water-works, **47**; High School, **87**; Established, **57**; High School First commencement, **59**; Home-Week Fair, **83**; Incorporated, **52**; P&LE station, **85**; Pittsburgh Wall Paper Company, **31**; Providence Hospital, **83**; Town plot laid out, **22**; Typhoid fever, **101**; U.S. Armory, **46**
Beaver Falls Art Tile Company, Limited, **66**
Beaver Falls Car Works, **58**
Beaver Falls Chemical Company, **63**
Beaver Falls Colonization Society, **33**
Beaver Falls Cooperative Glass Company, Limited, **59**
Beaver Falls Cutlery Co., **51**; Chinese workers Arrived, **55**; Chinese workers leave, **57**; Closes, **64**; Philadelphia Centennial, **56**
Beaver Falls Gas Co, **54**
Beaver Falls Glass Company, Limited, **65**
Beaver Falls Iron Company, **64**
Beaver Falls Paper Company, **61**
Beaver Falls Planing Mill Company, **58**
Beaver Falls Steel Works, **56**
Beaver Female Seminary, **41**
Beaver Gazette, **23**
Beaver Point, **38**
Beaver River, **24**, **103**
Beaver Times, **56**
Beaver Valley Brewing Co, **77**
Beaver Valley Chamber of Commerce, **96**
Beaver Valley Christian Academy, **127**
Beaver Valley Country Club: One of oldest golf courses in Western PA,, **78**
Beaver Valley Electric Company, **72**

Strolling Through Time: A Chonology of Beaver County, PA History to 2016

Beaver Valley Electric Light & Power Co, **66**
Beaver Valley Expressway, **121, 122, 124, 126**
Beaver Valley General Hospital, **41, 71, 95**; Merger, **121**
Beaver Valley Geriatric Center, **117**
Beaver Valley Glass Manufacturing Company: AKA Dinkey Glass Works, **61**
Beaver Valley Hebrew Religious School, **89**
Beaver Valley Hotel Corporation, **97**
Beaver Valley Interchange of the PA Turnpike: Opened, **114**
Beaver Valley Intermediate Unit, **124**
Beaver Valley Journal, **102**
Beaver Valley Mall, **123**
Beaver Valley Motor Club, **84**
Beaver Valley Motor Coach Company, **96**; Temporary Pittsburgh route, **108**
Beaver Valley News, **62**
Beaver Valley Providence General Hospital: formed, **121**; merged iwth Rochester Hospital, **124**
Beaver Valley School of Nursing, **95**
Beaver Valley Street Railway Co., **64, 69**
Beaver Valley Times, **56**
Beaver Valley Traction Company, **69, 73, 74, 75, 91**
Beaver Valley Transit Authority, **129**
Beaver Valley Water Co, **77**
Beavertown: Laid out, **16**; Renamed Beaver, **26**
Bedford County, **9**
Beeler's Blockhouse, **11**
Bell of Pennsylvania: PhoneCenter Store, **129**
Bennett, Betty Lee: Youngest solo flight, **115**
Beth Jacob Congregation: Aliquippa-Woodlawn, **90**
Beth Samuel Congregation: Ambridge, **89**
Bethel Methodist Episcopal Church: New Sewickley Twp., **59**
Betters, Chuck, **148**
Bible Society: First established, **34**
Bicentennial Celebration: 1776, **127**
Big Beaver: Blockhouse, **15**; Abandoned, **16**; Blockhouse Trading Post; Indians massacred by Brady, **15**; Boat Club, **104**; Glacier, **1**; Tornado, **132**; Township, **51, 81, 87**; Township to Borough, **117**
Big Knob Grange: Organized, **103**
Black sky over county, **114**
Blackhand Queen: Jenny DeLucia, **91**
Blackhawk School District, **123**
Blackledge, Cora, **115**
Blake, David, **52**
Blount House: Early hotel in New Brighton, **37**
Boles, John: Bolesville, **25**; First boatyard, **25**
Bonbright, John & William: Starch factory, **35**
Borough Township, **123**
Bott, Emil, **82**
Bouquet, Colonel Henry, **8**
Boxer Rebellion: breaks out in China, **74**
Boyd, Thomas, **57**
Brady, Sam, **12, 15**
Brady's Run Brickworks, **78**
Brady's Run Land Company, **78**

Brady's Run Park, **127**; Opens to public, **113**
Bridge: 1836 wooden covered, **63**; 1910 double stack, **86**; Aliquippa-Ambridge, **98**; Between Beaver & Rochester, **117**; Between Brighton & New Brighton, **24**; Cleveland & Pittsburgh, **62**; Cleveland & Pittsburgh Railway, **46**; Covered wooden, **32**; Covered wooden toll, **32**; East Rochester – Monaca, **117**; Fallston, **147**; Fallston Bridge, **63**; Ft. Wayne RR, **97**; Hell Gate in New York, **88**; Henry Mancini, **137**; Over Beaver River at Sharon, **67**; P&LE railroad first locomotive, **57**; P&LE RR, **62**; PFW&C railroad, **50**; Rochester Monaca, **72**; Rochester-Monaca; Toll removed, **80**; Shippingport, **120**; Tenth Street Bridge, **68**; the last covered, **112**; Vanport Bridge, **122**; Verrazano Narrows Bridge, **120**; Veteran's Memorial, **146**; Wolf Lane, **23, 62**
Bridgewater, **25, 26, 32, 56**; Consolidated with Sharon, **52**; St. John African Methodist Ep. Church oldest in county, **29**; Stone's Point, **26**
Bridgewater Crossing Development: Chuck Betters buys, **148**; County buys park, **148**
Bridgewater Gas Co., **62**
Bridgewater Historic District: National Register of Historic Places, **138, 153**
Brighton, **22, 34, 71, 164**
Brighton first post office: John Dickey's store, **24**
Brighton Hot Dog Shoppe, **118**
Brighton Township: Formed, **24**; Historical Society, **139**
Brodhead, Colonel Daniel, **11**
Brown, John, **25**
Brown, Pfc. Timothy R., **140**
Bruien, James: Escaped slave and Civil War veteran, **74**
Brush Creek Park: Opened, **127**
Bryan, William Jennings: Speaks at Beaver, **82**
Burkhardt, Christian: Laid out Baden, **33**
Burns, H.M.: lumber yard Fallston, **29**
Burr, Aaron, **21**
Bush, President George W.: Visits Control Concepts, **139**
Buttermilk Falls: Homewood, **53**

C

Camp Fombelina, **118**
Camp Johnson: First for African American youth, **106**
Camp, J. Gordon: Plane crash, **119**
Cannel Coal: First mentioned, **17**
Capital Airlines DC-3: Crash landed in cow pasture, **113**
Carnegie Free Library, **77**; National Register of Historic Places, **132, 153**
Carter, President Jimmy: Vetoes Legion Ville bill, **128**; Visited Aliquippa High, **128**; Visited Beaver Falls, **129**
Catholic, **16**; First Mass, **5**; First Mission, **7**
Center Township, **90**; First Wal-Mart, **136**; Plaza, **126**
Central District and Telegraph Printing Company: Earliest telephone service, **59**; Merges with Bell Telephone, **92**
Central Valley School District: Merger, **143**
Cephas, Dr. Charles R., **118**

Chadwick, Dr. A.E., **122**
Chamberlin, B.B.: First postmaster New Brighton, **38**
Chamberlin, Dr. E.K: Fallston & Brighton Gazette., **32**
Charlie No Face: Ray Robinson, **132**
Chief Pakanke: Chases away Father Virot, **7**
Chippewa: First school building in, **29**; Roads built, **96**
Chippewa Indians, **13**
Christ Church: Fallston, **38**
Christ Episcopal Church: New Brighton, **39**
Christ Evangelical Lutheran Church: Baden, **43**
Christ Temple Church of God in Christ: Beaver Falls, **96**
Church of God: New Brighton, **42**
Civil War, **50**
Civilian Conservation Corps, **102**
Clabaugh, Rev. J.W.: Homewood, **52**
Clay, Henry: Visits, **37**
Clements, Kim, **129**
Cleveland & Pittsburg: Crew foils robbery, **100**; Safe recovered from river, **75**
Cleveland & Pittsburgh: Beaver station fire, **48**
Clinton, President Bill: Visits Ambridge High, **136**
Clow, James: Abolitionist, **25**
College Hill Borough: Organized, **70**
Collins, Col. Charles Read: Confederate commander, **48**
Colonial Steel Company, **75**
Colonial Theater, **86**
Colt Industries, **133**
Colvin, Mary: Last Indian attack, **15**
Commercial Sash and Door Company, **76**
Concord Methodist Episcopal Church: North Sewickley Twp., **31**
Concord Presbyterian Church: Economy Township, **64**
Congregation Beth El: Beaver Valley, **110**
Connoquenessing Creek, **32**
Constable brothers: Laid out Brighton, **22**
Conway: Airfield, **94**; Airport first airmail flown out of county from, **105**; Formerly known as Agnew, **60**; Incorporated, **77**; Rail yards Pennsylvania Railroad, **66**
Conway – Freedom Boulevard, **96**
Cook, Captain David S., **49**
Cook, George Washington, **43**
Cook's Ferry, **43**
Cook-Anderson farm, **129**
Co-operative Flint Glass Company, Limited, **59**
Cooperative Foundry Association, **54**
Coulter, Jonathan, **19**
Covert, Jim, **131**
Coxey, Jacob: Coxey's Army, **71**
Craig Manufacturing Company: Freedom, **67**
Creach, Papa John, **137**
Croghan, George, **5**; 1751 visit to Logstown, **5**
Crow Island: Buried by J&L, **120**
Crucible Steel, **56, 87, 88, 128**; Closed Midland plant, **130**
Cuccinelli, Matthew, **141**
Cumberland County, **5**
Curtiss-Wright, **107**; Bus line, **108**

D

Dando Brickyard, **90**
Dannals, Thomas S.: Confederate prisoner, **47**
Darlington, **21**; Polo Club, **104**
Darlington Brick Company: Closes, **142**
Darlington Cannel Coal Railway Company: Formed, **40**
Darlington Free Presbyterian Church, **36**
Darlington Township: Formed, **36**
Darragh and Stow Foundry: Flood; Sharon, **29**
Darragh, Major Robert: First building in Sharon, **21**
Daugherty Cemetery: First Catholic cemetery, **20**
Daugherty Township: Formed, **71**
David Littell House: National Register of Historic Places, **133, 153**
David, George, **146**
Davis, Ann B.: Brady Bunch, **135**
Dawes & Myler: New Brighton, **72**
Dawes Manor, **89**
Dawson, Benoni, **14, 16**; Laid out Georgetown, **16**
Dawson, Nicholas: Early settler on North Side, **16**
Daylight Savings Time: 1942, **109**; Robert Garland, **91**
De Blainville, Pierre Celeron, **5**
De Bonnecamp, Rev. Joseph Peter, **5**
Delaware Indians, **4, 5, 7, 13**; Adopt Zeisberger, **9**; migration, **3**; Shingas King of, **6**; Tamaqui succeeds Shingas, **8**
DeLeon, Count Maximilian: New Philadelphia Society, **29**
Demand and Response Transit, **132**
Depreciation: Certificates, **12**; Depreciation Lands, **13**; Donation Lands., **16**
Dillon, Henry: measured Abraham Lincoln, **45**
Ditka, Mike, **131**
Doncaster House: Rochester, **55**
Dorsett, Tony, **136**
Dorsey, Verna: County's first black state policewiman, **125**
Douglas Whisler Brick Company: Beaver Falls, **73**
Douthitt, Joseph: Douthitt House built, **30**
Downie, Robert Magee: Keystone Driller, **58**; Keystone Steam Driller Company, **61**
Drake, Dr. N. Bell, **85**
Driver Improvement School, **121**
Dukovich, Theresa Ferris, **134**
Dungan, Levi: Earliest settler, **10**
Dunlap Mansion: National Register of Historic Places, **129**
Duss: John, **78**; Susie, **78**

E

Eakin, Captain Howard Jr., **119**
Eakin, Nathaniel: First murder trial, **22**
Earheart, Amelia: Visits Geneva College, **103**
Earthquake: 1886, **65**
East Bridgewater, **38**
East Liverpool (Ohio) City School District, **136**
East Rochester, **83**

Strolling Through Time: A Chonology of Beaver County, PA History to 2016

Eastvale, **19**, **20**, **73**; Eastvale Bridge Built, **121**; Formerly named Fetterman, **70**
Eclipse Bicycle Company, **69**
Economy Borough: Disembodied head found, **146**
Economy Historic District: National Register of Historic Places, **132**, **153**
Economy Oil Field, **68**; Peak production reached, **85**
Economy Park: Opened, **116**
Economy Savings Institution, **52**
Economy Works, **52**
EconomyBorough, **117**
Ed Schaughency: broadcaster, **129**
Eighteenth Pennsylvania Infantry: Recruiting record, **91**
Electa Smith: First pay school Beavertown, **19**
Ellicott, Andrew, **13**, **14**; Ellicott Line, **13**
Ellwood City, **80**, **92**; Annexes 76 acres, **119**; First hospital, **85**; First trolley, **83**; Forge Company, **85**; Historical Society, **136**; Hotel Oliver, **69**; Opens Veteran's pool, **114**
Ellwood Shafting and Tube Company: First factory in Ellwood City, **72**
Ellwood Stone Company, **75**
Elverson, Thomas: *First pottery business*, **40**; First pottery plant in New Brighton, **46**
Empire Axe & Hoe Works, **53**
Emrick, Mike "Doc", **143**; U.S. Hockey Hall of Fame, **144**
ESB Financial, **147**
Evangelical Association: Freedom, **35**; Rochester, **42**
Evangelical Lutheran Church: Freedom, **37**

F

Fairport, **38**
Fairview tower: Microwave relay, **113**
Fallston, **17**, **22**, **34**; Academy; Built, **29**; Canal groundbreaking celebration, **29**; Cholera epidemic, **31**; Established, **26**
Fallston & Brighton Gazette, **32**
Fallston Fire Company, **78**
Felician Park, **63**
Felician Sisters of North America, **119**
Female Reform Society: New Brighton, **34**
Fessenden, James, **52**
Fetter, Henry: Kenwood School for Boys, **41**
Fetterman Bridge: Built, **58**; Demolished, **121**
Fetterman, N.P., **32**
Fillmore, Vice President Millard, **38**
Finished Specialty and Machine Company, **76**
First Baptist Church: New Brighton, **51**; Rochester, **55**
First Christian Church: Beaver Falls, **63**
First formal football league, **79**
First Methodist Episcopal Church: Beaver Falls, **56**
First Methodist Protestant Church: Beaver Falls, **53**
First Moon Township, **23**
First National Bank of Beaver Falls, **64**
First Presbyterian Church: Bridgewater, **36**; New Brighton, **31**; Rochester, **56**
First Sunday School Association, **51**

First United Presbyterian Congregation: Beaver Falls, **53**
flood, **63**, **82**, **103**, **109**, **110**; *1852*, **40**; 1861, **46**; 1865, **49**; 1884, **32**, **62**; 1996, **138**; First pumpkin flood, **22**; Hurricane Alice, **125**; Hurricane Ivan 2004, **141**; Second pumpkin flood, **29**; St. Patrick's Day, 103
Fombell, **118**; Bridge stolen, **116**
Forbes, General John, **7**
Ford, President Gerald: Visited Aliquippa, **127**
Greene Township, **23**
Fort Dunmore, **11**
Fort Duquesne, **6**
Fort McIntosh, **12**, **13**, **126**; Abandoned, **15**; built, **11**; Deserters shot, **14**; National Register of Historic Places, **126**, **153**; Timbers used, **19**; Treaty of, **13**
Foster, Thomas: River Hotel, **20**
Foster, William H.: Homewood postmaster, **46**
Foulkes family: Attacked at sugar camp, **12**
Foulkes Mill: Little Beaver Creek, **17**
Foulkes, Neal: Early settler on north side, **16**
Four Mile United Presbyterian Church: Ohioville, **23**
Franciscan Manor, **121**
Francona, Terry, **140**
Frank, Anne: dies, **110**
Frank, Dr. James, **130**
Frankfort, **15**
Frankfort Springs: Established, **35**; Frankfort Springs Hotel, **32**; telephone company, **83**; Vance Hotel, **32**
Frankfort Springs Academy, **30**
Frankfort Springs Hotel: Dungan, James, **32**
Franklin Township, **24**; Established, **38**
Frazier, Tamar, **25**
Freedom, **30**, **51**; Bentel & Co.Bank robbery, **64**; Incorporated, **33**
Freedom Casket Company, **67**
Freedom Oil Works, **58**
Freedom Savings & Trust Co., **100**
Freemasonry: First lodge in county, **16**
French Point Street Railway: Ambridge, **81**
Friedenstadt, **8**, **10**; First baptism, **9**; First church dedicated, **9**
Friendship Ridge, **145**
Fry, Henry Clay: H.C. Fry Glass Co., **77**
Fugitive Slave Act of 1850, **38**

G

Gagarin, Major Uri: Frist man in space, **118**
Gardner, Alexander: Allison Photograph, **52**
Garfield, President James: Fell off canal boat, **36**; Funeral train, **60**; Nominee stops in Beaver Falls, **59**
Garrett, Harry L.: First African-American attorney, **112**
Gateway Rehabilitation Center: Center Township, **124**
Gee Bee Store, **126**
General Anthony Wayne Chapter of the Sons of the American Revolution, **106**
Geneva College, **143**; First basketball game held, **70**; Hosts cadets, **109**; Relocated, **60**

Strolling Through Time: A Chonology of Beaver County, PA History to 2016

Georgetown, **14**, **15**, **16**; Native American sites, **133**; River Hotel, **20**
Georgetown Island, **136**
Gibb, David: Still house Hookstown, **42**
Gibson, John: Trading post at Logstown, **9**
Gillman, Franz, **78**
Gist, Christopher, **6**
glaciers, **1**
Glasgow, **37**; Incorporated, **41**; Sanford C. Hill lays out, **32**
Glasgow, Rev. Ezekiel, **24**
Glass, Robert Roland: Drafted by Confederacy, **45**
Glasser, John, **24**
Globe Fire Brick Works: New Brighton, **36**
Gnadenhutten and Schoenbrun, **10**
Goosby, Edith B.: First African American notary, **113**
Goss, April, **148**
Gould, Marcus T.C.: Died, **44**; New Brighton Female Semiinary, **30**
Grace Evangelical Lutheran Church: Rochester, **41**
Grand Army Day: Rock Point Park, **70**
Grandview Electric Street Railway, **75**
Great Western File Works, **52**
Greenwood Institute, **42**
Greenwood, Grace, **40**; Marriage, **41**; Moves to New Brighton, **34**
Greer, Guion: First county treasurer, **21**
Greersburg: Greer, George, **25**; Greersburg Academy, **20**, **32**, **126**, **153**; Greersburg Resolution, **32**; Incorporated, **25**
Greersburg Academy: Closes, **57**; Given to the LBHS, **125**; National Register of Historic Places, **126**; Sold to NYP&C Railroad, **62**
Grimshaw, William: Homewood, **29**
Grove Cemetery: Dedicated in New Brighton, **44**

H

H. C. Fry Glass Co, **77**
H. T. & J. Reeves, **50**
H.M. Myers & Company, Limited, **52**
Hague, Captain John W., **47**
Hamilton, James: First murder trial, **22**
Hamilton, William L.: One of the first pottery industries, **34**
Hand, General Edward: Commander for Squaw Campaign, **11**
Hanna, Louis B.: North Dakota governor, **89**
Hannastown, **10**
Hanover Township, **14**, **15**; Oil Fields, **66**
Harmony Electric Co.: Merger with Pennsylvania Power, **100**
Harmony Society, **22**, **25**, **26**, **30**, **37**, **44**, **50**, **51**, **52**, **56**; Dissolves, **78**; Establish Economy, **25**; George Rapp died, **37**; Sold all land in Beaver County, **78**
Harmony Township: Formed, **39**; Montmorin surveyed., **14**
Hartman Manufacturing Company: Ellwood City, **70**
Hartman Steel Company, Limited, **62**
Hartman, H.W., **70**
Hartman, Henry: Buys Beaver Falls Railroad, **67**
Hartman, William, **54**
Headland, Reverend Isaac Taylor: became missionary to China, **68**
Heckwelder, John: Moravian Missionary, **7**
Heinz, H.J., **51**
Helvedi, Francis: Monaca's first settler, **23**
Hemphill, Joseph, **19**
Henry, William: First county sheriff, **21**
Hickman, Charles: Cheats gallows, **87**
Hill, Sanford C: Laid out Glasgow., **32**
Hills Department Stores, **139**
Hindenburg, **104**
Hog Island: buried by J&L, **100**
Holy Trinity Greek Orthodox: Ambridge, **90**
Holy Trinity Roman Catholic Church: Ambridge Miracle at, **134**; Diamond Jubilee, **131**
Homewood, **29**, **43**, **46**; Formed, **86**; Railroad station, **48**
Hookstown, **42**; Air Force T-33, **115**; Fever Epidemic, **35**; known earlier as Nineveh, **35**
Hoopes, Joseph: U.S.S. Kearsage, **50**
Hoopes, Townsend & Co., **20**
Hopewell Township, **97**; Formed, **23**; Mysterious box, **83**
Hopkins, Gregory Scott, **145**
Howard Stove Company: Beaver Falls, **51**
Howells, Pastor Henry, **127**
Hubbard, Bakewell & Company, **53**
Hughes, Mimi: Swims Ohio River stops at Baden, **143**
Hunter & Code refinery: First in county, **44**
Huntington Bank: Merged with Sky Bank, **142**
Hutchins, Thomas: Surveys Point of Beginning, **14**

I

Ice Age: Begins, **1**
Imbrie, Rev. David, **23**
Imperial Glass Company: Beaver Falls, **74**
Independence Township, **112**; Formed, **37**
Industry: Village of, **32**
Industry borough: Incorporated, **118**
Industry Presbyterian Church: Industry Twp., **50**
Ingram-Richardson Mfg. Co., **75**, **81**, **110**; First porcelain range, **87**
Interstate 376, **143**
Iris, Donnie: Hall of Fame, **147**; Jaggerz, **120**
Irish potato famine: Relief for, **37**
Isaac Wilson & Co: Town plot for Beaver Falls, **22**
Isaly's, **123**
Izenour, George Charles: Stage lighting system, **112**

J

J&L, **141**
J&L Steel: Mercantile store Woodlawn, **86**
J. H. Knott & Company: Flour mill, **61**
J. S. Mitchell & Sons: Beaver Falls, **72**

J.C. Russell Shovel Company: Aliquippa, **69**
Jackson, President Andrew, **26**
James Beach Clow House, **134**, **153**; National Register of Historic Places, **25**, **134**
James Nelson house: First UGRR station, **24**
James, George "Tookie", **139**
Javens, Connie Tuccinard: First female treasurer, **136**
Javens, Evelyn Faye: First female mayor, **119**
Jerry's Curb Service: Opens in Bridgewater, **113**
Jewish, **54**
John Conway's Bank: Second bank in Rochester, **54**
John T. Reeves & Company, **52**
Johnny Appleseed, **33**
Johnson, David: First Protohontary, **21**
Johnson, Laura: First female juror, **95**
Joines Radio Communications: New Brighton, **120**
Joncaire: French agent, **4**
Joncaire, Philippe Thomas de: French trader, **5**
Jones & Laughlin Steel, **81**, **84**, **87**, **109**, **122**, **126**; Aliquippa Works, **109**; Becomes J&L Specialty Steel, Inc., **133**; Fastest rolling mill, **112**; First oxygen furnace, **117**; Woodlawn boulevard, **97**
Jones, Ezekial: and wife Hanna first settlers North Sewickley Twp., **20**; First Coroner, **21**
Joseph Graff and Company, **53**
Junction Park, **70**, **84**, **88**, **105**; Built by Beaver Valley Traction Co., **73**

K

Kane Road Drive-In, **148**
Kelbaugh, Leroy, **104**
Kennedy, John E.: Seaplane crash, **110**
Kennedy, President John F.: Assassinated, **120**; visits Aliquippa, **119**
Kenwood School for boys: Demolition, **145**; New Brighton, **41**
Kerr, David: Early settlers on King's Creek, **11**
Keswick Pottery, **78**
Keyser, William M., **57**
Keystone Bakery, **48**, **131**
Keystone Chemical Works, **66**
Keystone Glass Company, **73**
Keystone Pottery Co.: Fire, **71**
Keystone Steam Driller Company, **58**, **61**, **117**; Skimmer, **88**
Keystone Tumbler Company: Rochester, **71**
Kier, S.M., **44**
King, Dr. Martin Luther: Killed, **122**
King's Creek, **10**, **11**; United Presbyterian Church, **15**
Kipling, Rudyard: Vistied Beaver, **67**
Kmart: Rochester closed, **146**
Knott, Harker & Company, **63**
Kobuta plant, **109**
Kolter, Joe: Sentenced, **138**
Koppel: Glaciers, **1**; Koppel, Arthur, **87**; Orenstein-Koppel Company, **87**; PHB&NC, **90**; Town for sale, **104**

Koppel Industrial Car and Equipment Company: Moves to Mckees Rocks, **104**
Koppel Steel, **81**; Bought by TMK IPSCO, **143**
Kossuth, Louis: Hungarian Patriot, **39**
Kristufek Agency, **76**
Kunselman, Deborah, **142**
Kurek, Jan: War shield, **90**

L

La Salle: Explored Ohio River, **3**
Lacock, Abner, **21**; Cemetery; Rochester, **47**; Laid out Darlington, **21**; Senator, **23**
Lake Monongahela, **1**
Lanam, Jack: East Liverpool Hist. Soc., **14**, **118**
Land Act: Sale of vacant public lands, **15**
Landslide on Constitution Boulevard, **109**
Lapic Winery, **128**
Laughlin Memorial Library, **99**
Law, Ty, **146**
Lawrence County: Formed from part of Beaver Co., **38**
Le Chevalier De Cambrary: Designed Fort McIntosh, **11**
Leech, Richard & wife: Open 2nd female seminary in N.B., **33**
Leet, Daniel: Laid out Beavertown, **16**
Legion Ville, **16**; Denied National Park status, **128**; National Register of Historic Places, **126**, **153**; Railroad finds body, **48**
Legionville: bronze tablet, **91**; Soldier shot, **16**
Letteri, Joe, **116**
Lewis, Meriwether: Corps of Discovery, **21**
Licker, John, Jr.: Plane Crash with J. Gordon Camp, **119**
Lincoln, President Abraham, **45**; Assassinated, **49**; Beaver County votes, **48**; Votes cast in Beaver County, **44**
Linn, Robert: Beaver mayor, **141**
Lippincott, Sarah Jane: Grace Greenwood, **40**
Little Beaver Historical Society: Incorporated, **119**
Little Beaver Township, **36**
Logan, Andrew: Beaver Gazette, **23**
Logan, James: Publisher Western Argus, **24**
Logan, Mingo Chief: Hunting camp Rochester, **9**; Logan's Town Rochester, **9**; Town, **38**
Logstown, **4**, **5**, **6**, **7**, **8**, **9**, **16**, **57**, **82**, **140**; Associates formed, **133**; burned by Scaroudy, **6**; French buildings, **6**; French fort, **6**; French trading post, **5**
London Company, **3**
Loxley, Nancy, **137**
LTV Steel Corporation, **126**, **139**; Closes Aliquippa Works, **132**; Sold Midland Specialty plant, **133**

M

Mancini, Henry, **137**; Conducts Aliquippa HS band, **130**; performs at CCBC, **128**
Mansfield, Ira: Robin Hood Club, **49**
Maple Syrup Festival: First pancake dinner, **128**
Maravich, Pistol Pete, **133**

Mariano, Amber Brkich, **128**
Marion Township, **38**; Formed, **36**
Marriage: First same sex marriage, **145**; licenses same sex couples, **145**
Marsh, Grant: Steamer Far West Custer massacre, **56**
Mathers, Betty, **25**
Matthew Stanley Quay House: National Register of Historic Places, **126**
McBeats, N.B.F.: Frankfort store, **24**
McCabe, Sergeant Joseph: Lee's surrender, **49**
McCallister, William: Laid out Baden, **33**; Village of Industry, **32**
McCarl Industrial Museum, **143**
McClure, David: Early missionay, **10**
McClure, Denny, **19**
McClure, Hughes O.: First electric car, **94**
McCool Tube Company, **71**
McCool, William: Patented cold draw machinery, **54**
McCullough, Dr.: First physician on southside, **22**
McDermott International Corporation: Announced plant closings, **133**
McElhaney, George: Indian scout, **12**
McGinnis, Edward: Frankfort Mineral Springs, **28**
McGuire Memorial Home, **119**
McGuire, James: First Catholic Settler, **16**
McIntosh, General Lachlan: Commanded Fort McIntosh, **11**
McIntyre, Captain: Wyandot raid, **12**
McKane, Dr. Alice Woodby: First African American female physician in Georgia, **48**
McKee, Alexander: Lived opposite Logstown, **8**
McKinley School, **54**
McKinley, John, **54**
McLaughlin, Neal: Early settler on north side, **16**
McLaughlin's blacksmith Shop, **75**
Mechanics Fire Company: New Brighton, **34**
Medical Center of Beaver, **129**
Medical Center of Beaver County: creation through merger, **124**
Melchior, Isaac, **14**
Mercer School: Closes, **115**
Mercur, Elise, **72**
Merrick Art Gallery, **122**, **131**, **153**; Established, **59**; National Register of Historic Places, **131**
Merrick, Hanna and Company: Iron passenger cars, **42**
Merrill Lock & Dam #6, **153**; National Register, **129**; Opened, **79**
Metheny, Moses: Metheny tavern, **32**
Methodist Church: Sharon earliest, **25**
Methodist Episcopal Church: Baden, **43**; Beaver, **26**; Freedom, **34**; Georgetown, **29**; Glasgow, **51**; Homewood, **52**; New Brighton, **33**; Rochester, **51**
Metric Metal Works: Produced gas meters, **66**
Metropolitan Brick Company: closes, **130**
Michael Baker, Jr., **117**; Opened first office, **107**
Midgeley, Thomas: Creator of tetraethyl lead, **90**
Midland: First Fourth of July parade, **128**; First National Bank, **81**; Midland School District, **136**, **147**; Midland School District Tuition Agreement, **148**; Telephone Service, **88**; Toyland, **87**
Midland Improvement Company, **87**
Midland Steel Company, **81**, **87**
Miles, Major General Nelson: County centennial, **74**
Mill Creek Presbyterian Church, **15**; Oldest established church, **13**
Mill Creek Valley: Agricultural Association, **75**; Fair, **64**; Hookstown, **65**; Hookstown Fair, **64**
Miller, Dobson & Trax, **52**
Miller, William: First African American mortician, **99**
Minerva: First newspaper in county, **22**; John Berry Publshed, **22**
Model T Ford, **83**
Moltrup Steel Corporation, **89**; Striker killed, **104**
Moltrup, Merle, **98**
Monaca, **25**, **56**; Centennial, **107**; Federal Works Agency, **107**; First settler Helvedi, **23**; Parade, **93**; Public library, **102**; Public schools, **78**; pump house, **106**
Monaca Community Hall of Fame, **136**
Monacatootha, **69**
Monongahela people, **3**
Monongahela River: Pre-glacial, **1**
Monterey, **37**
Montgomery Island Lock and Dam, **103**; Elizabeth M sinks, **141**
Montmorin: town never built, **14**
Moon Township, **90**; annexed to Monaca, **100**
Moore, James, **14**
Moore, Jesse: First judge 6th District, **21**
Moore, Judy, **137**
Moore, Thomas: Early settler in Greene Twp., **10**
Morado Park: Built by Beaver Valley Traction, **73**; Last trolley run, **105**
Moravia, Lawrence County, **8**
Morgan, John Hunt: Confederate cavalry, **48**
Morus Multicaulis, **32**, **44**
Moslener, Louis Jr.: First countian killed in WWII, **108**
Mount Gallitzin Academy, **74**
Mt. Carmel Presbyterian Church, **16**
Mt. Pleasant Presbyterian Church: Darlington, **17**
Murdocksville, **12**
Mutual Union Brewing Company, **80**

N

NAACP, **137**
Namath, Joe, **122**
National Bank of New Brighton, **42**, **64**
National Glass Company, **54**, **71**, **73**
National Tube Company, **80**
Native American site 36BV9, **118**
Navy fighter jet crash, **112**
New Bethlehem United Presbyterian Church: Hopewell Twp., **49**
New Brighton, **26**, **42**, **73**, **84**, **97**, **137**; blockhouse; built and occupied, **15**; Female Seminary, **34**; First graded public school, **42**; First publc school house, **31**;

Historical Society, **122**; Incorporated, **33**; Oldest brickyard on Oak Hill, **29**; Public Library; Opened, **121**; Telephone service began, **66**; Typhoid Fever, **101**; YMCA first outdoor pool, **89**
New Galilee, **25**; Frazier, Pompey, **25**; Incorpporated, **51**
New Philadelphia: Keil believed to be Christ, **36**
New Philadelphia Society, **30**
New River Gorge Bridge: American Bridge, **120**
New Salem Presbyterian Church: Ohioville, **17**
New Sewickley Township, **34**, **36**, **41**; Formed, **20**
New Sheffield, **97**; Academy closed, **90**
New York-Pittsburgh Company, **76**
News-Tribune, **98**
Nicholson File Works, **52**
Nicholson, James, **25**
Nicholson, Thomas: Frankfort Springs Academy, **30**
Noble, Thomas, **51**
Norfolk Southern Railway: Derailment, **142**
North Branch Presbyterian Church: Center Twp., **31**
North Sewickley Academy, **49**; Established, **36**
North Sewickley Church Academy, **39**
North Sewickley Township, **92**; Formed, **20**
North Shore Railroad, **63**; Spur to Wallace City abandoned, **85**
Northern Lights Shopping Center, **116**, **145**
Noss Family Band, **96**

O

Oak Grove Cemetery: Freedom, **47**
Obama, President Barack: Visit to Beaver, **145**; Visits Monaca, **143**
Ohio Company, **5**
Ohio River, **17**; Plane crash 1927, **98**; Plane crash 1944, **110**; Plane crash 1978, **128**
Ohio Township, **21**, **24**, **118**
Ohioville, **16**, **21**; Incorporated, **118**
Oil, **44**
Old, 22
Old Brighton: Renamed Beaver Falls, **51**
Old Brighton Paper Mill Company, **31**
Old Economy district, **125**
Old Economy Village, **94**, **122**, **153**; Fire, **30**; National Register of Historic Places, **122**; New visitor center, **140**
O'Leary, John P., **119**
Olive Stove Works, **55**
Olympic Torch Runs, **131**
Ondrusek, Mark: Beaver Super, **135**
Oriental Theater: Opened in Rochester, **100**
Ormes, William Patrick: Early oil well, **44**
Our Lady of Fatima School: Opened in Chippewa, **116**
Our Lady of Fatima Shrine: Ambridge war memorial, **115**

P

P&LE: Last passenger run, **132**; Monaca crash 1901, **76**; Woodlawn boulevard, **97**

P.M. Moore Company: J&L Employee housing, **87**
Paleo-Indian period, **2**
Pappan, Lou: Pappan's Family Restaurant, **120**; Pappan's Family Restaurant bankruptcy, **142**
Parilli, Vito "Babe", **122**
Park, James I.: Quarry, **62**
Park, John H., **63**
Parsons, Major Gen. Samuel H.: Drowns in Beaver River, **15**
Passavant Memorial Home: Rochester, **47**
Passavant Memorial Hospital, **18**
Passavant, Dr. William, **47**
Patricia, Italy, **96**, **149**; Sister city with Aliquippa, **149**
Pattens, Finlens, Swan & Company: County's first oil well, **44**
Patterson Dam, **20**, **26**
Patterson Heights: Airfield; Opened, **92**; Incline, **71**; Incorporated, **73**
Patterson Township: 1st board of commissioners, **95**; First school, **22**; Formed, **34**; police force formed, **126**
Patterson, James, **44**; Builds dam, **26**
Patuc, Joseph F.: First county volunteer WWII, **107**
Payne, William: Last execution in county, **79**
Peirsol Academy, **56**
Peirsol, Scudder, **56**
Pendleton, Captain Gilbert: Fire brick works, **42**
Pendleton, Colonel Joseph: Camp Pendleton, **90**
Pendleton, Joseph: Fire brick works, **42**
Penn Beaver Hotel: Rochester, **97**
Penn Bridge Works: New Brighton, **51**
Penn State Beaver: Brodhead Cultural Center, **127**; Opened, **121**
Penn State Special Metals, **142**
Penn, William, **4**
Pennsylvania – Virginia boundary stone, **118**; 1785, **13**; 1883, **61**
Pennsylvania Canal: Ground breaking, **29**
Pennsylvania Cyber Charter School, **139**
Pentecost, Joseph and Mary: First deed recorded, **21**
People's Water Co., **71**, **77**
Peoples Electric Street Railway Co, **70**
Perry, Commodore Oliver Hazard, **23**
Pettibon Raccoon Golf Course, **123**
PHB&NC, **100**
Phelps, Wilbur N.: First Degree Carnegie Tech, **101**
Phillips & Betz: Laid out Freedom, **30**; Relocated to Freedom, **30**
Phillips & Graham: Boat builders; Phillipsburg, **25**; Sell Phillipsburg, **29**
Phillips, Alice: Titanic survivor, **87**
Phillipsburg, **25**, **30**, **56**; Incorporated, **34**; M.E. Church, **50**; Renamed Monaca, **69**; Solder's Orphan School, **49**
Phillis Island, **136**
Phoenix Glass: Began operations in Phillipsburg, **60**; Destroyed by fire, **62**; plant, **128**
Pioneer Pottery Company, **50**

Strolling Through Time: A Chonology of Beaver County, PA History to 2016

Pittsburgh & Lake Erie Railroad: Beaver Station 1897, **72**
Pittsburgh & Ohio Railroad: Beaver Station, **39**
Pittsburgh and Lake Erie Passenger Station: National Register of Historic Places, **135**, **153**
Pittsburgh Hinge & Chain Factory: Beaver Falls, **64**
Pittsburgh Seamless Tube Company: Beaver Falls, **79**
Pittsburgh Tool & Wire Company, **76**
Pittsburgh Wallpaper Company: New Brighton, **74**
Pleasant Hills Wesleyan Methodist School, **128**
Poe, Andrew: Battle with Indian, **12**
Point of Beginning, **13**, **14**; National Register of Historic Places, **122**
Pontiac's Rebellion, **8**
population, **20**, **23**, **25**, **29**, **34**, **39**, **44**, **53**, **60**, **68**, **74**, **84**, **94**, **100**, **106**, **114**, **124**, **129**, **135**, **139**, **143**
Porter, Andrew, **14**
Post Office: Aliquippa, **70**, **102**; Baden, **40**; Conway "Agnew", **60**; Darlington, **29**; Fallston, **27**; Frankfort, **20**; Homewood, **46**; New Brighton, **38**; Phillipsburg/Monaca, **42**; Smth's Ferry, **31**; Woodlawn, **57**
Post, Christian Frederick, **7**
Potter Township, **88**; County poor farm, **40**; Secret avialtion fuel dump, **107**
Powers, Abraham: Methodist church, **22**
Presbyterian Church: Frankfort Springs, **31**; Freedom, **35**; Glasgow, **38**; Hookstown, **41**
Presentation of the Blessed Virgin Mary: Midland, **82**
Presentation School, **98**
Providence Baptist Church: North Sewickley Twp., **20**, **64**
Providence Hospital, **77**; Merger, **121**
Pugh family: Flour mill; Fallston, **21**
Pugh, Joseph: Pugh & Bacum's Sash Factory Fallston, **29**
Pulaski Township: Formed, **41**

Q

Quay, Matthew Stanley: Awarded MOH, **66**; Died, **78**; Earns MOH, **47**; Elected to Senate, **65**; House, **126**
Quigley Catholic High School, **122**
Quinn's Rope Walk: Monaca, **23**

R

R.E. Chambers Company, **92**, **101**
Raccoon Creek, **10**; Recreational Demonstration Area National Register, **133**; State Park, **28**, **110**
Raccoon Township, **30**
Railroads; P&LE, **86**; Ellwood Short Line, **69**; New Brighton and New Castle Railroad, **63**; Ohio & Pennsylvania first rail train from Allegheny City, **39**; Ohio & Pennsylvania RR ground breaking, **37**; Ohio and Pennsylvania; Extended from Pittsburgh, **38**; P&LE, **86**, **94**; P&LE builds Aliquippa Park, **60**; P&LE Fallston Station, **86**; P&LE moves passenger station, **86**; P&LE station West Aliquippa, **88**; P&LE to Youngstown completed, **58**; Pittsburgh and Western Railroad, **69**

Rank, Rev. Jacob, **42**
Rapp, Gertrude, **28**
Ray W. Snyder Elementary School, **118**
Reaping machine: First in county, **38**
Reardon's Run, **12**
Reddick, Judge John H.: Burial on state lines, **28**
Reeves, John, **71**
Reeves, Mary, **22**
Reformed Presbyterian Church: Little Beaver Congregation of, **22**
Reformed Presbyterian Congregation of Beaver Falls, **56**
Reno, Rev. Francis: One of the earliest settlers in Rochester, **18**
Republican commissioners: Attain Majority, **148**
Rhema Christian School: Hopewell Twp,, **130**
Richardson, Dr. Harrison H.: Polar Explorer, **105**
Richmond School, **124**
Riddle, George: First will, **21**
Ride, Sally: First woman in space, **131**
Ringling Brothers Barnum and Bailey Circus, **84**
Rittenhouse, David, **13**
Riverview Electric Street Railway, **73**
Robert Marjanovich: Served with Chetniks, **111**
Roberts, Col. Richard P., **48**
Roberts, John, **25**
Robertson, Archibald: Steam papermill; Brighton, **26**
Robinson, Ray, **132**
Rochester, **41**; Beaver CountyTeachers meeting to organize, **39**; Borough; Formed, **38**; first steel swimming pool, **125**; Heritage Society, **147**; Hospital, **73**; Incorporated, **38**; Lodge #229; Formed from St. James lodge, **23**; Public Library, **95**; Ttelephone exchange, **74**
Rochester - Monaca bridge, **99**; 1897, **72**; torn down, **132**
Rochester & Monaca Electric Street Railway, **75**
Rochester Electric Company, **68**, **72**
Rochester Flint Vial and Bottle Works, **58**
Rochester Flouring Mills Company, **61**
Rochester Hospital, **129**; merger with Beaver Valley Providence General Hospital, **124**
Rochester Manufacturing Company, **41**
Rochester Township, **38**, **83**; created, **34**
Rochester Tumbler Co., **54**; Works, **73**
Rock Point, **36**, **39**, **142**; Amusement Co., **63**; Nature Area, **142**
Rocky Spring United Presbyterian Congregation of New Galilee, **26**
Rome Monument Works: Michael Dioguardi starts, **102**
Romigh School: New Sewickley, **72**
Rutherford, Robert: First Virginia patent, **11**

S

Sabo, Specialist Four Leslie Jr., **144**
Salaya, Ralph: Apollo 13, **123**
Salem Church, **16**
Salvation Army, **63**

San Rocco Festival, **96**
Sandy and Beaver Canal, **41**; Completed to Bolivar, Ohio, **37**
Sawkunk, **4, 7**; Second Village, **7**; Smaller one, **7**
Scaroudy: burns Logstown, **6**
Scassa, Alex Sr., **127**
Schade, Agnes L.: First single female Lutheran missionary, **68**
Schulte, Bea, **137**
Scott, Rev. John Witherspoon: Died in White House, **70**
Service Creek Reservoir, **114**
Service Theological Seminary: Eudolphia Hall, **17**
Service United Presbyterian Church: Second oldest church, **15**
Sewickley Township: Their first school board, **31**
Shallenberger, Oliver: Wattsmeter Invented Wattsmeter, **71, 101**
Shannopin: 1902 explosion, **77**; 1908 explosion, **83**; Dynamite explosion, **72**; Name changed to South Heights, **84**; Nitro explosion, **66**; South Heights, **84**; Standard Oil Co., **65**; Train riot, **69**
Sharon, **52**
Shawnee Indians, **4, 5, 17**
Sheets, Eli: First judicial hanging, **47**
Shelby Steel Tube Company, **80**
Shell Chemical Company: Buys Horsehead site, **147**; Considering site, **144**; Official announcement, **149**
Sherlock, William: Transportation Secretary killed, **127**
Sherwood Brothers Pottery, **58**
Shingas, **8**; Delaware King, **6**; Dies, **8**
Shippingport, **85**; atomic plant, **116**; Ferry, **43, 120, 121**
silkworms: Mulberry tree, **32**
Sisters of Charity, **77**
slavery, **10, 12, 19, 32, 33, 36, 39, 74**; Anti-slavery convention held New Brighton, **39**
Sloan, Dr. James: Opened Frankfort Springs Academy, **30**
Smith, Fulton C.: First countian killed in WWI, **92**
Smith, Joseph M., **29**; Laid out Homewood, **43**
Smith, Samuel, **31**
Smith's Ferry, **31, 44, 45**; James Clark first house, **15**; Petroglyphs, **3, 83**
Snow Shovel Riding Contest, **121**
Snowstorm: 1940, **106**; 1941 train derails; sabotage suspected, **107**; 1950 Thanksgiving, **114**
Social Security, **106**
Soldier's Orphan School in Phillipsburg, **50**; Destroyed by fire, **56**
Soldier's Orphan School of North Sewickley, **49**
Soldiers and Sailors Memorial, **75**
Sons of Israel Congregation: Midland, **92**
South Beaver Township, **21, 24**; Glaciers, **1**
South Heights, **84**; First school opened, **63**
Southside Historical Village, **137**
Spang-Chalfant, **107**; Labor riot, **102**; Opened Ambridge plant, **89**; Purchased by Armco, **89**
Spanish Flu, **92**
Spencer, Niles: Post office mural, **102**

Speyerer :& McDonald Bank: First bank in Rochester, **53**
Spratt, Edward J.: First motor ambulance, **87**
Spring Water Brewery, **52**
Squaw Campaign, **11**
St. Lukes Episcopal Church: Georgetown, **24**
St. Blaize: Midland, **82**
St. Cecelia's Roman Catholic Church: Second Catholic church in county, **41**
St. Cecilia Parish: Rochester, **64**
St. Clair Borough, **70**; Incorporated, **51**
St. Cyril and Methodius Church: New Brighton, **97**
St. Elijah Serbian Orthodox congregation: Aliquippa, **89**
St. Felix Catholic Church: Freedom, **81**
St. George's Serbian Orthodox: Midland, **98**
St. James's Lodge: First Masonic lodge physically in county, 23
St. John the Baptist Catholic church: Baden, **50**
St. John the Baptist School: Baden, **119**; Monaca, **115**
St. John's Lutheran Church: Built by Harmony Society, **26**
St. Joseph Lead Co., **100**
St. Joseph School, **89**
St. Joseph's Cemetery, **29**
St. Luke's Protestant Episcopal Church: Georgetown, **20**
St. Mary's Catholic Church: Beaver Falls, **44, 55**; School Beaver Falls, **67**
St. Nicholas Russian Orthodox Church, **138**
St. Paul's Episcopal Church: Ohioville, **28**
St. Paul's Evangelical Lutheran Church: Rochester, **51**
St. Peter & Paul Church: First R.C. church in county, **33**
St. Peter's German Lutheran Church: First pipe organ installed, **38**
St. Peters Evangelical Church: Phillipsburg, **30**
St. Philomena School: Beaver Falls, **117**
St. Rose of Lima Catholic Church: Darlington, **45**
St. Stanislaus School, **123**
St. Theresa School: Opened in Koppel, **114**
St. Theresa's Catholic Church: Koppel, **54**
St. Veronica's and Divine Redeemer., **123**
St. Veronica's High School, **140**
St. Vladimir Ukrainian Orthodox: Ambridge, **96**
stagecoach stop between Pittsburgh and Cleveland, **25**
Standard Connecting Rod Company, **76**
Standard Fire Clay, **78**
Standard Gauge Steel Company: Beaver Falls, **69**
Standard Horse Nail Works, **54**
Standard Slag Company, **133**
Stanton, Edwin: Harmony Society case, **37**
Stanton, Elizabeth Cady: Passed away, **77**
Steinfeld, Dr. Jesse, **123**
Steubenville East Liverpool & Beaver Valley Traction: Last run, **105**
Stoll, Esther: Prima Donna, **98**
Stone, Adam: Remains found, **148**
Stoops, Jennie: Rescued by Sam Brady, **12**
Stubert, Joseph: First Postmaster Aliquippa, **70**
Stucky, Melba: First female lawyer, **95**
Sullivan, John L.: Ex-Champ visits Majestic, **85**
Sullivan, Stella Burge: First female licensed pilot, **100**

Strolling Through Time: A Chonology of Beaver County, PA History to 2016

Sunday, Billy: Beaver Falls, **88**
Swearingen Cemetery, **15**
Sylvanian Hills Christian School, **129**
Synagogue of the Congregation Tree of Life: Rochester, **92**

T

Tabernacle Baptist Church: Beaver Falls, **92**, **94**
Taft, President William Howard: Visits Heath Manor, **91**
Tamaqui, **8**
Tanacharison, **5**, **6**
Tannehill, Ray: New Brighton, **123**
Tatalovich-Rossi, Teri, **142**
Taunt, Lieutenant Emory: Kenwood School/Greely Expedition, **63**
Taylor, Dr. R.T.: Beaver College, **67**
Taylor, President Zachary: Visits Metheny Tavern, **39**; Visits Old Ecomony, **38**
Taylor, Rev. W.G., **50**
Taylorcraft: Mauro, Ben, **113**
Teacher's Association: Rochester, **39**
The Daily Times, **56**
The Holy Ghost Russian Orthodox: Ambridge, **82**
The Valley Glass Company, **65**
Thiel College: Founded, **50**
Thomas Calhoun: Ambushed at Beaver Creek, **8**
Thompson, Colonel Joseph H.: Medal of Honor WWI, **92**
Tomlinson's Run Presbyterian Church: Greene Twp., **31**
Tonti, Joseph: World's strongest upside down man, **117**
tornado: 1985, **132**; Center Township, **124**
Townsend Company: Relocated, **26**
Townsend, Baird and Company: Incorporated, **32**
Townsend, David, **17**; Fallston mill, **22**; Flour mill, **26**; Laid out New Brighton, **26**, **33**
Townsend, Mary, **22**
Townsend, Robert, **30**
Toy, James Madison: First Native American baseball player?, **65**
Travers Engineering Company, **101**; Amusement rides, **92**
Treaty of Fort Stanwix, **13**
Treaty of Greenville, **17**
Trent, William: French building at Logstown, **6**
Trevelline, Victor & Francis, **118**
Trinity Episcopal Church: Rochester, **39**
Trinity Evangelical Lutheran Church: St. Clair, **52**
Trobe, Gertrude: Radio personality WBVP, **113**
Trobe, Harold: Helped Jewish refugees, **138**
Tubman, Harriet: Passed away, **89**
Tuscarawas Trail, **8**
Tuscarora Plastics, **119**
Tuskegee Airmen, **147**

U

Ubalto, John: Crimean War, **62**
UFO Chase, **121**

Union Building & Loan: Bridgewater, **121**
Union Drawn Steel Co., **76**; Beaver Falls, **66**
Union Water Co., **70**, **77**
United Hospital: former Beaver Valley Providence General Hospital, **129**
United Presbyterian Church: Beaver, **40**; Hookstown, **36**
United Presbyterian Congregation of Camp Run: Franklin Twp., **60**
United States Sanitary Manufacturing Co, **77**
United States Steel Ellwood, **80**
Urista, Thomas: Crash landed in front of train, **105**
USAirways: Abandons Pittsburgh Hub, **141**; Flight 427 crash, **137**

V

Valley Electric Company, **72**
Valley Ice Company, **72**
Valvoline Oil Company: Freedom, **117**
Van Reed, Jacob: Still house, **42**
Vanport, **107**; Electric Street Railway, **75**; Township, **123**
Veon, Mike, **143**; Released on parole, **147**
Vera, Captain J. Adams, **47**
Veteran's Memorial, **146**
Vicary, Captain William: Builds mansion, **25**; Lays out St. Clair, **33**; Mansion on National Register of Historic Places, **126**, **153**
Viele, Arnout: Explored Ohio Valley, **4**
Virot, Father Calude Francis: Catholic misson at Sawkunk, **7**
Vujnovich, George: WWII Rescue, **110**

W

Wagner Act, **104**; Supreme Court Decision, **104**
Wagner, Henry: Wagner's Brewery, **59**
Walker, Dwan, **144**
Walker, George, **141**
Wallace City, **68**
Wallover Oil Company, **45**
Wallover, P.M.: Oil refinery, **45**
Wal-Mart, **126**, **145**
Walton, Denver, **144**
War Manpower Commission, **110**
War of 1812, **23**
War Production Board: L-85, **108**
Warhola, John, **144**
Washington County, **12**, **14**, **52**
Washington, George, **6**, **8**
Water Cure, **42**; Founded, **37**; Phillipsburg, **50**
Watts Mill: Bridge, **153**; Road Bridge National Register of Historic Places, **134**
Watts Mill, **17**
Wayman Chapel A.M.E. Church: New Brighton, **29**
Wayne, General Anthony, **16**, **17**
WBVP: First county station, **113**
Webber, Rev. Henry, **49**
Webster, Henry and Henley, **25**

Weiser, Conrad, **5**
Welfare Office: Opened in Rochester, **105**
WesBanco, **147**
West Aliquippa, **89**; Brewery, **80**; Dr. Jesse Steinfeld, **123**; Mancini Bridge, **137**; New county jail, **43**
West Augusta, **11**
West Mayfield, **95**; West Mayfield Christian School, **128**
Western Argus, **24**
Western Beaver Junior-Senior High School, **119**
Western Star newspaper: Started by Bigler & Denlinger, **35**
Westmoreland County, **10**
Weyand, Michael, **56**
White Eye's Town: old Sawkunk, **7**
White Mine: First strip mine in America, **92**
White Oak Flats, **16**
White Township: Founded, **65**
White, Thomas: First mill in county, **12**
White, Timothy B., **43**
White, William E., **86**
Whitla Glass Company, Limited, **65**
Wide Awakes: Republican marching club, **42**
William B. Dunlap Mansion, **129**, **153**
William Miller & Sons, **52**
Williams, Ennion: Land agent, **17**
Williams, Lauryn, **141**
WillowBrook Lake Resort, **114**
Wilson: Dr. Fred, **96**; Dr. Ruth Early female physician, **96**
Wilson, Barker & Gregg: Iron blast furnace, **22**
Wilson, Hall, **27**
Wilson, Judge J. Sharp, **80**
Wilson, Lewis "Hack": Baseball, **100**
Witherspoon, Rev. J.M., **49**
WMBA: Founded, **117**
Woceshoski, Stanislof: Electric chair, **91**

Wolf, John: Flour mill, **17**, **38**
Women's Christian Temperance Union: Beaver, **61**; Beaver Falls, **62**; Rochester, **61**
Wood, James: Homewood named after, **43**
Woodlawn, **97**; Academy, **59**; Highland School, **85**; Park purchased, **81**
Woodlawn & Southern Street Railway Company, **87**
Woodlawn Street Railway Company: Last run, **104**
Woodruff, Jemuel: Oldest Mason, **74**
Woodson, Richard: Kidnapped back into slavery, **39**
Woolaway, Thomas, **119**
Wright, Alexander, **16**
WRYO radio: Goes off air, **115**; Rochester Twp., **113**
Wyandot Indians, **5**
Wychoff Steel, **131**

Y

YMCA: New Brighton, **69**
Yohogania, **11**
Young Ladies' Christian Temperance Union: Beaver Falls, **63**
Young Men's Christian Association: Rochester, **65**
Young Woman's Christian Temperance Union: Beaver, **63**
Young, Candy: World record hurdles, **129**
Youngstown and Eastern Railroad: Oldest operating short line, **149**

Z

Zeisberger, Rev. David: Moravian Missionary, **9**
Ziegler, William: Forms Royal Chemical Company, **55**
Zion Church: Fireballs, **57**

Made in the USA
Columbia, SC
20 November 2017